Harper College Library

3 2158 00498 0379

W9-BPL-816

QUICK

Date Due

RNING

BRODART, CO.   Cat. No. 23-233   Printed in U.S.A.

Quick Hits for Service-Learning

SUCCESSFUL STRATEGIES BY AWARD-WINNING TEACHERS

Edited by

M. A. COOKSEY and **KIMBERLY T. OLIVARES**

INDIANA UNIVERSITY PRESS

Bloomington and Indianapolis

This book is a publication of

Indiana University Press
601 North Morton Street
Bloomington, Indiana 47404-3797 USA

www.iupress.indiana.edu

Telephone orders   800-842-6796
Fax orders   812-855-7931
Orders by e-mail   iuporder@indiana.edu

© 2010 by Indiana University Faculty Colloquium on
Excellence in Teaching

All rights reserved

No part of this book may be reproduced or utilized in any
form or by any means, electronic or mechanical, including
photocopying and recording, or by any information storage and retrieval system, without permission in writing
from the publisher. The Association of American University Presses' Resolution on Permissions constitutes the
only exception to this prohibition.

⊖ The paper used in this publication meets the mini-
mum requirements of the American National Standard for
Information Sciences—Permanence of Paper for Printed
Library Materials, ANSI Z39.48-1992.

Manufactured in the United States of America

Cataloging information is available from the Library of
Congress.

1 2 3 4 5 15 14 13 12 11 10

HARPER COLLEGE LIBRARY
PALATINE, ILLINOIS 60067

CONTENTS

4 Global Studies and Local Outreach to Exceptional Populations   67

5 The Study of History, the Social Sciences, and the Arts   91

INDIANA CAMPUS COMPACT DIRECTORS' WELCOME

Welcome to *Quick Hits for Service-Learning*, the fifth volume in the Quick Hits series, sponsored by the Indiana University Faculty Colloquium on Excellence in Teaching (FACET) in conjunction with Indiana Campus Compact (ICC).

Founded in 1993, ICC is a network of over 40 college and university campuses in Indiana that supports higher education's efforts to develop students into well-informed, engaged citizens. By providing programs, services, and resources, ICC serves as a catalyst for campuses and communities to improve people's lives through service-learning and civic engagement initiatives. One way in which ICC serves as a change agent is to work directly with faculty on the development or enhancement of service-learning courses. In 1995, ICC introduced the Faculty Fellows' Program to allow faculty members from a wide variety of disciplines and across institutional types to come together to refine their service-learning courses while working collaboratively on a group project to advance the field of service-learning. Over the last 15 years, over 100 fellows have participated and, in cohorts of eight faculty members per year, have taken on a number of projects. This fifth volume, Quick Hits for Service-Learning, is one such project.

Quick Hits for Service-Learning was born from the 2007-2008 ICC Faculty Fellows' cohort. The eight Faculty Fellows served as the original editorial board for this project during the 2007-2008 academic year. We would be remiss if we did not acknowledge the many hours they contributed to this project, including the main concept behind this volume – to create a tangible, practical, hands-on resource focused on the development of a service-learning course through the ingredients one should consider while fully baking one's ideas into reality. The 2007–2008 Faculty Fellows included:

- M.A. Cooksey (Senior ICC Faculty Fellow), Indiana University East
- Marcie Coulter-Kern, Manchester College
- Jacquelyn Frank, University of Indianapolis
- Judith I. Gray, Ball State University
- J.R. Jamison (Advisor), Indiana Campus Compact
- Mark Malaby, Ball State University
- Ingrid Rogers, Manchester College
- Julien Simon, Indiana University East

Our two editors of this volume, M.A. Cooksey and Kimberly T. Olivares (FACET), have worked over the last two years continuing to bring the fellows' idea—this publication—to fruition. The organization of the chapters by our editors was done intentionally to showcase the depth and breadth of discipline areas that have developed innovative strategies to involve students in the process of serving to learn and learning to serve. The submissions to this volume from around the globe truly highlight experiences and suggestions from educators to educators on the development of a service-learning course. As an organization that strongly believes that students are developed through service-learning experiences into well-informed, engaged citizens, we are proud to sponsor this volume and to introduce you to *Quick Hits for Service-Learning*.

Margaret Carnes Stevens
Executive Director

J.R. Jamison
Associate Director

WELCOME TO
QUICK HITS FOR SERVICE-LEARNING

The *Quick Hits* series of publications has arisen to address contemporary challenges of teaching and learning. While initial volumes were authored by members of the Indiana University Faculty Colloquium on Excellence in Teaching (FACET), subsequent volumes have been authored by a wider range of contributors. The FACET organization seeks to recognize outstanding leaders and practitioners of teaching and learning and advance educational success of students. This mission embraces not only traditional didactic teaching, but the myriad of new pedagogies and, more strikingly, the new modalities and contexts for teaching. The evolving expectations today for students includes engagement with the broader community beyond institutional walls. It is clear the richness of education is not only the fundamental content of courses and its application, but in situ contact of student and community. In the previous volume, *Quick Hits for Educating Citizens*, its focus addressed new expectations and outcomes in this context, including associations with the American Democracy Project. The current volume of *Quick Hits for Service-Learning*, edited by M.A. Cooksey and Kimberly T. Olivares, addresses the addition of service-learning to our curricula in a pragmatic and straight-forward manner. In the tradition of other volumes in the series, what are the direct actions of faculty to advance the cause of teaching and learning? This volume provides palatable and clear strategies to aid faculty in exploring the addition of this valuable addition to the panoply of student activities.

Teaching and learning are clearly evolving not only in practice, but in context. One only need look at the additional expectations our stakeholders are coming to expect. This is a refreshing evolution that expands content issues to application and consequence. For a large share of traditional faculty, challenges exist to readily understanding how they might be a part of this evolution. The current volume attempts to rationalize and directly provide insight into how this might be achieved. With suggestions that address course-specific examples through projects, readers can sample the incredible diversity of roles and actions to improve institutional connections to communities and students.

This *Quick Hits* volume is certainly in keeping with our series and will provide fresh perspectives on the importance of educating our students within the context of civic engagement. This is the natural extension to our new paradigms and reflects a contemporary and progressive viewpoint. Faculty in all disciplines should find this an engaging treatment of "Service-Learning."

David J. Malik
University Director, Faculty Colloquium on Excellence in Teaching, Indiana University
Chancellor's Professor of Chemistry and Chemical Biology, Indiana University Purdue University Indianapolis

About FACET
The Faculty Colloquium on Excellence in Teaching (FACET) was established as an Indiana University Presidential Initiative in 1989 to promote and sustain teaching excellence. Today, FACET involves over 500 full-time faculty members, nominated and selected through an annual campus and statewide peer review process.

FACET is a community of faculty dedicated to and recognized for excellence in teaching and learning. FACET advocates pedagogical innovation, inspires growth and reflection, cultivates the Scholarship of Teaching and Learning and fosters personal renewal in the commitment to student learning.

EDITORS' INTRODUCTION

"College is a time you'll explore. You are going to do things you've never done before, and you are going to meet people from all over the world." This is what our parents told us the day we went off to college. The only new things we really hoped to find were new ways to have fun, and the only new people we really hoped to meet were new friends—especially boys. But as always, our parents were right. We did do new things we had never done before, and we did meet people from all over the world.

College is still a time for our students to explore—for them to do things they have never done before, and to meet people from all over the world—including other worlds within their close proximity—like those of different ethnicities, social classes, even sub cultures within their own communities. It is into these worlds that service-learning and civic engagement allow students to travel and to explore, and the educations they receive and the lessons they glean within these living, learning laboratories is an experience far richer than that they could receive when their studies take place in the classroom alone.

This publication is a compilation of roadmaps—possible pathways down which we may journey with our students, the details of the trip to be fleshed out by you, the classroom teacher. The articles here are presented as examples of ways to excavate the nooks and crannies of our disciplines, encouraging the development of field expertise and professional skills in our students. You may then adapt their content and direction to your campus and your community. They are descriptions and directions offered for your reference and study as you map out your more specific, curricular plan. Please feel free to contact the authors for more details on their projects; contact information for each of the authors is located in the back of the edition.

Many scholars have come together to make this publication possible, and we wish to thank them all for their excellent contributions.

M. A. Cooksey
Director of Service-Learning
Senior Lecturer in Humanities

Kimberly T. Olivares
FACET Administrative Manager

The Education of Children and Youth

Introduction

Jeffrey B. Anderson
Professor, Teacher Education
Director Academic Service-Learning Faculty Fellows Program
Seattle University

A national study that included all institutional members of the American Association of Colleges for Teacher Education (AACTE) in the U.S. found that 59% of responding campuses integrated service-learning experiences into the preparation of their teacher candidates, and 39% prepared teacher candidates to use service-learning as a pedagogy with their future K-12 students. Numerous rationales for the use of service-learning were offered, with the most frequent being the belief that engagement in service-learning would be one of the most effective methods to prepare new teachers to successfully teach students from ethnically and economically diverse backgrounds.

Even with this fairly wide spread adoption of service-learning, there still remains, however, confusion regarding distinctions between service-learning and the traditional student teaching internship, with many teacher educators believing that the two are the same. In order to advance service-learning in pre-service teacher education, key decision makers need to understand how service-learning and student teaching internships are distinct. The difference is seen in the intentions behind the each of the practices. Student teaching is provided, primarily, to benefit teacher candidates by giving them an opportunity to develop professionally as they apply methods and theories they have learned in their university classrooms. Service-learning can allow for the same professional development, but also places equal emphasis on addressing genuine community-identified needs. Additionally, service-learning places explicit emphasis on strengthening the civic responsibility of the teacher candidates involved. With these benefits in mind, it is easy to see that well implemented service-learning experiences early in the pre-service teacher's education, can provide a foundation that will expose candidates to many of the issues that they will later encounter as student teachers and in-service teachers, as well as help candidates determine if the K-12 classroom is the right professional destination for them.

A second issue also creates confusion regarding the use of service-learning with teacher candidates. Service-learning can be used to assist teacher candidates to meet the goals of their professional courses, ranging from understanding theories of educational psychology to appreciating the diverse cultural backgrounds of their future students. While an appreciation of student diversity is the most frequent use of service-learning in teacher education, some teacher educators argue that preparing future teachers to use service-learning as a pedagogy with their future K-12 students is an even more important outcome. These service-learning advocates note that each new teacher can enhance the education of from 25 to over 100 K-12 students in just one year by facilitating service-learning activities for them, thereby educating these students about diversity in their own communities and helping them explore and meet pressing community needs.

Teacher education programs are well placed to facilitate the inclusion of service-learning into both the K-12 and higher education curricula. For example, if a program annually prepares 200 new teachers to use service-learning and 30% of them actually implement this approach, the result would be 60 K-12 classrooms in which students experience service-learning. In addition, many teacher education programs have formed equitable, collaborative relationships with K-12 schools, and as a result, have the potential to establish K-higher education service-learning partnerships that effectively address the needs of K-12 schools and their wider communities, along with the needs of teacher education programs.

The examples of service-learning projects in this chapter demonstrate that implementing service-learning in pre-service teacher education is not that different from service-learning in K-12 schools and in other disciplines at the university level. As the following examples demonstrate, through service-learning, pre-service teachers can learn about:

- Pressing community needs, cultural compentency, and the changing demographics of America's classrooms (Faux; Colby, Bercaw, Clark, and Galiardi; Hasslen and Mitchell-Agbemadi; Malaby and Clausen; Donovan)
- Developing partnerships (Smith, Robinson, and Barber; Malaby and Clausen; Bleicher, Buchanan, and Correia)
- Teacher preparation and dispositions (Smith, Robinson, and Barber; Malaby and Clausen; Bleicher, Buchanan and Correia; Dowell; Donovan; Watson, Barber and Smith; King and Reder; Carson)
- College access (Hasslen and Mitchell-Agbermadi)
- Teaching techniques (Ironsmith and Eppler)
- Literacy (Ironsmith and Eppler; King)
- Child development (Cemore)
- Philanthropy and service (Rogers)

However, teacher educators face unique challenges as they seek to enhance the teacher education curriculum through the integration of service-learning. In order to prepare graduates to implement service-learning, programs must go beyond using service-learning as a teaching method. They must provide students with explicit instruction in the use of service-learning pedagogy, and field experiences in which teacher candidates engage in service-learning design, implementation, reflection, and assessment working closely with experienced K-12 teachers, their students, and other community members.

Reference

Anderson, J.B. & Erickson, J.A. (2003). Service-learning in teacher education. *Academic Exchange Quarterly,* 7 (2), 111-115.

MEETING THE NEEDS OF CHILDREN

TAMMY FAUX
WARTBURG COLLEGE

Keywords: child welfare, at-risk youth, resiliency, after-school program, early childhood education, social work, learning disability, behavioral disability

Introduction

Service-learning is theory in action. Students who take a course titled *Meeting the Needs of Children* engage in approximately twenty-five hours of service-learning during a general education course implemented by the social work department. This class uses service-learning to encourage the application of child welfare theories and concepts through participation in an after-school program and a junior high special education classroom.

Project Description

Meeting the Needs of Children (MNOC) is an introductory level course. The typical demographic of the class consists of equal parts early childhood education, social work, and students from a variety of other majors who have interest in working with children. The course emphasizes systems theory and focuses on the needs of children as individuals, as members of families, and as members of society. Core concepts include identification of "at-risk" children and the augmentation of "resilience" factors.

Service-learning is incorporated throughout the semester. Students participate in two different projects. Students are paired with an eighth- grade child who has a learning or behavioral disability label. The students meet with their partners every Friday during the regularly scheduled MNOC course time slot. Students develop a positive relationship by serving as tutors and mentors over the course of the semester.

MNOC students are also required to work at the Salvation Army's after-school drop-in program a minimum of five times for at least two hours each session. Students play games with the children, provide supervision for activities, and assist with serving the evening meal. The students' primary assignment is to go to the program and "play." While they are interacting, the MNOC students serve as role models and help to provide necessary structure for the children.

Project Timeline

Both service-learning components run concurrently throughout the term. The first two weeks of the course provide students with their initial exposure to the key concepts of resilience and at-risk factors. Students are also introduced to service-learning concepts.

MNOC students are introduced to their eighth-grade partners at the end of the second week. Nine additional sessions are scheduled. Most sessions focus on tutoring, with every fourth session offering a social activity in place of tutoring. The tenth and final session is a closure activity featuring food and games. Each meeting time is scheduled for the same day of the week during the same time.

Participation in the after-school program begins during week three of the course; students sign-up for five sessions that fall outside of the MNOC class period. There are approximately 40 opportunities to participate. Ideally, three to five students fill each available time slot.

Steps for Implementation

Project planning begins several months prior to the term with the development of a relationship with personnel at the chosen sites. Careful assessment of the needs of the children and the program sites ensures a reciprocal relationship. Evaluating the partnerships at the conclusion of the semester is a key to continuing to improve the relationships and learning experiences.

The course uses one third of its scheduled meeting time for the school partnership. Students learn theories and concepts during the first two classes each week, and apply the learning during the service-learning day. This schedule requires the instructor to be concise and well organized in the structure of the in-class portion of course content.

The instructor must prepare students for their experiences by introducing them to anticipated characteristics of the children in the programs, and to the structure and purposes of the programs themselves. The professor accompanies students to all activities at the junior high and serves as a facilitator. The after-school program only requires attendance by the instructor for the first couple of sessions. Peer introductions are used in subsequent sessions. Significant effort is required in order to handle scheduling, transportation, and special situations throughout the term.

Outcomes/Assessment

Reflection is a crucial component of service-learning. This course provides multiple opportunities for reflection using individual journals, small group discussion, and class discussion. Students complete a structured journal entry after each experience. These reflections have five elements. Students write about how they planned for their experience, describe the day's events, identify what they would change about the experience, give a detailed connection to course concepts, and describe a conversation they had with someone outside of the class about these experiences. Short class discussions occur approximately once a week to discuss project events. Additionally, their connections to real-life circumstances through these projects can be used as case studies to introduce new concepts in the course.

Service-learning project assessment hinges primarily on the content of the individual journals. Attendance and positive participation are expected; however, this is not enough to indicate appropriate synthesis of theory and action. Two-thirds of the project grade is determined by evaluating journal content, and the remaining one-third in a final summary paper completed at the end of the class. Writing content must show thoughtful reflection of the student's experience and strong connections to course material. The service-learning project represents one-third of the entire course grade.

Many students enter the class with a belief in individual blame for risk factors. They have little experience working with low-income or minority children, and have minimal working knowledge of programs that reach out to children in these situations. The service-learning projects, combined with classroom content focusing on risk and resilience, promote an evolution to a broader view. The ultimate outcome of these experiences is that students believe that all members of a community have a responsibility to meet the needs of children.

Conclusion

An embedded service-learning experience helps students connect course concepts to real-world experiences. The opportunity to apply theories to experiences with children results in a deeper understanding of the theories. Repeated opportunities to demonstrate connections between course concepts and service-learning experiences result in functional and lasting knowledge. The additional planning for an intensive service-learning course is worth the effort when students demonstrate a meaningful change that places themselves into a community that is responsible for its children.

FROM COMMUNITY SERVICE TO SERVICE-LEARNING: A PROGRAM PERSPECTIVE

SUSAN COLBY, ANN MARIE CLARK, SHARI GALIARDI
APPALACHIAN STATE UNIVERSITY

LYNNE BERCAW
CALIFORNIA STATE UNIVERSITY

Keywords: program model, teacher candidates, pre-service teachers, citizenship, democracy

Introduction

Preparing students for active participation in a democracy is a goal of higher education. As globalization and diversity increase, how to better prepare students to meet the challenges of the 21st century is a topic of discussion at many universities. Amidst these discussions, the elementary education faculty at a comprehensive university in the southeast in conjunction with the University's ACT Office (Appalachian & the Community Together, www.act.appstate.edu) added a community service/service-learning component to their undergraduate program, *The 20/20 Program: Bringing Community Issues Into Focus* (http://www.ced.appstate .edu/departments/ci/programs/2020/). The rationale for this program is based on changing demographics in society and, specifically, the K-12 classroom. The predicted enrollment in elementary schools shows the number of children of color is increasing (Banks, et al., 2005), while prospective teachers have limited interaction with cultures outside

of their own (Ladson-Billings, 1996; Nieto, 2000). Through community service and service-learning, students interact with other cultures and engage in active citizenship in their communities.

Program Description

The 20/20 Program provides community service/ service-learning experiences over the course of an entire undergraduate program. Essential to the success of this program is the integration of course content, field experiences, and leadership. Students transition from participating in community service as sophomores, to experiencing service-learning as students in their junior year, and, finally, to leading a service-learning project as classroom teachers while seniors. The mission of the 20/20 Program states:

> The Elementary Education 20/20 Program at Appalachian State University strives to prepare teachers

to be active participants in the life of their school and community. Our program seeks to empower future teachers to work toward social justice through an ethic of caring, commitment, and conscience.

Project Timeline

Prospective teachers begin with twenty hours of community service in two non-profit, non-religious organizations. This fosters awareness of complex issues that the community faces and the service agencies available. Students seek pre-approval for their community service sites from the 20/20 Program coordinator. Upon completion of their service, students submit a short reflection with a log showing hours worked, activities conducted, and the signature of an organization representative.

The second phase of the program consists of twenty hours of service-learning completed in two upper level courses, approximately 10 hours per course. In *Learner Diversity*, the first course, students examine stereotypes and become aware of their own thinking and their families of origin, on issues of ethnicity, race and bias. Service-learning projects cover a wide range of activities, including family literacy initiative for migrant families in a rural school; coordinating and implementing Special Olympics for the county; working with homeless shelters to provide food and other necessities; and leading activities for children placed in a shelter for abused women. In addition to participating in discussions over the course of the semester, students write three reflections about their experiences: (a) an anticipatory reflection outlining their expectations and feelings; (b) a mid-semester reflection where challenges are discussed; and (c) a final reflection where they often reveal changes in their thinking.

The second course in the sequence is *Social Studies in the Elementary School Curriculum*. This course is part of five methods courses and a field placement that directly precedes student teaching. For the last five weeks of the semester, prospective teachers are placed in K-6 classrooms where, along with other responsibilities, they are expected to lead children through a service-learning project. Students learn how to develop and implement an age-appropriate project, to connect the project to the curriculum, and to design appropriate reflection activities for children to learn from their experience. Projects include developing a local garden; sending care packages to the troops; and organizing school-wide activities such as canned food drives or recycling centers.

Steps for Implementation

For the first 20 hours of community service, students seek preapproval for their community service sites from the 20/20 Program coordinators. Students may use the university database developed by ACT to choose appropriate sites. Upon completion of their service, students submit a short reflection with a log showing hours worked, activities conducted, and the signature of an organization representative. The final 20 hours are completed as part of the two courses designated as service-learning courses.

Outcomes/Assessment

Data collected from 2004 to 2006 provide evidence that the program is effective in its mission. In an average academic year, 400 sophomores participate in community service activities; 200 juniors participate in service-learning projects; and 200 seniors implement service-learning in their field placements. School-based projects actively engage 4000 children per year.

Students enrolled in the two courses complete extensive surveys at the end of the semester. Data from the *Learner Diversity* course provide evidence that service-learning has increased students' knowledge about issues/concepts presented in class, has broadened their understanding of social issues that affect their community, and has allowed them to acquire/practice skills useful in their future careers. Because of their experiences, students feel a greater sense of responsibility for the community. Data from the second course provide evidence that students perceive they are well-prepared to use service-learning in the classroom, they are more comfortable with service-learning as a pedagogical tool, and they plan to use service-learning in the future. Most importantly, students believe the children they interacted with benefited from involvement in their service-learning project.

With an emphasis on transitioning from community service to service-learning, students in this program evolve in their understanding, attitudes, and abilities.

Conclusion

Based on the findings above, the 20/20 Program is successful in preparing teachers to be active participants in their school and community, and at empowering future teachers to work toward social justice. With an emphasis on transitioning from community service to service-learning, students in this program evolve in their understanding, attitudes, and abilities. This progression enables candidates to recognize the needs of communities, respond to those needs, and help apply the pedagogy of service-learning in a wide variety of situations (The International Partnership for Service-Learning and Leadership, 2008).

References

Appalachian & the Community Together. (2008). Appalachian State University, ACT Retrieved May 31, 2008 from from http://act.appstate.edu/index.php?&MMN_position=5:5

Banks, J., Cochran-Smith, M., Moll, L., Richert, A., Zeichner, K., LePage, P., et al. (2005). Teaching diverse learners. In L. Darling-Hammond & J. Bransford (Eds.), *Preparing teachers for a changing world: What teachers should learn and be able to do* (pp. 232-274). San Francisco, CA: Jossey-Bass.

Ladson-Billings, G. (1994). *The Dreamkeepers: Successful Teachers of African American Children.* San Francisco, Calif.: Jossey-Bass.

International Partnership for Service-Learning and Leadership. (2007). IPSL Declaration of Principles. Retrieved May 31, 2008 from http://www.ipsl.org/advocacy/declaration-of-principles.html

Nieto, S. (2000). *Affirming diversity: the sociopolitical context of multicultural education* (3rd ed.) New York, NY, Longman.

DISCOVERING SELF IN SERVING OTHERS: CUIN 302 AT PIEDMONT HEALTH SERVICES

THOMAS J. SMITH AND ELIZABETH A. BARBER
NORTH CAROLINA AGRICULTURAL AND TECHNICAL STATE UNIVERSITY

DIANE ROBINSON
PIEDMONT HEALTH SERVICES AND SICKLE CELL AGENCY

Keywords: university/community agency partnership, teacher education/dispositions and cultural competencies

Introduction

CUIN 302 Service-Learning at North Carolina A&T provides semester-long opportunities for pre-service teachers, school counselors, or social workers to develop cultural competencies for working successfully across diversity. A partnership grew from concern that early field experiences place students in settings in which misconceptions about diverse, poor, and immigrant children may be reinforced, rather than critically examined. At the same time, Piedmont Health Services and Sickle Cell Agency (PHSSCA) needed to implement a diabetes outreach program to meet community needs, but lacked the staffing to do so.

> CUIN 302 provides scaffolded experiences in which students can field-test their preconceptions about diverse individuals to develop more accurate understandings.

To meet overlapping needs, A&T and PHSSCA joined forces to support students in exploring their socio-cultural identities, recognizing the situatedness of all identities, and respecting others whose life circumstances differ from theirs. PHSSCA is located across the street from A&T, but worlds away from the backgrounds of most students.

Project Description

CUIN 302 provides scaffolded experiences in which students can field-test their preconceptions about diverse individuals to develop more accurate understandings. At PHSSCA, students work with people who cannot afford health care, may be sickle cell, diabetes or HIV/AIDS clients, may inject illegal drugs, or earn livings as commercial sex workers.

A series of readings and experiences, crafted by instructors and the agency's Community Health Educator (CHE), facilitate student reflection and development. Through weekly group meetings and conferences with individuals, the agency CHE mentors students toward the sense of efficacy, identity, moral development, ability to work with others, leadership, communication skills, real-world knowledge application, complex understandings, problem analysis, critical thinking, and career development promised in the literature on service-learning (SL). Students enter as students, but leave self-assured and self-determined.

Project Timeline

Weeks 1–3:
Class meets on campus. Instructors model best practice teaching strategies while providing readings and reflections to ground student definitions of SL and cultural competence.

Week 1:
University instructors share overview of PHSSCA experience.

To introduce selves and initiate students' first experience of looking inward, instructors share "Where I'm From" poems (Christensen, 2000) and invite students to draft their own.

Students read about child SL (Seo, 2001; Rusch, 2002; Hoose, 1993; Schwager & Schuerger, 1999) and respond with Text-to-Self Connections.

Students complete the Multicultural Efficacy Scale.

Week 2:
Students share and revise drafts of "Where I'm from" poems, discuss and draft resumes.

Students read teacher accounts of SL projects (Wade, 1997) and make Text-to-Text Connections.

Week 3:
Students read about the development of cultural competencies (Gay, 2002; Ladson-Billings, 2001) and make Text-to-World Connections.

Students edit "Where I'm from" poems and add a photo, for the PHSSCA Bulletin Board.

Students edit resumes and prepare sections of their SL Agreements.

Week 4:
From this week on students meet at PHSSCA.

Students present "Where I'm from" poems and resumes to agency CHE.

CHE guides "getting to know you" activity, talks briefly about the agency history and purpose, and distributes information about sickle cell disease.

CHE and instructors give assignments:
Read bell hooks' "Solidarity with the Poor," and respond by writing "I Used to Think, But Now I Know" poems.

CHE makes appointments with students to negotiate their SL Agreements and coordinate schedules.

Week 5:
Agency workers present on conducting community outreach.

Students discuss "Solidarity with the Poor," and share "I Used to Think, But Now I Know" poems.

CHE gives assignments:
Read about strategies for SL with children (Lewis et al., 1991; Lewis, 1995; Teaching Tolerance; Rethinking Schools).

CHE and students negotiate SL Agreements and schedules, based upon individual skills, learning goals, and agency needs. Across the ensuing weeks the CHE leads weekly group meetings, and she and agency personnel transform students into high-functioning staff members.

University instructors make weekly visits to the agency to participate in outreach activities, join in-group meetings, or drop in on students.

Week 6:
Students begin their individual work schedules.

At group meeting students discuss conducting SL with children, and select a bilingual children's book (i.e., Diego, or All The Colors We Are) for use in a SL unit. Students have 2 weeks for this project, are encouraged to work together.

Weeks 6–15:
CHE and students conduct outreach in local neighborhoods, parks, and businesses. Meticulously prepped for every task, students undergo extensive role-playing before contact with the public.

Student SL Agreements largely determine their tasks and experiences. CHE partners student apprentices with agency personnel as they learn to handle everything from client intake interviews to preparing HIV/AIDS prevention "goodie bags" during 30+ hours of service.

Students create health brochures on client reading level, plan and coordinate with local churches and YMCA, and locate materials and staff health fairs.

Personal Connections Reflection Guides and journaling help students anchor moments in which transformations take place for de-briefing with CHE and instructors.

Selected readings and responses support students in making connections between PHSSCA experiences and their professional development courses.

Facts-Questions-Feelings responses structure reflections on how to socially integrate a severely disabled child (Kissinger, 2005).

Students explore textbook bias (DeRose, 2007), and reflect on a Black educator's accomplishments (Peterson, 2007).

Mid-term:
Social-Cultural Identity Papers, and Exit Slips on how it felt to write these, take students deep into the roots of their own biases. Later they read about identity formation in children and youth (Roots for Change, 2003).

Week 16:
At a celebration the CHE prepares the students' favorite

foods while they share changes, surprises, and turning points across the term.

Implementing a University-Agency Partnership

Select an agency partner based on opportunities it offers for meeting course objectives and student developmental needs. Consider the depth of the agency's commitment to students, the opportunities available for student learning, and location. Make face-to-face contact, share objectives, and negotiate support for students and co-teaching, where possible, with agency staff. University instructors and agency CHE meet at the end of each term to review outcomes. Planning is collaborative, ongoing.

Outcomes and Conclusion

To track development toward more culturally competent practice, students complete entering and exiting Multicultural Efficacy Scales (Guyton & Wesche, 2005), entering and exiting the field surveys, and write final reflection papers. A rubric guides evaluation of course written materials. Successful completion of assignments results in grades; students not meeting expectations receive an "Incomplete" and return to the agency to complete expectations. Agency outcomes include launching a diabetes outreach program, additional staffing and new perspectives, and the ability of youth to reach out successfully to potential clients in need of services.

Across the term students undergo profound changes. At first they demonstrate their over-socialization to public education: reserved, they whisper, avert their eyes, remain inside themselves like preteens at the first school dance. Instructors invite them to take roles in the housekeeping chores of running a college course, but most decline, unwilling to risk.

These behaviors recur when students role-play their "diabetes screening pitches" as they prep for their first encounters with agency clients. Students introduce themselves, shake hands, explain their purpose, distribute materials, and answer client questions. Even within the cloistered agency setting students whisper, avoid eye contact, and sit tongue-tied like wallflowers.

After outreach, after students have approached potential clients on the street, stood at their front doors, chatted with them on park benches about coming into the agency for needed screenings and services, they are transformed. Coming back from fieldwork loud and animated, we hear them long before we see them. Back in the agency, students sit on the edges of chairs, lean forward, smile, make eye contact, and talk and talk. No longer lost in the audience, students emerge as seasoned actors, confident, standing center stage of their own lives.

References

Christensen, L. (2003). *Reading, writing, rising up*. Milwaukee: Rethinking schools.

DeRose, J. (2007). History textbooks: Theirs and ours. *Rethinking schools*, http://www.rethinkingschools.org/archive/22_01/ours221.shtml

Gay, G. (2002.) Preparing for culturally responsive teaching. *Journal of teacher education*, 53, pp.106-116.

Guyton, E. & Wesche, M. (2005). The multicultural efficacy scale. *Multicultural perspectives*, 7 (4), 21-29.

Hoose, P. (1993). *It's our world, too!* Boston: Little, Brown

Kissinger, K. (2005). Holding Nyla. *Rethinking schools*, http://www.rethinkingschools.org/archive/19_03/nyla193.shtml

Ladson-Billings, G. (2001). Teaching and cultural competence. *Rethinking schools online*, http://www.rethinkingschools.org/archive/15_04/Glb154.shtml

Lewis, B. (1995). *The kid's guide to service projects*. Minneapolis: Free Spirit.

Lewis, B., Espeland, P. & Pernu, C. (1991). *The kid's guide to social action*. Minneapolis: Free Spirit.

Peterson, B. (2007). The passing of a great BLACK educator. *Rethinking schools*, http://www.rethinkingschools.org/archive/22_01/asa221.shtml

Roots for Change. (2003). Overview of the development of ethnic, gender, disability, and class identity and attitudes in children and youth. *The early childhood equity alliance's journal*, 1, 2-5.

Rusch, E. (2002). *Generation fix*. Hillsboro, Oregon: Beyond Words.

Schwager, T. & Schuerger, M. (1999). *Gutsy girls*. Minneapolis, MN: Free Spirit.

Seo, D. (2001). *Be the difference: A beginner's guide to changing the world*. BC: New Society.

Wade, R. (1997). Empowerment in student teaching through community service learning. *Theory into Practice*, 36(3), 184-191.

To meet overlapping needs, A&T and PHSSCA joined forces to support students in exploring their socio-cultural identities, recognizing the situatedness of all identities, and respecting others whose life circumstances differ from theirs.

PREPARING FOR THE FUTURE: A COLLABORATION BETWEEN URBAN STUDENTS AND PRE-SERVICE TEACHERS

ROBIN HASSLEN
BETHEL UNIVERSITY

VERONA MITCHELL-AGBEMADI
BETHEL UNIVERSITY/FROGTOWN/SUMMIT UNIVERSITY

Keywords: diversity, teacher preparation, recruitment, mentoring, tutoring, pre-service teachers, college preparation, minority

Introduction

In an era of teacher shortages, changing demographics, externally imposed standards and high-stakes testing, the recruitment, retention, and nurturing of resilient teachers who can teach and advocate for all children is imperative. That is the goal of this service-learning project, along with the preparation of underrepresented groups of public school students for college.

Through this partnership between a small, private university and an urban public school system's Advancement via Individual Determination (AVID) tutoring program (www.avidonline.org), middle and high school students are exposed to college students who mentor, tutor, talk about college experiences, and invite them to campus. For most of the AVID students, this is their first exposure to university students; forming these relationships encourages them to recognize their own potential and enhances their desire for a college education.

Project Description

The AVID Program in this urban Midwest school district is an in-school academic support program for grades 7–12 that prepares students for college eligibility and success. AVID places academically average students in advanced classes, preparing these predominantly minority and low-income students (none of whom have a college-going tradition in their families) for college. One of the most critical components of the AVID program is the tutor. In the partnership with the public schools' AVID program, this small private university provides tutors. Although often working together across cultures, tutors and AVID students are able to find a common bond in recognizing the importance of education.

Project Timeline

The AVID program for middle and high school students begins within three weeks of the beginning of the school year. At the same time, prospective tutors complete an in-class training session in the Socratic method of tutoring and questioning during the first week of the semester and sign up to commit to 1–2 hours/week of tutoring for the term. New tutors are added each semester with a new section of EDU 317; however, some tutors choose to continue their AVID participation despite the completion of the service-learning requirement.

Steps for Implementation

Prior to the beginning of a semester, the EDU317 professor and the AVID Director determine dates for training and school tutoring time schedules. College students participate in the training and then sign up for the schools and time slots that meet their schedules. While it is necessary for pre-service teachers who are predominantly white and middle-class to understand how to relate to and teach all students, it is often perceived as threatening to them to be placed in field experiences in diverse classrooms. The experience of AVID tutoring is an opportunity to interact with underrepresented students who have potential to attend college and lack only the self-confidence needed to pursue such a goal. For college students, interacting with small groups of AVID students is both a professional and a personal experience that can result in richer understandings and deeper relationships.

Outcomes/Assessment

The university's service-learning coordinator assesses all experiences. Several of the findings from the Spring 2008 EDU317 university service-learning student survey revealed that 78.8% of 22 students (i.e., tutors) agreed that because of the interaction that the course provided, they had a workable understanding of the needs and problems facing the communities in which the AVID students resided; 69.7% of the tutors had a better understanding of cultural diversity; and 93.3% of the tutors reported that they achieved a new level of comfort (nonexistent prior to the service-learning experience) working with various racial and ethnic groups. For the EDU317 course, the service-learning experience is awarded a number of points based on the students' attendance, quality of experience, and reflections as noted in their reflective journals. In-class opportunities exist for processing with the professor and AVID staff. "Community-based learning experiences that are most productive are well-planned, linked directly to teacher education, and involve guided reflection" (Sleeter, 2008). The EDU317 service-learning experience, now in effect for two years, is very meaningful to students, one of whom wrote:

> Working with AVID this semester has been a great experience. It has been a great opportunity to work on the front lines with some of the information I have learned through college. This experience has encouraged me in further pursuing working in diverse school districts and urban areas. I have found it both challenging and rewarding. I have learned a great deal about myself and through interaction, about the real needs and issues facing urban youth. It has given me knowledge and experience that goes beyond the classroom. I have come to a better understanding of the need for relationships with students, and the need students have to be encouraged and motivated as they face challenges and sometimes injustice outside the classroom. This experience has given me the opportunity to work in a school that I maybe wouldn't have been placed in for any other field experience, but one that I think has been so formative to my education. It is an experience that I think has better prepared me for being an educator.

When AVID students were asked what was the most helpful element of the program, the number one response was tutors! Over 60% of the 473 students from the 2005-06 cohort did not know a college student personally before their tutors started.

Conclusion

Service-learning is about reciprocity and reflection. It is more than an experience, or simply a service to others. This particular collaboration has resulted in greater student awareness, acceptance and appreciation of diversity, and of inequities and community, all of which have been defined by Boyle-Baise (2002) in a description of multicultural service-learning. Often the EDU317 service-learning is the earliest experiences that the mostly Caucasian college students have with urban students. The fact that these AVID students are serious about their education and excited about prospects of college destroys some stereotypes that the tutors have about urban learners. Most students finish the semester recognizing that the service-learning experience was perhaps the most significant aspect of the course. A student wrote:

> My time with AVID has been invaluable to me as a future teacher. I worked with some students who never anticipated that they could excel academically for the simple reason that they never knew anyone who had. Others lacked the knowledge of why it is important to be well educated, and how being knowledgeable in an academic field can be advantageous for them in terms of their profession. It was very rewarding for me to work with these students, and I am very grateful for this experience. I know for certain that this has altered the way I will teach in the future.

References

Boyle-Baise, M. (2002). *Multicultural service-learning: Educating teachers in diverse communities.* New York: Teachers College.

Sleeter, C.E. (2008). Preparing white teachers for diverse students. In   M. Cochran-Smith, S. Feiman-Nemser, & D.J. McIntyre (Eds.), *Handbook of research on teacher education: Enduring questions in changing contexts, 3rd Ed.* (pp. 559-582). NY: Routledge.

LEARNING TO READ AND READING TO LEARN: A SERVICE-LEARNING SEMINAR ON THE PSYCHOLOGY OF READING

MARSHA IRONSMITH AND MARION EPPLER
EAST CAROLINA UNIVERSITY

Keywords: reading, tutoring, elementary-school children, psychology, after-school program, research, social policy

Introduction

In our seminar on the psychology of reading, students tutor elementary-school children. We discuss research on reading and relate students' tutoring experiences to the research. Using insights gained from teaching this course and from the service-learning literature, we offer strategies for a successful service-learning course.

Project Description

Senior psychology majors tutor third-, fourth-, and fifth-graders attending an after-school program for children at-risk for academic failure. Our goals for the course are two-fold: (a) to increase children's reading performance and their motivation to read, and (b) to more actively engage Psychology majors in learning about research and social policy.

Project Timeline

The after-school program runs from November to May, and our course runs from January to April. Our students begin tutoring during the second week of classes. They tutor once a week for 27 total hours, finishing right before end-of-grade tests.

Late in the semester, we invited a reading specialist to provide students with resources and ideas for effective tutoring. These students felt gratified that an expert validated ideas they had generated on their own.

Steps for Implementation

Planning Course Activities

An important academic goal is to integrate students' service-learning work into the course. Reflection through class discussion and journal writing encourages students to discover links between service experiences and academic material. Class discussion also allows students to process anxieties about service. Our students worry that they will make mistakes while tutoring, or that they are responsible for children's performance on high-stakes tests. We begin every class by asking if anyone has tutoring issues to discuss, which takes substantial time at first. Gradually, discussion of service experiences becomes more academically focused. Students recognize how research helps us to understand the reading process and to generate effective tutoring strategies.

Journal writing allows students to engage in reflection without the pressure of having to organize their thoughts on the spot and facilitates ongoing dialogue with the instructor. Our most reserved student shared thoughtful observations in his journal. He discussed how his child got distracted when reading challenging books, frequently stopping to invent elaborate stories about his family. Rather than becoming exasperated at the boy's distraction tactics, our student noticed the connection to articles we read describing socio-cultural differences in language environments and the role of oral traditions. However, this was an exception to the general rule that students use superficial analyses in journal writing. They need detailed feedback and writing prompts to help them think more deeply about how service experiences and course readings inform each other.

Tutoring comprises 20% of the course grade. Quality of class discussion (20%) and journal writing (20%) comprise another large portion of the course grade. Students also answer study questions that facilitate mastery of the readings (20%). Their favorite assignment is an oral and written review of a children's book (5%). The remaining 15% is an integrative final project. Groups of students are assigned roles and tasks, such as President (formulate national plan to address achievement gap), Secretary of Education (formulate plan to modify No Child Left Behind legislation), or University Dean of Education (suggest research-based revisions to curriculum for elementary school teachers).

Developing Community Service Relationships

When choosing service placements for students, match service activities to specific course content. Although students derive many benefits from service-learning courses, academic benefits depend on how well volunteer experiences are integrated into the course. This course focuses on cognitive and perceptual factors underlying the development of reading, effects of home environments on literacy, interventions, and social policy implications. Students find this research abstract and challenging. However, the service-learning component brings course content to life. Students learn to read with a purpose, searching for clues to help with tutoring, identifying children's reading problems, and eventually seeing how research informs practice.

Service-learning courses should meet identified community needs, but student volunteers also require some autonomy. Lack of autonomy can negatively impact what students gain from service-learning. We require all our students to work in the same setting, but they have independence regarding what they do while tutoring, including working on subjects other than reading. One student helped a child who had no assistance at home to complete a science project—and he won a prize at the science fair! Autonomy encourages students to be creative, plan their activities, be resourceful when solving problems, and take greater responsibility.

Strive to create positive, mutually beneficial relationships between instructors, students, and community partners. Students often encounter circumstances contrary to their idealistic expectations, so instructors should provide background information to help students understand the broader context. We model respectful interactions through our own participation in service side-by-side with the students. Faculty service strengthens bonds with community partners and helps when circumstances change. Our school was assigned a new principal just before the course began, but relationships established with school staff during our volunteering preserved the partnership through the transition.

Outcomes/Assessment

In this reciprocal relationship, we provide the school with tutors, and the school provides our students with valuable hands-on learning experiences. Service-learning represents a social contract between instructors, students, and the community. Therefore, it is important to document the benefits for all participants. Doing so may also serve as a tie-in to research programs.

Most service-learning research has focused on benefits to college students. We use journal entries and academic assignments to measure how tutoring enhances understanding of research on reading. However, effects of service-learning extend beyond course content to include personal development. As part of our research program, we document quantitative changes in students' achievement motivation goals, motives for volunteering, racial attitudes, and community service efficacy.

Less research focuses on benefits of service-learning to the community. However, providing program evaluation strengthens the partnership. Many community agencies depend on funding sources that demand evidence of efficacy. Our research assesses changes in children's achievement motivation goals and reading scores as a function of being tutored.

Conclusion

To ensure that service-learning is rewarding for all participants, instructors should (a) closely match the service-learning placement to course content, (b) develop assignments that encourage reflection and integration with course material, and (c) assess benefits for both students and community agencies. Students may find service-learning requirements burdensome, but our students enthusiastically endorse the experience as a meaningful learning tool. Faculty may find service-learning courses labor-intensive, but we enjoy teaching students who are more engaged in learning. With adequate guidance from instructors, students achieve richer understanding of course material while providing valuable community service.

UNDERSTANDING PLAY AT THE DISCOVERY CENTER

JOANNA J. CEMORE
MISSOURI STATE UNIVERSITY

Keywords: play, community engagement, development, science, civic values, civic responsibility

Introduction

Service in a play class came as a surprise to some students as they sat in the first day of the course "Play as Development." How are play and service connected? In the four years this course has been taught as service-learning, it has gone through continual changes. What works best for the students learning of the academic content? What is the most beneficial service to the community? And what experiences help students live the value of civic responsibility? These are the questions that guided the implementation of the service-learning project with a local science center.

Project Description

Students learned about the intricacies of play, assessed the needs of the science center, and created project ideas that would improve the amount of play and the quality of play at the science center. They did this by making exhibits more developmentally appropriate, more accessible, more attractive, and more ably facilitated by the staff of the center. Project ideas were disseminated through actual implementation of a project or a presentation on how the center could implement the project ideas.

Project Timeline

The first day of class, students are introduced to the university definition of service-learning that includes academic content, service to the community, and reflection (Citizen-

ship and Service-learning, n.d.). In essence, they will use their experiences to learn the course content and to help the community, and they will use multiple levels of reflection throughout the semester. Their projects begin the first day and run through the end of the semester.

During the second class period, the director of the Citizenship and Service-Learning office from the university meets with the class to explain the history of service-learning at the university and in the state. At this time, the director also discusses requirements such as hours needed and paperwork.

At the fourth meeting of the class, the education director of the science center comes to introduce the goals and mission of the science center, and what the students can expect when they visit the center. The students then meet at the science center to take a tour of the areas of the center in most need of help.

Students spend time in class discussing possible ideas following the visit. Two weeks later, the education director is back in the classroom where students share their ideas and receive feedback on their project ideas. After this exchange students are encouraged to continue brainstorming ideas. A few weeks later, the students form groups based on similar ideas to implement at the center. This semester six groups were formed, ranging from 2–5 students in each.

While students were provided in class time throughout

the semester to meet, the majority of the project was done out of class, per the directives of service-learning at their university (15+ unpaid, out of class hours). Each group met individually with the instructor of the course throughout the semester, and each student wrote reflections. The instructor read reflections throughout the semester to facilitate understanding and handling of the projects.

Steps for Implementation

To successfully execute this kind of teaching, planning is essential. The instructor needs to have a good relationship with the community partner, clear objectives, a clear plan for implementation, and effective reflection exercises in place.

The instructor spends a lot of time at the center outside of class time and communicating with the staff throughout the semester. Establishing a positive relationship with the community partner prior to the semester beginning helps this process go more smoothly and builds trust.

The instructor does not need to know the specifics of the project prior to the beginning of the semester, but she does need to know the purpose of the activity; what the students are supposed to experience, do, and learn. One of the biggest challenges is encouraging the students to do their own thing. Students typically want to know exactly what they need to do, and how. This project is different. The students create the projects themselves with checkpoints along the way to help them feel secure and ensure they are on the path to achieving the goals.

Effective reflection occurs on many levels. In this case, the students reflected in groups during class, as a class during progress discussions, with the community partner, and individually through written reflection. The most effective written reflection process this instructor used was a weekly journal that lasted five weeks of the projects' planning and implementation. Students were given copies of North Carolina's Service-learning Reflection Framework (Ash & Clayton, in progress). This framework guided students in reflection while allowing freedom to meet varied experiences. For example, each reflection began with a description of the experiences objectively, and then students answered one question from any of the three sections: (a) personal perspective, (b) civic perspective, and (c) academic perspective. Each section had 6–17 questions to choose for reflection. By the end of the semester, they needed to address each of the three areas at least once.

Outcomes/Assessment

The guiding questions for the project implementation are the guiding questions for assessment including academic learning, beneficial service, and civic values. Student objectives were measured through assignments, exams, process, presentations, reflections, group evaluations, community partner input, and instructor observation. This project is designed for the student to be the "expert" while working with the community partner. The students' understandings of the concepts show clearly in these interactions. The community partner is a valuable assessor of this project.

Civic responsibility was assessed through the reflections, presentations, and a pre-/post-test (an adapted version of the Virginia Tech Service-Learning Participant Profile and Service-Learning Evaluation {James-Deramo, 1998}). The pre-/post-test shows what most engaged students and their perceptions of their own learning.

Conclusion

Service-learning is a valuable way to teach that requires constant attention from the instructor to keep things moving effectively. It can be difficult at times for the students, the community partners, and the instructors. Even with the difficulties, time commitments, and obstacles, overwhelmingly the sentiment expressed from those involved was "it was worth it."

References

Ash, S. L., & Clayton, P. H. Teaching and Learning through Critical Reflection: An Instructor's Guide. Sterling, Virginia: Stylus Publishing. In progress.

Citizenship and Service-Learning (n.d.). *Definition of service-learning.* Retrieved January 5, 2007 from http://www.missouristate.edu/casl/

James-Deramo, M. (1998). *Pre- and Post-Course Questionnaire.* Blacksburg, VA: Service-learning Center at Virginia Tech.

The guiding questions for the project implementation are the guiding questions for assessment including academic learning, beneficial service, and civic values.

‖‖‖

THE SCHOOLS AND COMMUNITY PROJECT

MARK MALABY AND JON M. CLAUSEN
BALL STATE UNIVERSITY

Keywords: pre-service teachers, town/gown, social justice, social classification

Introduction

School administrators in the town where this project took place desire greater engagement between teachers and the communities where they teach. Similarly, a central tenet of our departmental mission statement is to instill in our students an awareness of social justice issues that are demonstrated through hands-on, immersive projects that provide service to the community. It was natural, then, to develop a partnership between our department and the local school district to work toward a deep understanding of the local community.

Project Description

The Schools and Communities project sends pre-service teachers into the local community during the semester prior to student teaching to learn about the lives of students and their families in this urban, high-poverty area.

At the beginning of the project students are divided into four teams and charged with exploring the qualities of (a) the school, (b) the economic lives of the residents, (c) residential and recreational life, and (d) the local values and ethics that are strongly held by community members. Over the course of the project, the students work to develop consistent themes, problems, successes, and areas of potential growth that at the end of the semester can be presented back to the local community. To facilitate these presentations, we develop a website and a DVD to document our findings.

Project Timeline

Prior to the beginning of the semester, students are sent an introductory e-mail and a link to the course handbook, which contains an overview of the course, prior projects, testimonials, weekly schedules, and answers to frequently asked questions.

During the first two weeks, students discuss preconceptions about the school and district they will be studying, attend presentations on local history and Q&A sessions with local school administrators, and tour the school.

Between week three and week twelve, student teams conduct research in the district.

Between week twelve and week fourteen, teams compile their research and prepare for presentations to the community.

During finals week, students gather at the school to present their research to faculty, staff, local community members, parents, and elected officials in a presentation lasting one to two hours.

Student Roadblocks

Since the vast majority of our education students are white, middle-class, and have little experience with poverty and racial diversity, this project can be seen as threatening. Early visits with local teachers and administrators, a school tour and neighborhood exploration, and historical and demographic research are all employed in order to provide a deeper and therefore less threatening context for the students involved.

Additionally, the scope of the project can be overwhelming for students. The development of a course pack that contains step-by-step tutorial and demonstrations will assist greatly in easing these concerns.

Community Roadblocks

There is a large divide between the university community and the local community along class and racial lines. Community members often feel that the University is condescending to the townspeople and are often initially suspicious of the motives of the research teams. The values of developing relationships with local gatekeepers and liaisons such as local business owners and community leaders cannot be overstated. There is also a fear within the schools that this project will be highly judgmental, which can lead to guarded responses from teachers and principals. A faculty member visit with the school faculty and staff regarding the project and its desire to assist the schools will do much to alleviate these concerns.

Steps for Implementation

Prior to start of project:
1. Contact local school administrators, explaining the program and outlining the benefits. Get necessary permissions.
2. Develop technical support team (often available within the University) for website or DVD production.
3. Develop a course handbook outlining all aspects of

the project, including rationale, tutorials, forms, and desired outcomes.

4. Meet with principal of school being studied in the upcoming semester to explain project and go over concerns.
5. Write a letter to students just prior to start of the semester giving them a glimpse into the project. Send them the handbook and an enthusiastic greeting!

During the project:
6. Have a guest with deep ties and knowledge of the neighborhood being studied visit the class. (We used the Assistant Superintendent, a life-long resident who is deeply immersed in the local community.)
7. Meet with the school faculty to introduce them to the project and ask for their support.
8. Offer tutorials for the necessary technology, including camera work, library archive research and database analysis (the DOE and Census websites are good starting points).
9. Set up presentation dates and times for a presentation, at the school, or research findings.
10. Have the students turn in their projects at least two weeks before the presentation date. Spend the rest of the semester practicing the presentation refining and combining the info into a central document.

After the project:
11. Gather feedback from the school after the presentation.
12. Reflect on successes and failures and revise for next time.
13. Work with administrators to determine next area being researched.
14. Return to step 4 and begin again.

Outcomes/Assessment

Student class evaluations have risen 20% since the inception of this project. Teachers and administrators in Muncie schools have expressed strong support for the project. There have been no dissenting voices so far.

Research framework for students

Research Side (How do I find it?)
■ Identify the questions and needed information–"What would a new teacher need to know about the school, businesses, neighborhoods and residents to teach at this school?"
■ Defining strategies to answer questions–"Where do I need to go to answer these questions?"
■ Locate and access resources–"Where can I go to conduct the interviews and find the data?"

Process Side (What do I do with it?)
■ Use the info–"How do I read the data?"
■ Synthesize Themes–"Out of all this information, what needs to be told?"
■ Dissemination–"How am I going to tell it?"

Conclusion

While the startup requirements for this project are rather high, the payoff is the chance to transform your teaching while providing a real service to local schools. By the end of the project, the students have built a real relationship with the local community, which is based on accurate information. The hope is that they will continue this work in their future careers.

Plan on a full semester in preparation before beginning the project, and use that time to make the local connections and set up the necessary technological support.

...developing relationships with local gatekeepers and liaisons such as local business owners and community leaders cannot be overstated.

A SERVICE-LEARNING MODEL FOR PRE-SERVICE TEACHER PREPARATION

ROBERT E. BLEICHER, MERILYN C. BUCHANAN AND MANUEL G. CORREIA
CALIFORNIA STATE UNIVERSITY CHANNEL ISLANDS

Keywords: community/university partnerships, town and gown, reflection, pre-service teachers, field experience

Introduction

"This experience allowed me to see myself in the future. Before, being a teacher was all in my head, but now I can actually see myself as a teacher." —Derek

This article describes a service-learning course, Introduction to Elementary Schooling (EDUC 101), which aligns a clear statement of community partner needs with student learning outcomes. With careful planning this service experience is neither contrived for student convenience nor are student learning outcomes add-ons to that experience. Reflection is fundamental in connecting service experiences to learning outcomes.

Project Description

Multiple sections of the course are conducted at two elementary schools involving nearly 600 elementary school children, 60 university students, and 30 classroom teachers. In participating classrooms, the teacher and two university undergraduate classroom tutors (CTs) form a team. CTs provide tutoring one morning each week for three hours over a 13-week period. Immediately following the classroom experience, all CTs meet with their professor at the site for an hour to debrief their experiences.

Project Timeline

Through our experience, we feel that planning a service-learning course minimally requires three months, although our project took about five months to arrange. As we have evolved into the sixth year of our partnership, modifications have been implemented. Below is an outline of the initial timeline.

1. **Faculty meetings with colleagues:** Determine a range of possible field experiences appropriate to helping students achieve program learning outcomes (two weeks).
2. **Department Chair/Dean meeting:** Discuss workload, FTE, tenure, and liability issues needing to be considered for a "non-traditional" field based, off campus course (two weeks).
3. **Contact possible community partners:** Discuss their needs and align with student learning outcomes (one month).
4. **Community partner meetings:** Work through the chain of management described below; collaborate with classroom teachers to revise student learning outcomes and parameters of the service experience to maximize benefits to both partners (two months).
5. **Course syllabus:** Finalize and route it through the university's new course approval process (one month).

Steps for Implementation

Planning a service-learning course is premised on forming a strong community-university partnership. There are many steps to course implementation. The following covers the essentials to ensure success:

- Start with the people who manage the workplace in which students will be placed; in our project, the district superintendent and principals;
- With the managers' permission, begin discussions with the people in charge of the work site in which students will be doing their service field experiences; in our project, the classroom teachers;

- Plan on several meetings (if you're not getting tired of meetings, you probably have not called enough!);
- Work with the university advising staff so that students come to the new course understanding the philosophy of service-learning and with reasonable expectations.

Outcomes/Assessment

At a minimum, a service-learning course should help students develop skills and attitudes in two broad areas, learning to serve and serving to learn.

Learning to Serve
- Increase motivation, challenge participants to reflect/think critically about and learn from their experiences, and enhance understanding of real-world complexity
- Develop a spirit of service
- Meet needs the community finds important

Serving to Learn
In a service-learning course, learning outcomes require close alignment with the service experience. As an example, the learning outcomes for students in EDUC 101 include:
- Tutor K-5 children and demonstrate sensitivity to diverse learners' needs;
- Reflect on interactions with children by keeping a journal and participating in-group discussions;
- Describe and interpret the role of the classroom teacher in meeting the social, emotional, and cognitive needs of children;
- Discuss various classroom practices including models of organization, instruction and methods to meet diverse learners' needs.

In a university course, written and oral assignments require assessment. But in the case of a service-learning course, assessment should also involve collecting evidence that students have developed substantial skills and attitudes related to the learning to serve outcomes outlined above. We advise a combination of both open-ended, more qualitative data and quantitative surveys. Our most cogent data source was electronic journals in which CTs responded to reflection writing prompts (Correia & Bleicher, 2008). We also collected Likert-scale surveys about professional dispositions and work ethic from both CTs and their supervising teachers. As a pre-measure, we collect background information from students about their experiences in a school setting and their notions about teaching from a "draw myself as a teacher" activity. In addition, having more than one section allowed for rich discussions among the three instructors about the course, the school setting, and the CTs' experiences.

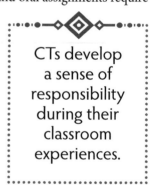

CTs develop a sense of responsibility during their classroom experiences.

The evidence we have collected indicates that CTs feel they experience what teaching involves in a real-world classroom setting. There is frequent mention of developing a "real" understanding of teaching compared to more theoretical ideas formed through "traditional" courses and previous brief visits to classrooms. Also, it is evident that CTs develop a sense of responsibility during their classroom experiences. As the project progresses, CTs demonstrate a keen focus on assisting children in the classroom.

Faculty teaching this course meet regularly to discuss possible course improvements. We discuss CTs' progress and identify challenges, areas for improvement, and successes of the project. We elicit formal and informal feedback from classroom teachers and principals about how our project can be improved. We also meet with professors teaching service-learning courses in other disciplines to share ideas and practices.

Conclusion

EDUC 101 has successfully run for six years. The impact on our students has been profound. Factors that were strongly affected through the program were the attitude and beliefs of the CTs, particularly confidence and self-esteem. According to the teachers and principals, as well as direct observations by the course professors, the extra tutoring and pro-social interactions with the university students have increased the children's learning. Such outcomes and conclusions are beneficial and can be expected from a service-learning course that has been carefully crafted.

References

Correia, M. G. & Bleicher, R. E. (2008). Making connections to teach reflection. *Michigan Journal of Community Service Learning,* 14(2), 41-49.

REACHING CHILDREN AND FAMILIES OF NATURAL DISASTERS THROUGH SERVICE-LEARNING

RUSSELL L. CARSON
LOUISIANA STATE UNIVERSITY

Keywords: natural disasters, after-school programming, underserved youth

Introduction

From earthquakes to tsunamis, hurricanes to tornadoes, and volcanoes to wildfires, natural disasters can happen in every region of the US. As recently as the fall of 2005, this country was reminded of the catastrophic impact when one strikes. Hurricanes Katrina and Rita were powerful tropical storms that forced hundreds of thousands of Gulf Coast residents to search for new homes (Wikipedia, 2008). While some turned to families and nearby friends, the majority were evacuated to government-funded, travel trailer communities for short-term housing relief (DHS, 2006). The repercussion was one of crisis and vulnerability, and demanded a menu of service responses to those affected. As demonstrated in this article, service-learning projects can be one form of university assistance that can help families and children regain the health and livelihood they once knew before a natural disaster. A service-learning project that successfully accomplished this goal was Lifetime Exercise and Physical Activity Service-learning (LE PAS).

Project Description

In conjunction with several educational initiatives offered by local, state, and Louisiana State University (LSU) service providers, LE PAS was established as an after-school program devoted to attending to the myriad of physical and social needs of youth displaced after the 2005 hurricanes to Renaissance Village (FEMA-run, 550+ travel trailer living community). The primary purpose of LE PAS was to promote the importance of regular, lifelong physical activity with displaced K-12 youth through structured, cooperative, fun-filled outdoor activities. Equally, LE PAS provided future allied health professionals (e.g., physical education teachers, physical therapists, fitness directors, rehabilitation specialists, etc.) hands-on experience planning, implementing, and observing (inherent cognitive, social, and physical processes) interactive human movement. LE PAS was the first opportunity for many college students to work (a) with a youth population, and (b) in an impoverished setting, allowing them to broaden their career skill set in ways beyond a classroom-only approach. The project was initially geared for K-5 children, and later expanded to include teens.

...allowing them to broaden their career skill set in ways beyond a classroom-only approach.

LE PAS was conducted on a large outdoor play area (including two playgrounds, a turf-covered gathering area, and a water play area), every Monday through Thursday for 60–90 minutes, immediately following a collaborative after-school tutoring program. Activities included a wide range of aerobic/rhythmic movements, cooperative challenges, and lifetime sports. Paid LE PAS instructors (i.e., graduate assistants and former LE PAS undergraduate students) were on site each day to oversee and lead activities as needed. LE PAS was primarily integrated as a semester-long assignment in two courses: Lifespan Motor Development and Curriculum Construction in Physical Education (Carson, 2008).

Project Timeline

LE PAS was certainly not developed overnight. Several steps were followed that might be useful to other faculty seeking to establish a service-learning project. For this reason, they are presented in general terms below.

1. Arrange an individual meeting with your university's service-learning office (or equivalent). In one hour, you will leave with information galore regarding examples of successful service-learning courses, list of networking opportunities (e.g., conferences, listservs, faculty scholars, etc.), possible funding sources and journal outlets, potential community partners, and more. For an example, refer to LSU's Center for Community Engagement, Learning, and Leadership (http://appl003 .lsu.edu/slas/ccell/ccell.nsf/index).

2. Reach out to colleagues who have or are implementing a service-learning project. They can provide you with valuable hands-on information such as "do's and don'ts" and "best-kept secrets" that might help you mold and shape your project's plans.

3. Wait for a disaster to strike. Well, not really. Natural disasters may strike intermittently, but crisis situations are everywhere and worthy of well-orchestrated service-learning projects. Contact national (e.g., Americorps; http://www.americorps.org/), state (e.g., Campus Compact; http://www.compact.org/) or local (e.g., big buddy programs; http://www.bigbuddyprogram.org/ us/) service providers for a crisis near you.

Steps for Implementation

1. **Give it a catchy name.** It not only aids in identifying your project, but can excite students, community partners and grant agencies too. LE PAS, meaning "the step" in French, was purposefully conceived to do just that!

2. **Familiarize yourself with the service-learning site.** Get acquainted with the entry procedures, available facilities and resources, on-site personnel, etc., and clearly explain to the community partner the services your project intends to provide. Also, early in the semester, devote a class period to do the same with your partici-

pating students. This way, they know how to get there and what to do once there, both of which can help reduce their initial concerns and be reflection topics for class discussions.

3. **Logistics, logistics, logistics.** Every service-learning project will have unavoidable logistical issues that must be dealt with each semester. For LE PAS, they were scheduling students for each session, getting students to and from the site, and obtaining and transporting needed equipment. Map out a plan of attack for your project and be ready to make adjustments over time.

4. **Enjoy it!** Once your project is rolling, get out there, observe, and interact with your students in action, and reward yourself by joining in the fun and civic learning that you helped create.

5. **Whenever and however possible, spread the word about your project.** Local news stations, university websites, and service-learning offices can kindly spotlight your project. Also, try to disseminate your project at conferences and in scholarly journals.

Outcomes/Assessment

The goal is always to produce a long-lasting, successful project. Identify outcomes (i.e., personal, social, learning, career) that you feel demonstrate service-learning success (Eyler, et al., 2001), and find ways to assess them (e.g., reflections via the ORID model, valid questionnaires, anecdotal evidence) among your college students and participating community partners (Shoemaker and Dill, 2008). For example, throughout its six-semester existence, LE PAS enlisted a total of 141 undergraduate service-learning students, and served an average of 28 K-12 children and 12 teens a day.

The goal is always to produce a long-lasting, successful project.

Conclusions

As the projected paths of storms can shift and redirect their course, so can service-learning projects. LE PAS was never implemented the same way across two consecutive semesters. Therefore, a final of piece of advice: remain flexible and patient with the ever-changing tides of service-learning, especially when developing a project in the aftermath of a natural disaster.

References

Carson, R. L. (2008). Introducing the Lifetime Exercise and Physical Activity Service-Learning (LE PAS) Program.

Journal of Physical Education, Recreation and Dance, 79(1), 18-22, 35.

Eyler, J. S., Giles, D. E., Stenson, C. M., & Gray, C. J. (2001). At a glance: *What we know about the effects of service-learning on college students, faculty, institutions and communities, 1993-2000 (3rd ed.).* Retrieved July 31, 2008, from http://www.servicelearning.org/pubs/index.php

Shoemaker, J., & Dill, R. (2008). *Service-learning faculty partner handbook.* Retrieved July 31, 2008, from http://

appl003.lsu.edu/slas/ccell/facultyinfo.nsf/$Content/Handbook+for+Faculty?OpenDocument

U.S. Department of Homeland Security, Federal Emergency Management Agency. (2006, August 30). *Hurricane Katrina – One year later.* Retrieved February 22, 2006 from http:// www.fema.gov/hazard/hurricane/2005katrina/anniversary.shtm

Wikipedia. *Hurricane Katrina.* Retrieved July 2008 from http://en.wikipedia.org/wiki/Hurricane_Katrina

INVENTING PEDAGOGY AND METHODS: OPPORTUNITIES FOR SERVICE AND LEARNING IN THE PREPARATION OF PRE-SERVICE TEACHERS FOR URBAN CLASSROOMS

MARGARET-MARY SULENTIC DOWELL
LOUISIANA STATE UNIVERSITY

Keywords: urban classrooms, teacher preparation, post-Katrina, literacy, reading program

Introduction

Teacher preparation programs grapple with the complicated and intricate issues surrounding preparing white teachers to work effectively with children of color and their families in public school systems in urban areas. Disconnection can occur and tensions can surface in classrooms around issues of ethnicity, culture, race, and socioeconomic difference (Andrews, 1993; Delpit, 1994 & 1995; Anyon, 1995; Cazden, 1996). Tensions that arise as a result of dissonance between teachers and the cultural orientation of classrooms and children's home culture affect learning and teaching (Au, 2006). To help address this disconnect, universities and school districts partnering in teacher education preparation should explicitly address the educational impact of culture, ethnicity, and economic difference in urban systems by incorporating Academic Service-Learning (AS-L) components in teacher education coursework. Urban school systems are often portrayed as crumbling infrastructures and characterized by inadequate resources and low reading scores. Using literature and providing access to books is a cornerstone of reading development (Neuman, 1999; Smith, Constantio, & Krashen, 1996).

A sustained body of research suggests accessing reading material readily, frequently, and in abundance increases fluency (Allington, 2001; Armbruster, Lehr, & Osborn, 2001), influences vocabulary development (Snow, Burns & Griffin, 1998), and promotes comprehension (Guthrie, Schafer, Vaon Secker & Alban, 2000). In order for children to learn to read and to improve reading proficiency, they need time to read independently daily (Morrow & Gambrell, 2000; Shefelbine, 2000). Classroom libraries provide the access to literature and the environment that contributes to reading competence.

Project Description

Oftentimes, access to quality literature is denied urban children. Post-Katrina, the New Orleans area faced both frightening and fascinating challenges as it recovered, rebuilt and underwent a rebirth in terms of educational reform. Nowhere was that more apparent than in education. When Abramson Science and Technology Charter School opened in August 2007, they didn't have electricity, much less a library. Still running on generators as late as December 2007, stocked bookshelves were a dream in a school contained in temporary trailers and surrounded by demolished or condemned buildings. The national average of access to books for school aged children is 22 books to every child; in the greater Los Angeles area the number drops to 5 books per child (Ruurs, 2008). At Abramson in New Orleans East in 2007, there were 0 books per child.

As an assistant professor of reading education at Louisiana State University (LSU) in Baton Rouge, I was aware immense needs existed in the fledgling Recovery School District (RSD) created just prior to Katrina. Recognizing a carefully crafted, implemented, and monitored course-imbedded service opportunity could help prepare education majors to teach in an urban environment while greatly supporting a recovering school such as Abramson, the Abramson Book Project was conceived (see www.lsu.edu/coe/books).

The goal of this project was two-fold: (a) establish classroom libraries for all K-8 classrooms and teachers who taught language arts at Abramson, and (b) involve undergraduate teacher education majors enrolled in a required methods course with opportunities to apply knowledge of quality and culturally appropriate books. That goal represented a target amount of 7,600 books.

Table 1.1. Timeline of Activities for the Abramson Book Project.

7/2007	assessed public school needs, met with school administration, shared project
8/2007	conducted in-service at school, informed colleagues of project, gained support
9/2007	web site website, distributed poster, book lists created, met with Lab School faculty
10/2007	began collection, sorting, delivery of books, visits/faculty meetings @Abramson
11/2007 – 2/2008	collection, sorting, delivery of books, visits/faculty meetings @Abramson
3/2008	collection, sorting, delivery of books, met with Abramson elementary/LA faculty
4/2008	collection, sorting, delivery of books, visited Abramson with spring class & Dean
5/2008	final delivery of books to Abramson, created College bulletin board, sent thank you's

Steps for Implementation

1. Prior to the beginning of any service project, assessing the needs of service providers and recipients is paramount.
2. My next step was to meet with Abramson's administration in July 2007, a month prior to classes beginning. I also secured an enthusiastic champion in the Dean of our college. Garnering support from the entire college faculty ensured success to meet the project goal of 7,600 books.
3. In August, I conducted a morning in-service with the entire Abramson faculty, then worked with elementary and language arts staff during the afternoon. By the time fall 2007 classes began, a web site and posters advertising the project were available.
4. In September, students enrolled in my methods course created lists of preferred books for classroom libraries in an effort to guide donations of new and gently used books.
5. By October, donations began to pour in as my fellow instructors and professors encouraged their students to donate books. I met with Lab School staff to pitch the idea and coordinate donations. As part of course activities, students sorted donated books for Abramson classrooms. Class discussions of donated books went far beyond, 'Is this age appropriate?' We discussed inclusion of books about religion, firearms, war, and weaponry, even the history of gangs. I transported all books to Abramson. In October, I made two visits to Abramson, visiting and delivering during regularly scheduled faculty meetings. Ever mindful of Abramson's own school calendar, I made two deliveries during December, coinciding with faculty meetings, and began visiting individual classrooms.
6. In January, I unveiled the project to the students enrolled in the spring semester class. Their response was extremely enthusiastic. During January and February, I made two monthly visits, delivering books, visiting classes, and attending faculty meetings. The Dean's former colleague from Oklahoma collected, donated, and personally delivered over 2,000 books while attending the ASCD conference in March in New Orleans.
7. On April 7th, all but one LSU student made the trip to New Orleans East and Abramson. The administration greeted LSU students and after unloading a truck load of books, assigned students to individual classrooms for some hands-on fieldwork. Abramson faculty were appreciative of the extra assistance and LSU students reveled in seeing the fruits of their labor displayed in classrooms and being accessed by students. Table 1.1 highlights the projects timeline.

Outcomes/Assessment

Engagement, involvement, and sustainability are the earmarks of successful service-learning projects. Such measures can be slippery and difficult to assess. Throughout the entire project, students enrolled in my assigned courses enthusiastically sorted books according to the range appropriate to specific grade levels. Classroom conversations were rich and generative regarding the place of literature in language arts instruction and opportunity to access literature. One of my departmental colleagues became involved assisting with sorting. The entire departmental secretarial staff, along with the Dean's administrative assistant, continually scouted for boxes for delivery. Considering that moving books from Baton Rouge to New Orleans East was occasionally problematic in inclement weather, my chair made sure the project was supplied with enough plastic garbage bags to cover all those boxes of books. And one student, enamored with her visiting experience, approached me wanting to explore options to student teach at Abramson.

This project epitomized the essence of academic service-learning, collegial collaboration, and community involvement. The entire College of Education enthusiastically assisted as a community of learners and supporters, and both service providers and recipients of the service received mutually beneficial, reciprocal benefits. The final number of books delivered to Abramson was 8,665 books, surpassing the established goal by 1,065 volumes.

Conclusion

This project exemplified academic service-learning, both provider and recipients were involved, the benefits were mutually beneficial and through the project, a strengthened community emerged. Most of the students in the course were from white, middle-income families and educated in private or parochial schools—a stark contrast to the demographics of the student, teacher, and administration at the Abramson school, which consists mainly of African-American, Vietnamese, and Hispanic students. Through their work and involvement, LSU students expanded their cultural horizons and frames of reference while strengthening preparation for teaching in one of the most challenging urban environments in the nation, all while providing a valuable service. The Abramson students received much-needed books, while university entities assisted with the vital rebuilding of a community school.

References

Allington, R. (2001). What really matters for struggling readers: Designing research-based programs. New York: Addison-Wesley.

Armbruster, B., Lehr, F. & Osborn, J. (Eds.). (2001). *Putting reading first: The research building blocks for teaching children to read.* Washington, D.C.: The National Institute for Literacy.

Andrews, L. (1993). *Language exploration and awareness: A resource book for teachers.* White Plains, New York: Longman.

Anyon, J. (1995). Race, social class and educational reform in an inner-city school. *Teachers College Record, 97*, 69-94.

Au, W. (2005-06). Conversations on quality: An interview with Gloria Ladsen-Billings. *Rethinking schools, 20,* 36-37.

Cazden, C. (1996). How knowledge about language helps the classroom teacher–or does it? In B. Power and R. Hubbard (Eds.), *Language Development* (pp. 8-15). Englewood Cliffs, New Jersey: Prentice Hall.

Delpit, L. (1994). Seeing color. In B. Bigelow, L. Christensen, S. Karp, B. Miner & B. Peterson (Eds.), Rethinking Our Classrooms: Teaching for Equity and Justice (Vol. 1: 158-161). Milwaukee, Wisconsin: Rethinking Our Schools, Ltd.

Guthrie, J., Schafer, W., Vaon Secker, C. & Alban, T. (2000). Contributions of integrated reading instruction and text resources to achievement and engagement in statewide school improvement program. *Journal of Educational Research, 93:* 211-226.

Morrow, L. & Gambrell, L. (2000). Literature-based reading instruction. In M. Kamil, P. Mosenthal, P.D. Pearson, & R. Barr, (Eds.). *Handbook of Reading Research* (pp. 563-586). Mahwah, NJ: Earlbaum.

Neuman, S. (1999). Books make a difference: A study of access to literacy. *Reading Research Quarterly, 34:* 286-311.

Ruurs, M. (2008, February/March). Two programs put books in children's hands *Reading Today,* 31.

Shefelbine, J. (2000). *Reading voluminously and voluntarily.* New York: The Scholastic Center For Literacy and Learning.

Snow, C., Burns, S. & Griffin, P.(Eds.) (1998). *Preventing reading difficulties in young children.* Washington, D.C.: National Academy Press.

Smith, C., Constantio, B., & Krashen, S. (1996). Differences in print environments for children in Beverly Hills, Compton & Watts. *Emergency Librarian,* 24: 8-10.

MEETING THE CHALLENGE OF IMPLEMENTING SERVICE-LEARNING WITH IN-SERVICE TEACHERS

JUDY DONOVAN
INDIANA UNIVERSITY NORTHWEST

Keywords: graduate students, teacher education, in-service teachers, diversity, pre-service teacher, race, class, gender

Introduction

An online graduate course, Issues in Education: Race, Class and Gender, was completed by in-service teachers. The goals of the course were to have students increase their awareness of educational inequities involving race, class and gender; recognize and examine their beliefs; and identify ways to promote social justice in schools. Because practicing teachers often view the educational system through a lens derived from personal experience, a required service-learning assignment was designed to expand their viewpoints.

Project Description

Student Instructions:
- The service-learning assignment requires you to choose a school or non-profit organization serving PK12 students. To maximize benefits, select a site where you will be exposed to individuals of a socioeconomic class, gender or race/ethnicity with whom you do not normally interact.
- To find your site, utilize the class discussion forum, e-mail classmates, and actively look for service-learning activities in your school you can offer classmates. If you have made a strong effort and are unable to plan your service-learning activities by Week 4, contact me for help.

Assignment Description:
1. Find an appropriate site at which to perform service, and create a service plan. In your plan, identify the educational organization, the demographics of the school (race, income levels, test scores), and the site person who will oversee your service-learning. The Service-learning Plan is due in week 4.
2. Plan a minimum of 10 hours performing service. Service is defined as activity which benefits members of the organization you are working with. Observation, while valuable, does not count toward service hours. Most activities which involve direct interaction with students do qualify, such as chaperoning, tutoring, coaching, and teaching. Spread the required hours over a minimum of four visits. Complete two hours by the end of week 6.
3. Log your experiences in your journal, including dates, times, and activity description. Entries in your service-learning journal must chronicle your on-site experiences, and relate to course materials, assignments and discussions.

Steps for Implementation

Before the course begins, plan the service-learning activity to meet learning outcomes. Contact local schools and agencies to find placement sites, or plan to rely on students to find their own site. Be prepared with a few sites students can utilize on weekends (community centers, YMCA, etc.) for those who cannot find a placement. Include a notation that the course has a service-learning component in the schedule of courses and the institution registration website. Explain the assignment during the first class meeting. Allow students plenty of time (at least a month) to set up their placements. Have a letter ready explaining the assignment (for principals and classroom teachers who ask students for this). Reassure students periodically that they can find the time and their learning will be worth the effort. Conduct evaluation during and after the class with students, measurement of learning outcomes, and community partners.

Project Timeline

The timeline in Table 1.2 lists the major tasks comprising the service-learning assignment. Students may wonder how, as full time teachers, they can spend time in another school setting. The instructor may suggest placement sites which can be utilized before or after work hours, such as a Native American Center, YMCA or Boys and Girls Club.

In week 4, students submit the Service-learning Plan, which details placement specifics (planned activities, people involved), and contrasts their service-learning site with their home school.

In week 6, students submit the first of several focused journal reflections, which relate the service-learning to the coursework. The last week of class students reflect on and assess the service-learning.

Table 1.2. Service-learning Timeline.

Timeframe	Task	Responsibility
Before course	Research placement sites	Instructor
First day of class	Communicate assignment	Instructor
First month of class	Find placements	Students
Week 4	Service-learning Plan	Students
Week 6	Complete 2 hours at site	Students
Throughout semester	Complete 10 hours at site	Students
Last week of semester	Service-learning evaluation	Students
	Final journal entry	Students
Last week of semester	Contact site supervisors to verify hours, determine benefits to site	Instructor
After course	Evaluate student experiences, revision	Instructor

Table 1.3. Comparison of Schools Example.

	Urban School	Rural School
Enrollment	493	531
Free Lunch	81%	5%
Ethnicity:		
White	3	494
Hispanic	208	25
Black	275	4
Multi-racial	6	3
Asian	0	5
Test Scores	Passed 39%	Passed 75%
Single Parent	27%	10%
Median Income	$26,538	$45,799
Below Poverty	24%	9%

Outcomes/Assessment

The final exam and course evaluation measured course success. Final exam results reveal students examined their beliefs, and plan to work for social equity in their classrooms, schools and communities. Aggregate course evaluations scores were 4.67 of 5.0, indicating high levels of student satisfaction.

> The evaluation results indicate 95% of the students rated the service-learning "very worthwhile" or "worthwhile" and many commented that the assignment changed them personally and professionally.

Benefits of the service-learning experience were measured through the service-learning evaluation and the last journal entry. The evaluation results indicate 95% of the students rated the service-learning "very worthwhile" or "worthwhile" and many commented that the assignment changed them personally and professionally.

In the last journal entry, students wrote about what they had learned through service-learning. Themes emerged which indicate the experience exposed students to different points of view, revealed racism and sexism still exist, related class readings to the real world, and raised awareness of inequities.

Student comments:

- Service-learning has been a very positive experience for me. I was able to focus in on the issues faced by young women in our culture, and observe my own blindness to things that were just a daily part of my middle class "whiteness." How difficult was it for me to see issues in race when I was so much a part of the majority there…
- It is essential for us to get out into the world and truly see the issues we've been discussing. It's so easy to brush off their importance when we're not face to face with them.
- I found myself thinking of our forums, readings, and assignments while at my service-learning site.
- In theory I gained valuable knowledge and learned about uneven playing fields, gender gaps, stereotypes, racism, glass ceilings, poverty; but the hands on observation put a face to the theory.

Conclusion

The service-learning assignment helped students achieve course goals, through increased awareness of issues of power, resources and equality in education. Factors which worked with the service-learning to make the course a success include students' choosing their placements, the online format of the class freeing hours for service-learning, reflective journal assignments, and the richness and candor of online discussions.

The service-learning assignment described can be modified for other disciplines, as many areas of study have an "issues" or "ethics" discipline specific class. Service-learning helps students who have worked as professionals find a new lens to examine their volunteer site, and their no-longer-as-familiar workplace and community.

ENCOURAGING YOUTH PHILANTHROPY

INGRID ROGERS
MANCHESTER COLLEGE

Keywords: foundation, philanthropy, YES initiative, millennial, youth, community

Introduction

Young people often possess unique visions of how to improve the world around them but lack the financial means to make these visions a reality. In North Manchester, Indiana, a program was created through a partnership between the university and the community to involve college students and high-school youth in philanthropic projects to enable them to pursue their dreams for the good of the larger community.

Project Description

The YES initiative (Youth Engaged in Service) invites high school students to submit a proposal aiming at improving the community they live in. This proposal is composed of a written application accompanied by a detailed explanation of their financial needs.

The projects are selected by a committee of university and community partners, with award winners receiving grants of up to $1000. Preference is given to projects that a) empower youth to plan and implement service projects to meet community needs; b) recognize and promote youth as volunteers; c) educate youth to become philanthropists; and d) foster youth-adult partnerships.

Timeline

This program works on a six-month cycle and is structured as follows:

First Month: Form an Advisory Board and recruit service-learning faculty partners
Second Month: Develop grant application materials and distribute it
Third Month: Meet with faculty using YES service-engagement component
Fourth Month: Guide youth in their proposals
Fifth Month: Distribute awards and aid youth in securing funds and supplies
Sixth Month: Celebrate projects with ceremonies and events

The application deadlines are October 15 or April 15. Once accepted, the project needs to be completed within six months.

Steps for Implementation

Step 1: Forming an Advisory Board
A group of people who share your enthusiasm for youth philanthropy is recruited. They flesh out grant guidelines, recruit youth to participate, evaluate proposals, and provide an administrative framework. This Advisory Board includes representatives from the local high school (teachers, students from all grades, and parents), the college (instructors and students), and the wider community (youth pastors, community foundation members, etc.). Board members commit to meet monthly the first year, then quarterly in subsequent years.

Step 2: Developing Grant Application Materials
To develop the grant applications materials[1] , we looked at other similar programs in Indiana, such as Youth as Resources (YAR), the KEYS program of Kosciusko County, and the Youth Philanthropy Initiative of Indiana (YPII). A number of national and state organizations have developed programs with structures, mission statements, and award processes that can serve as models too.

Step 3: Involving the College
The YES program fosters student engagement as part of several college courses in a variety of academic disciplines. The participating instructors tie the philanthropy program experiences to the learning objectives of their courses:

- Entrepreneurial Studies/Non-profit Management: Students assess community resources, do market research, survey the community for possible projects, find potential donors or YES candidates, and evaluate the benefits of the program.
- English and Composition Courses: Students draft and revise award applications, feature the program in college or town publications, write grants, and serve as teacher/mentor by helping high-school students edit and polish their manuscripts.
- Graphic Design. The first year, we collaborated with students in a graphic design course. The students developed a brochure for an initial program

---

1. The application materials (brochure, forms, and program description) for the YES initiative can be acquired by contacting the author.

presentation, including pictures, a brief program description, deadlines, and contact addresses. They also assembled a visually attractive packet that one could use for approaching potential donors. They crafted a logo to appear on all materials, using the YES acronym and suggesting youthful energy and excitement. Finally, they made T-shirts with the logo, for YES board members and YES winners.

Step 4: Guiding Youth With Their Proposals

College students help their youth peers through the following process:

- Identify a local need and talk about it with representatives of the agency or group they want to strengthen.
- Present their project at a YES board meeting for feedback. Based on this report the YES board advises the candidate, suggesting contacts or adult sponsors, pointing out pitfalls to avoid, and giving encouragement.
- Develop a detailed plan including a timeline and budget and a 250-to-500-word essay formulating their project idea. In this essay, they indicate when and where their project will take place and who they will work with.
- Find three adult sponsors who think the project is feasible, one of whom will write a letter of support.

The finished proposals are then evaluated by a review board and either selected as winners or sent back for further revision. The review board consists of a group of high school students representing each grade level, assisted by a college student and a YES board representative.

Step 5: Securing Funding

In order to raise the necessary money, YES board members present the program to various organizations, local businesses, and civic clubs (Rotary, Kiwanis, and Lions). This also raises community awareness about the initiative. Schools can apply for funds through the county's Community Foundation.

Step 6: Celebrating the Projects

Approximately two weeks after the selection of grant winners, the students are recognized at a public event attended by parents, sponsors, friends, and project participants, along with agency representatives, YES board members, and reporters from local newspapers. The winners receive a certificate and the achievements of the youth are reported in the media.

Outcomes/Assessment

The immediate outcomes of this project are the good deeds that result from students' funded projects. By participating in the YES program, students develop philanthropy awareness. Moreover, they gain increased communication skills, leadership ability, relational and team-building competency, grant-writing experience, personal satisfaction from helping the community, and self-confidence from seeing one's project to completion.

Millennials, the generation currently entering high schools and colleges, have been recognized to be more civic minded and concerned with the community they live.

Assessment is accomplished primarily through indirect methods. During the biannual celebration, the YES winners describe their envisioned projects. Those who have concluded the six months of the previous award cycle report on how they reached their goals and what the community gained from it.

The work of collaborating college students is evaluated by individual instructors through reflection papers and portfolios, among other means of assessing learning goals.

Conclusion

Millennials, the generation currently entering high schools and colleges, have been recognized to be more civic minded and concerned with the community they live in: "Millennial teens are hard at work on a grassroots reconstruction of community, teamwork and civic spirit" (Howe and Strauss 2000). The YES program provides them with a structure to unleash their creativity in identifying a need around them, devising a plan to address it and working in a team to successfully carry out the plan. Students involved in this program are therefore not mere executors but empowered agents of the changes to be made. And by engaging the entire community, their work becomes holistic.

Reference

Howe, N. & Strauss, W. (2000). *Millennials rising: The next great generation*. New York: Vintage Books.

||||||||||||||||||||||||||||||||||||||||||||||||||||||||||||||||||||||||||||||||||||||||||||||||||||||||||||||||||||||||||||||||||||||||||||||||

LEARNING TO TEACH THROUGH SERVING OTHERS: THE S.M.A.R.T. TUTORING AND ENRICHMENT PROGRAM

NATAKI WATSON, ELIZABETH A. BARBER, AND TOM SMITH
NORTH CAROLINA AGRICULTURAL AND TECHNICAL STATE UNIVERSITY

Keywords: teacher preparation, urban impact schools, pre-service teachers, tutoring, mentoring

Introduction

Beginning in the spring 2007 semester, 40–50 pre-service teachers from North Carolina Agricultural and Technical State University have tutored 70–80 children from a nearby highly impacted urban school as part of the S.M.A.R.T. Tutoring and Enrichment Program (Service, Mentoring, Achievement, Responsibility, Teamwork). These students are drawn from foundation-level education courses to work in pairs with groups of four to six children who are bused to the university twice weekly for two-hour literacy tutoring sessions. Children considered at risk for success on state standards tests are nominated by their school, and organized into groups based on reading levels.

Project Description

S.M.A.R.T. aims to help pre-service teachers develop the dispositions and skills for success in highly impacted urban schools. A major component of their preparation involves the use of service-learning as a pedagogy of empowerment. S.M.A.R.T. engagements breathe life into university course objectives for best practice literacy teaching. The leveled texts used for tutorial reading instruction consist of the finest in children's literature to reinforce state curriculum standards in the content areas (math, science, social studies). Acquisitions also include books that reflect the children's cultural heritages, support English language learners, and ground the service projects completed by tutoring groups across the term.

> Opportunities to serve others re-position children and tutors as helpers, not just recipients of service.

Opportunities to serve others re-position children and tutors as helpers, not just recipients of service. Experienced S.M.A.R.T. tutors provide input for ongoing program development, and take leadership positions within the program as site directors, peer mentors, and/or tutor trainers.

Project Timeline

1. **Prior to the semester:** Hold a half-day Saturday Start-Up Conference which opens with a get-to-know-you brunch at which tutors find a partner, and are assigned a reading level. Next, experienced tutors and program directors model the four components of a tutoring session—Read Aloud, Word Study, Guided Reading and Writing Workshop—within the context of a service-learning lesson plan.

2. **Weeks 1–2:** Tutors meet without tutees two hours twice a week for "Tutor Work Days" that consist of intensive training by peer leaders and program directors in the four components of the tutoring model, as well as in democratic group management techniques and service-learning as a literacy pedagogy. Tutors review the S.M.A.R.T. portfolios of their tutees and prepare lesson plans. Time is also reserved for school visits in which tutors observe tutees at work in their classrooms, and have lunch with them and their teachers.

3. **Weeks 3–4:** At the end of this preparation time of 3 ½ to 4 weeks, tutees arrive on campus for regular tutoring sessions which strategically take place in the Memorial Student Union on campus, and are presided over by peer site directors, a peer mentor for each reading level (1–5), and program directors. Tutors share responsibility for each session. At first, one tutors and the other takes detailed field notes, to split the difficult demands of both carrying out a session and observing child progress. Eventually, some tutor pairs merge the roles and both tutor at the same time.

4. **Weeks 5–14:** During the term students in the counseling track at the university do "counseling and guidance days," special education students and faculty provide support with strategies. Children get a campus tour that includes viewing robots in the College of Engineering (for which the university is famous), and visiting dorm rooms. During school holidays and on other days as needed, periodic "Tutor Work Days" allow times for guided reflection and ongoing tutorial support.

5. **Weeks 14–16:** At the end of each term, children self-assess using their S.M.A.R.T. portfolios, set future learning goals, and brainstorm strategies for reaching these. Whenever possible, tutors facilitate child portfolio conferences with their tutees' families, and meet

with school faculty to share input and plan together. A celebration at which children and tutors receive certificates of completion closes each term.

Steps for Implementation

Gaining full trust and collaboration of a partner school is critical to program success. Representatives of the University's Teaching Fellows Program met with an interested principal and extensive co-planning took place over a full semester prior to program implementation. Ongoing program evaluation and collaboration of the partners, respect, and a true desire to learn from each other characterize the university-school partnership.

Outcomes/Assessment

To date, three semesters of intensive tutoring have yielded gains for both tutors and children. Pre- and post-assessments and child portfolios allow tutors and tutees to reflect on accomplishments and to develop a strong sense of efficacy. The child-and-tutor learning communities that form each term consistently report gains in child word study, reading and writing levels, with our two partner elementary schools achieving Adequate Yearly Progress (No Child Left Behind

Act) for the first time in many years. However, with nearly one third of children changing schools each year, school success constitutes an ongoing struggle in which the university and its pre-service teachers have become high-functioning partners.

University tutors have demonstrated gains in commitment to their profession, and the development of peer leadership. Tutors tend to return each term to "check on" their tutees, and to take paid or volunteer leadership roles to the extent that the program is now largely student-led.

Conclusion

In its fourth semester, S.M.A.R.T. is a student-owned and student-led program. Tutors from previous terms now serve as Site Directors and Peer Mentors to assist in training, supervising, holding office hours, conducting Running Record assessments of children for whom we have no reading data, and program assessment and revision. Soon, S.M.A.R.T. will expand to follow tutees to their middle and high schools. On the last tutoring day every spring, the fifth-graders headed for middle school run back from the bus, teary-eyed, to hug us and beg that S.M.A.R.T. follow them. Soon we will be able to!

THE STORIES PROJECT: NURTURING CREATIVITY AND LITERACY THROUGH STORYMAKING

NANCY KING
UNIVERSITY OF DELAWARE

CLAUDIA M. REDER
CALIFORNIA STATE UNIVERSITY AT CHANNEL ISLANDS

Keywords: storytelling, storymaking, English learners, literacy, teacher education, pre-service teachers

Introduction

The Stories Project service-learning course developed from Dr. Nancy King's work in storymaking, structured to motivate children who were reluctant readers and writers (http://www.nancykingstories.com/index.htm). She designed and taught the course in the Honors Program at the University of Delaware as a first-year interdisciplinary colloquium for liberal arts students. UD students worked with children with learning differences from the College School. When Dr. Claudia Reder taught the course she was so impressed by the progress children made in reading and writing that she later incorporated The Stories Project into her Children's Literature course at California State University at Channel Islands. Her university students

worked with 4th–6th graders, many of whom were English learners and reluctant readers and writers.

Project Description

Folktales were chosen because they offer wisdom handed down from one generation to another, across cultures and time. Students told folktales after which children and university students made images in one minute or less with clay or fingerpaints from abstract prompts. They then wrote or dictated a new story based on the abstract prompts. Materials used: fingerpaints or washable paints in tiny pots, unlined paper, paper towels, non-hardening clay, and pencils.

The UD student also wrote a story for the child and put a copy of it in the child's book. At the end of the semester the children received their books at an Authors' Celebration where each "storypartner" read one story and shared their experience. Each storypartner chose one story for an anthology that was bound and put in the school's library.

> Their painted images of themselves "before" and "after" the project expressed the growth of creativity, suspension of judgment, and a willingness to respond spontaneously to the children's questions and responses.

Although Dr. Reder preferred a one-on-one partnership, the numbers of students shifted to meet the needs of children in the Homework Club. University students paired up to design lessons together and worked with several students at a time. After every session, each university partner posted a journal entry on the course blog. Students brought the children's folders to each session, and began every session by discussing what had happened the previous week.

In class, Dr. Reder modeled storymaking tasks. Selected websites and folktales were posted on Blackboard©. Students also created story maps and shared personal stories. College students kept children's folders, typed children's stories, and at the end, gave the children their bound books.

Project Timeline

Flexible: a full year or one semester with 10 sessions.

Steps for Implementation

1. Set up communication with people at each site.
2. Visit the site and explain project.
3. Person from site visits university students to discuss situation and expected professional conduct.
4. Model storymaking.
5. Participants sign a contract stating their commitment for the project's duration.
6. University students work at the sites.
7. Keep communications open during each week. Provide feedback.
8. Schedule periodic reflections and at the end of the project.
9. Closure: Authors Reading and Celebration.

Please note that working at just one site eases ongoing assessment through observation and discussion.

Outcomes/Assessment

We looked for a growing narrative imagination in all partners. University students found that most children who had written one sentence now wrote a page or more. UD students kept two journals: the first covered the ten sessions with their storypartners. Each entry included planning, actual experience, reflection, and the child's reaction. A final entry reflected on the total process, the making of the books of their writing and the child's, and what they had learned. The second journal detailed class experience, and what the student learned. In midterm and final papers, students used journal entries to support their measurement of how and what they had learned.

CSUCI students kept reflection journals, posted entries on Blackboard©, and wrote a reflection paper. Tableaux were also used as a reflection task. CSUCI students contributed to a group brainstorm to generate ideas for final papers (categories included fears, hopes, challenges, stories that worked, as well as frustrations) which were based on the service-learning model: "What? So What? Now What?" Their painted images of themselves "before" and "after" the project expressed the growth of creativity, suspension of judgment, and a willingness to respond spontaneously to the children's questions and responses.

Conclusion

When reflecting on why this project was successful, several things came to light. Dr. King noticed that storytelling, an interactive learning technique, helps to develop community and facilitates language usage and literacy. Dr. Reder enjoyed the intimacy of working at the site with her class because it altered the teacher/student interaction. Using a separate space meant students could create their own space in meaningful ways by designing the atmosphere, and building a rapport with children and each other. Here they could meet their professional selves. University students learned how to cope with issues such as violence in stories, children who initially spoke reluctantly, and mistrusted outsiders. The children became motivated to share their stories in their classrooms with their teachers. Prospective teachers developed tools to help meet literacy standards through storytelling. Children viewed their university partners as allies and mentors and many said, "You mean I can go to college?"

CIVIC AWARENESS, ENGAGEMENT, AND ACTIVISM

INTRODUCTION

MAGGIE C. STEVENS
EXECUTIVE DIRECTOR
INDIANA CAMPUS COMPACT

Faculty members enter into service-learning projects for many different reasons—a desire to increase academic learning, an intention to engage students in their communities, a plan to enhance personal or professional growth. All of these are noble reasons for bringing service-learning into the classroom; and as the entries in this chapter demonstrate, even when civic learning is not the primary outcome that you are working toward, it is often inevitable that it will occur when students are engaged in meaningful service-learning projects that include reciprocity and reflection. As these entries will demonstrate, civic learning is not limited to political science or history classrooms. It happens across disciplines every day.

In the preface to his book, *Civic Responsibility and Higher Education*, Erlich reminds us that in Dewey's *Democracy and Education*, there is not a prescribed curriculum or list of courses for students to enroll in to learn about democracy or citizenship. Rather, as Erlich says, "when one considers the book (*Democracy and Education*) as a whole, it is about how leaders of a school or educational system should shape all programs and arrangements, curricular and extracurricular, toward the goal of democracy." (vi)

Carpini and Keeter's (2000) article, *What Should be Learned through Service-Learning?* focuses on learning outcomes for service-learning courses in their own discipline, political science. They say,
    "Underlying the pedagogy of service-learning are the beliefs that a central mission of civic education
    is to produce active, engaged citizens and this mission is more likely to be accomplished by allowing
    young Americans to directly experience 'politics' as part of their education." (p. 635)

Again, while some may argue that teaching "politics" should not be on the agenda of classes in disciplines outside of political science, the examples that follow show not only why we should teach civic awareness, engagement and activism in the classrooms, but also how this can happen in disciplines including education (Spielman and Mistele), criminal justice (Nelson) and environmental science (Kalbach). The projects range from what one might consider "traditional activism" where students are learning about, evaluating and advocating for specific policy (Mobley; McIntosh) or bringing a voice to a problem that might otherwise be silenced (Maier and Gagne) to action-oriented activism where students are recycling trash bags to create new products (Kalbach).

Carpini and Keeter (2000) also talk about the opportunities and challenges that we encounter in service-learning. The submissions in this chapter share some of those challenges, but ultimately highlight the opportunities that present themselves for both intentional and unintentional learning through service-learning (Wehrle). Service-learning, when well implemented, brings the pages of a textbook and the words of a lecture to life. However, without proper reflection and discussion in the classroom, the service will be stagnant.

In order to ensure that students are able to take the theories and put them into action, they must be guided through intentional reflection. David Kolb's Theory of Experiential Learning provides a helpful framework for guiding students through this journey.

When examining service-learning in light of Kolb's learning theory, it is easy to see how one supports the other. Students often enter a class with preconceived ideas of the content and the application. Students start in the concrete experience stage of Kolb's cycle as they participate in the service-learning experience. They gather information through their experiences and interactions. Possibly during the service experience, but more often after the experience, students will move into the reflective observation stage where they will reflect upon the experience—as an individual (possibly during a car ride home and/or through journaling or some other form of guided reflection) and as a member of the community (in their classroom).

After these initial opportunities for reflection, students will move into the abstract conceptualization phase, where they will try to understand their experiences in light of their previous knowledge and the information that has been presented in the classroom. Students may struggle at this point because of the accommodation process that may be necessary to adapt some of their thinking to make meaning of the experiences.

Finally, students move into the active experimentation stage of the process. Bloom (1956) would refer to this as the point where synthesis and evaluation take place. At this point the students are creating new ideas and theories of how and why things work and getting ready to test new theories, and thus begin the cycle over. Hopefully the students will be able to visit the service site multiple times in order to move through this learning cycle more than once to continually challenge their previous thoughts and experiences and to gain a deeper knowledge and understanding of the theories and ideas presented in the classroom.

As you peruse this chapter and the examples of courses and service-learning projects highlighting, *Civic Awareness, Engagement, and Activism,* we hope that you will find examples of activities that could be implemented in your teaching and learning environments.

While we have one chapter focused on service-learning in teacher education programs, there are examples of teacher education classes in this chapter as well. These courses focus on the advocacy and community outreach that results from the service-learning projects. Spielman and Mistele's submission demonstrates how service-learning helped "preservice teachers learn about children and their communities while also becoming more civic-minded and gaining valuable knowledge and skills needed for teaching mathematics."

And finally, as Mironesco reminds us, service-learning not only helps our students learn and our communities grow, but as reflective practitioners, faculty will find that by using service-learning, it may change the way others teach and the way that the university views service.

References

Carpini, Michael X. Delli and Keeter, Scott. "What should be learned through service-learning?" *PS: Political Science and Politics*, 33(3). 635-639.

Erlich, T. (2000). *Civic Responsibility and Higher Education.* Westport, CT: The Oryx Press.

TEACHING POLICY ADVOCACY THROUGH SERVICE-LEARNING: PROJECT IMPLEMENTATION AND COURSE INTEGRATION

CATHERINE MOBLEY
CLEMSON UNIVERSITY

Keywords: policy, advocacy, Sociology, sustainability, homelessness

Introduction

The Breaking Ground service-learning project was implemented in my Policy and Social Change course during the fall semesters of 2001, 2003, and 2004. This sociology course is designed to inform students about the processes by which policy is developed, implemented, and evaluated. Through this course, I hope to broaden students' perspectives about community service to include advocacy and civic engagement as important routes for social change. The service-learning project, Breaking Ground, helped students to not only think about the "downstream" symptoms of social problems (and applying what one student called a "band-aid" approach to community problems), but also allowed them to understand the need to move "upstream" and tackle the causes of social problems. More specifically, the course and the service-learning project focused on the social problem of homelessness.

Project Description

In Fall 2001, students enrolled in my Policy and Social Change course established a unique learning community consisting of Clemson University students and faculty, advocates for the homeless, policy makers, and homeless and formerly homeless individuals. Through Breaking Ground, students established an "advocacy partnership" with the Upstate Homeless Coalition, a non-profit organization based in Greenville, SC that addresses the lack of affordable housing in the Upstate. Project activities included policy-related research on homelessness in South Carolina and the Upstate and organizing fundraising and awareness-raising activities for the Upstate Homeless Coalition.

The culmination of Breaking Ground occurred in mid-November (November 11–16) 2001, during National Hunger and Homelessness Awareness Week. Sponsored by the National Coalition of the Homeless and the National Student Campaign against Hunger and Homelessness, this event is designed to raise public awareness about homelessness (see http://www.nationalhomeless.org/getinvolved/projects/awareness/index.html for more information and resources about the awareness week). For this service-learning course, students worked with project partners to design an awareness-raising and fund-raising event for the upstate community. The resulting activities were:

- **Dine out for the Homeless Night:** Through this project, managers of four local restaurants agreed to donate a percentage of profits during the awareness week to the Upstate Homeless Coalition.
- **"Change for Social Change" Collection Effort:** Another team of students designed and created "donation jars" that were placed in various business establishments in Clemson for a two-week period, prior to and including the awareness week. The donations were given to the Upstate Homeless Coalition.
- **Awareness Week Food Drive:** This student team placed food collection boxes in Brackett Hall, the student unions, and several dormitories. Donations were provided to Clemson Community Care, a local food bank.
- **Tabling and Awareness Raising Events:** These events, which took place at the student unions, provided an opportunity for Clemson University students, faculty and staff to obtain materials and information on homelessness, to sign a petition letter to the Governor of South Carolina, and to view a short film on homelessness. More than 200 letters were signed and sent to the Governor.
- **Awareness Raising Events at local churches:** This student team sent a letter to area churches, asking the pastors, ministers, or other church leaders to dedicate sermons to the topics of homelessness and hunger and to consider donating a portion of their Sunday collection to the Upstate Homeless Coalition.

Project Timeline

Week 1: During the first week of class, I formally introduced the project to students. On the first day of class, I distinguished between service and advocacy, with a particular emphasis on the definition of service-learning. I also administered the pre-test assessment survey at this time.

Week 2: At the beginning of this week, community partners, including staff and clients, visit class to talk about the organization and its work. Students had completed readings on homelessness in the Upstate and were required to come to class prepared to ask questions of the community partners. At this time, students were assigned to teams to research various dimensions of homelessness. Topics addressed included the causes of homelessness, children and homelessness, homelessness in the Southeast, health care for the homelessness, homelessness in South Carolina, and student advocacy on the issue of homelessness.

Week 3: Students initiated their policy research (which continued through Week 13) and began to arrange awareness week activities (planning continues through Week 14). Community partners should be encouraged to participate in these planning sessions.

Week 6: Students began to establish media contacts, including on-campus newspapers and local newspapers. This helped to ensure early "buy-in" to the awareness week activities.

Week 7: I suggest inviting project partners to class so they can actively participate in the planning process. At this time, they can also provide additional information to students about homelessness in the Upstate. This visit allows students to ask additional questions and to verify what they are learning through the team research projects. Mid-term evaluations should also be administered at this time to allow for "fine-tuning" of both the project and the course. Holding a mini-celebration of mid-term accomplishments can help to rejuvenate student enthusiasm for the project.

Week 10–15: Continue to make media contacts by preparing formal press releases. Invite the media to class and to the campus events.

Week 11: Community partners should be invited to attend class to assist in planning for events.

Week 13: Students and partners implemented the awareness week activities. Project partners should actively participate in this phase of the project to the greatest extent possible.

Week 15: A Breaking Ground celebration was held during the last week of class; the media and project clients should be invited to this event. The post-test was administered to students on the last day of class.

Steps for Implementation

As illustrated in the timeline and described below, the project was designed to facilitate the implementation of the seven elements of high quality service-learning, as defined by Youth Service California: integrated learning, high quality service-learning, collaboration, student voice, civic responsibility, reflection, and evaluation (see www.yscal.org for more information). Additionally, Breaking Ground also incorporates the five stages of service-learning, identified by Kaye (2003) as essential for service-learning: preparation, action, reflection, celebration and assessment.

Three months prior to the project: Successful service-learning projects are characterized by advanced planning. I met with the project partners early on to learn more about

the agency's needs and to talk about the expectations for the service-learning partnership. I would recommend that an e-mail be sent to students who are pre-registered for the course to let them know that the course is a service-learning course; this can help to increase student commitment to the class. At this time, I also prepared and submitted my application to the Institutional Review Board (IRB) for approval of the assessment portion of the project. [1]

2–3 weeks before class: I met with community partners to review the final course timeline and expectations for the service-learning partnership. I also sent another e-mail to students enrolled in the course, with an update on the course plans and a reminder that the course was a service-learning course. At this time, I also ensured that the class survey has been approved by the IRB.

Throughout the semester (Weeks 1–15): A hallmark of this service-learning project was the continuous integration of course material with the service-learning project itself. That is, I tried to link nearly all of my lectures on the policy process, social change and advocacy to the Breaking Ground project. Also, students were asked to keep a reflection journal in which they either wrote open-ended journal entries or entries in response to specific questions about the course material or the service-learning project. I recommend ensuring that such reflection happens throughout the course, and not just at the midterm and the end of the semester.

Outcomes/Assessment

Project assessment consisted of pre-test and post-test surveys which covered several topics including self-efficacy, opinions about working in group projects, working with and learning from individuals from different race and class backgrounds, and beliefs about individuals who are homeless. An earlier article, published in Teaching Sociology (Mobley, 2007), provides detailed information about program outcomes. In summary, Breaking Ground students experienced several important outcomes that may be partially attributed to their participation in the project. Results suggest that students' perceptions about individuals who are homeless changed in a positive direction. That is, they were less likely to agree with negative stereotypes about individuals who are homeless after the project than they were at the beginning of the semester. And, Breaking Ground students were more likely to change these perceptions than were students enrolled in a non-service-learning course.

Conclusion

An important element of project sustainability is whether the model used to develop and implement Breaking Ground can be used in other contexts. While designed for a specific

---

1. A copy of the assessment tool is available from the author upon request.

course, the project can be used in many other disciplines and contexts. I plan to use the Breaking Ground model in my Environmental Sociology and Social Problems courses. The timeline of course and service-learning events could also be used during any semester that concludes with a large-scale event. For example, in spring, a similar project could be organized around Earth Day, which generally occurs in late April, around the fourteenth week of a regular semester.

Through their involvement in Breaking Ground, students engaged in concrete action to address a social problem, in this case, homelessness and the shortage of affordable housing. By working directly with clients, caseworkers and advocates, students participated in a real-world, grassroots public awareness project. And, working with clients as active partners had positive impacts beyond the project. As

I describe in the Teaching Sociology article, the students' more empathic beliefs about individuals who are homeless are important starting points for engaging in advocacy. That is, "the project may have been successful in "breaking ground" for students to engage in advocacy in relevant areas of their lives after graduation" (Mobley, 2007).

References

Kaye, C. (2003). *The complete guide to service learning: Proven, practical ways to engage students in civic responsibility, academic curriculum, and social action*. Minneapolis, MN: Free Spirit Publishing.

Mobley, C. (2007). Breaking Ground: Engaging undergraduates in social change through service learning. *Teaching Sociology, 35 ,125-13.*

||

SERVICE-LEARNING HAS A STATEWIDE IMPACT ON SEXUAL VIOLENCE

ELIZABETH MAIER
NORWICH UNIVERSITY

BOBBI GAGNE
EXECUTIVE DIRECTOR, SEXUAL ASSAULT CRISIS TEAM - WASHINGTON COUNTY, VERMONT

Keywords: sexual violence, courts, Criminal Justice, victim advocacy

Introduction

Victims of crimes of personal violence often feel isolated and confused. They normally do not know where to turn for assistance and do not understand how the justice system functions. In order to fill this void, criminal justice students at Norwich University created an informational booklet for victims. The booklet contained information on confidentiality, the role of a victim's advocate, wire warrants, relief from abuse orders, sexual assault nurse examiners (SANE), evidence kits, local assistance programs, and the justice system processes associated with reporting a sexual assault. The final product/booklet, "The Unknown Truth: Your Rights as a Sexual Assault Victim," was presented to the governor and distributed throughout the state.

Project Description

Fifty-five students enrolled in upper-division criminal justice courts courses created an informational booklet for sexual assault victims in Vermont. The instructor met with the university service-learning coordinator who introduced the instructor to the community partner. At the initial meeting, the community partner described the community's needs to the instructor and they determined an informational booklet would best meet those needs. The instructor and

executive director of the community partner met several more times to finalize the projects shape, create deadlines, and articulate the project expectations. The students were introduced to the project the first week of the semester. The community partner came to the course, introduced herself, and spoke about the community's needs. The students were made aware of project expectations and timelines. The students were allowed to choose what section of the booklet they would complete. Allowing each student to choose helped the students buy in to the project.

Students' progress was monitored by having group meetings in class. Additionally students had to complete several reflection assignments. Students' reflections on the project allowed them to analyze the project and realize how it related to the course. The community partner assisted students in locating information and was accessible throughout the project.

The students submitted their sections electronically to the instructor. It was then compiled into one document and edited by the instructor and community partner. It is important to have the assistance of the community partner. The community partner can enhance the content, assist with the editing, and order the information since he/she will know the specific jargon used by the community.

Timeline

The project took 13 weeks.

Week 1: instructor and community partner met and discussed the project

Week 2: project introduced to students

Week 3: students chose part of project they would complete and were given instructions

Week 4: students started collecting information

Week 5: progress report conducted in class and help was given to students needing assistance

Week 6: students completed a reflection assignment

Week 7: students continued gathering information and began writing

Week 8: students' progress checked in class

Week 9: students submitted drafts to the instructor and any problems were addressed

Week 10: students turned in their sections and a reflection assignment

Weeks 11–13: editing and compiling the final product

Steps for Implementation

1. Find a community partner to collaborate with on the project. The instructor should contact the university's service-learning coordinator, the local prosecutor's office, or law enforcement agency and ask them for the local victim's services organization.
2. Meet with the executive director of the community partner and discuss the community's needs and the project.
3. Create a plan of action for the project. The instructor, executive director and board members of the community partner should create the action plan together. This could simply be an outline, or it could be a very detailed spreadsheet specifying everything that needs to be done, by whom, and when.
4. Present the project to the students. Begin by explaining what service-learning is and how it relates to the course material. Present the project overview.
5. Discuss the project expectations and deadlines with the students.
6. Determine what type of word processing software should be utilized and type/size of font. If the final product is going to be printed, it is a good idea to contact the printer and find out what size font, margins, etc. he/she will need for the printing.
7. Monitor the students' progress. The community partner should allow time to respond to students' questions and assist students with locating information.
8. Collect each students' part of the project and compile it into one document.
9. The community partner and instructor proofread the document.
10. Send the document to the printer. For this project, the printing was donated by a local print shop; however, local, state, and federal grants exist for printing such projects. The finished product also can be displayed on the internet in PDF format.
11. Distribute the work.

Outcomes/Assessment

The booklet created by the Norwich students was first of its kind in Vermont. The reaction from the Vermont Network Against Domestic and Sexual Violence, the statewide office for the sixteen statewide programs, was very positive. They have made a commitment to mail the booklet out statewide and the sixteen programs have already received copies. Several victims have reviewed the booklet and say they feel it will give control back to the victim by explaining the process of the legal, advocacy, and medical systems, as well as explaining their rights as a victim that is what they often never know. This book will ensure victims are no longer just a witness in their own case without knowledge of the resources, which are located throughout Vermont.

As part of the service-learning requirement, the students were asked to complete several reflection assignments wherein the students shared their thoughts about the project. Students were asked to explain how the project related to the course; the ease or difficulty of locating information; the significance of the project to them. None of the students had participated in a service-learning project before this project. Their reflections revealed that they found the project enlightening and a welcome change from lecture. To learn about real-life issues and community needs was very appealing to them.

Conclusion

Both communities and students benefited from this service-learning project. The students learned about the court system and how it specifically relates to sexual violence victims. Communities in Vermont now have access to an informational booklet that explains the rights and resources available to sexual violence victims, and the police and court processes associated with reporting a crime.

TRASH BAGS TO HAND BAGS: AN ECOLOGICAL SERVICE-LEARNING PROJECT

LINDA M. KALBACH
DOANE COLLEGE

Keywords: ecological justice, sustainability, empowering, student driven project, reuse and recycle

Introduction

This article discusses a service-learning project that emerged from a course on sustainable living and grew into an entirely student-led organization. The project is simple, yet its multilayered elements connect it to a worldwide movement to ban plastic shopping bags and to empower local communities to turn items of refuse into saleable commodities.

Project Description

Trash Bags to Hand Bags is an ecological project whereby Doane College students teach others about the environmental perils of hundreds of millions of discarded plastic shopping bags and how to turn them into sturdy, reusable tote bags. It confronts the burgeoning mounds of bags and allows students to examine issues of consumer waste and economic sustainability, along with questions of ecological justice and community organizing. The project promotes individual creativity and intergenerational dialogue. Young children can work side by side with elders to turn refuse into an item of infinite creative possibilities, using nothing more than collected bags, an iron, scissors, wax paper and a sewing machine. (For construction instructions on the bags check out http://www.youtube.com/watch?v=cf7alw4RN5c.)

The current project started with a demonstration at Doane College by its Roots and Shoots chapter. It took off when a group of students from the Sustainable Living course decided to take the idea on the road. With the help of the college chaplain, the professor and five students conducted a workshop at a local community center in Lincoln, Nebraska. Working in concert with a VISTA volunteer, they developed a presentation about the environmental realities of the problem and worked with participants to make hand bags as an example of reusing a disposable resource. The F Street Community Center has a diverse membership and is located in an area of Lincoln that lacks many of the economic resources of other neighborhoods in the city. While discarded bags are an issue in every city, their eyesore is worse in locations where trash collection is less affordable.

This last point is particularly important since a component of the sustainable living course includes ecological justice. It is impossible for many poor communities to manage the problem, and the infusion of bags throughout Latin America, Africa and India by globalization and tourism is becoming a major health problem. They clog waterways and flood trash dumps. Land and marine animals consume and/or become entangled in the bags, which never decompose.

While there is no immediate cure for the magnitude of the problem, *Trash Bags to Hand Bags* has the potential to help communities chip away at the problem. They can promote elimination of the bags through local and national ordinances, an issue addressed in the student presentation along with the economic benefits of selling the tote bags. Although *Trash Bags to Hand Bags* focuses on making bags, the plastic once melted could be made into everything from raincoats to sandals and tarps. The ingenuity of local artisans and people well-versed in community sustainability will take the project to even greater dimensions than the Doane students can on their own.

Project Timeline

1. **Day one of class**—introduce basic project idea to students as one of several options and outline the key elements including potential community partners. Students begin considering curriculum ties including environmentalism, community activism, ecologically sustainable business ventures, "reduce, reuse and recycle."

2. **Project workdays**—time needs to be built into the course for students to collaborate and initiate contact with community agencies/centers, schools, youth groups, religious organizations etc. whose needs or interests align with the project. A formal presentation is crafted to meet the audience level, which will stress collecting the bags, working to ban their use, and teaching the elements of construction. Students will need to learn and practice making the bags including the creative opportunities.

3. **Presentation hours**—this amount varies depending on the level of the environmental talk, the complexity of the bags presented and the age level of the participants. The following recommendations are offered:

   Early elementary—(using simplest bag design)
   - **15 minutes** for "academic" introduction to teach the key ecologic pieces and demonstrate how to "cut the bags" and ready them for ironing.
   - **20 minutes** for students to cut the handles and bottoms off their bags, eight total—each tote has two sides.

- **10 minutes** of ironing PER every four bags melted together (The total time varies depending on the number of adults doing the ironing; it is not recommended this be done by young children.)
- **5 minutes** of sewing to connect the two sides and put in a hem (adults need to assist in this phase)
- **45 minutes** for students to decorate the bags and cut handle holes

All others age groups (production times vary depending on the complexity of bag design)
- **25–30 minutes** "academic introduction"
- **20 minutes** for students to cut off handles and bottoms of 12 bags; each tote will have two sides plus two sets of straps.
- **10 minutes** of ironing per every four bags melted together
- **45 minutes** of sewing to connect the various pieces. This portion of the presentation will vary greatly depending on the creative interests and the number of sewing machines available.

Steps for Implementation

Every service-learning project needs to be deeply tied to the content. Ensuring the fit is the first step, and following this an instructor needs to determine potential community part-ners. For *Trash Bags to Hand Bags*, partners must be willing to help collect and transform the bags and arrange future presentations. A debriefing session needs to follow each student presentation to discuss intersections with course content and to continue refining the project.

Outcomes/Assessment

Students journal on the academic and practical connections and participate in debriefing sessions. They are asked to consider the many interests and people woven together in the project, and what this says about the complexity of service work. They also consider what they learned about themselves as environmental activists. The greatest outcome is the extent to which the project sustains itself by expanding who will take the project themselves and present it to another willing group.

Conclusion

The student leaders are looking to launch this project overseas in countries whose pollution problem is greater, and who must make life work on fewer financial resources than the U.S. It will likely be these people who take the project to its greatest heights. They will use it not only to eliminate the bags, but also to create cottage industries as they craft the totes and other items made into saleable commodities.

FINDING ONE'S VOICE THROUGH POLICY ADVOCACY PROJECTS

DONNA MCINTOSH
SIENA COLLEGE

Keywords: student-community advocate, policy team advocacy, community-based advocacy, politics, legislature

Introduction

Those of us who teach policy courses want students to not only learn about the political process and advocacy strategies but to answer the call to action. Teaming students up for a semester with community advocates has been a win-win opportunity for both students and advocates. The students participate in real legislative advocacy agendas of their interest, and advocates gain much needed people power to mobilize for change.

Project Description

Teams of students work with community advocates on current policy issues during our state's legislative session. While students generally express not liking group assignments, in this project learning effective teamwork as part of a community coalition is an essential learning objective. Students learn about the importance of building political relationships and knowing when to negotiate, challenge, barter, and compromise. Students learn by immersion that legislation can pass overnight, or take years to move through the process.

Community advocates must be recruited and oriented well in advance of the course being offered. Often we brainstorm together what types of policy advocacy activities might be appropriate for students. Over the years, I have learned it is advisable that before recruiting advocacy organizations, check with students first if you can to see what their interests might be. It is not the role of the community advocate to try to first convince a student of the value system and position of the policy under study. Students have to be fairly sold on a position as part of teaming with a specific advocate.

I designate one of the three weekly class times as a "lab" in which students are out in the community with the advocates, or working on team tasks on campus. Students develop and periodically update a work plan in partnership with the community advocate and course instructor. Each student also submits a written analysis of the policy under study to ensure we all start off on the same page about our understanding of the policy. Throughout the remainder of the semester, students submit individual biweekly report of their team's progress.

Students have spearheaded postcard campaigns, conducted petition drives, arranged for public awareness presentations on campus, developed FAQ forms, conducted literature searches, designed and implemented community surveys, attended public hearings, participated in rallies, met with legislators, developed annual reports and other policy evaluation reports, and designed and distributed legislative action brochures, flyers and gimmick gifts. One year, students' work resulted in an additional state appropriation of $500,000 for homeless children.

Project Timeline

The project is semester-long and hits the ground running in the first week with students forming teams assigned to specific advocates. The teams are expected to make contact with their community advocates within the next week. After two meetings with the advocates, students are expected to have a schedule of meeting dates and times for the remainder of the semester. A work plan is generally submitted one month into the semester and updated periodically. Blackboard© has been an effective tool for the team and instructor to communicate, hang files, etc. The project is normally implemented within the state's legislative session, and thus students are educated in the classroom about this calendar and process.

Throughout the remainder of the semester, students submit the written policy analysis, a biweekly report, and engage in a range of policy advocacy tasks with their advocates.

In the past, a final team report has been required, but this has been foregone in favor of increased range of policy activities. Frankly, this project is more about students doing the real advocacy work in the community than writing papers about it.

Steps for Implementation

1. Recruit community advocates prior to the start of the semester and based on informal discussion with students about their interests.
2. Orient community advocates to the course and learning objectives, and discuss a range of policy activities in which students could participate. Be sure to let community advocates know of time requirements of students for this project.
3. Develop all the required instructions, forms, and assignments for the team project, including what is group graded and what is individually graded.

4. During the first week of class, have students self-select into teams based on their interests in the policy issues.
5. Distribute a schedule of project assignment due dates at the beginning of the semester, but be prepared to modify these dates depending on the startup and ongoing work of the teams.
6. Build in time for reflection with each team and as a full class and try to encourage what I call "cross-pollinating" of teams' work so that students get interested and involved in each team's efforts.
7. Maintain contact with the advocates throughout the semester.
8. The instructor should attend or participate in some of each team's activities.
9. Mediate any problems or concerns because there will be problems in any teamwork.
10. Seek input from the community advocates for the final grade. The last biweekly report submitted by students is a reflection of what they have learned about themselves and about policy from this project, as well as their recommended final grade for their work.

The best feedback comes from students who report that when other students on campus learn what they are doing in the community, they are envious.

Outcomes/Assessment

Students have participated in a full range of policy activities in partnership with community advocates and other professionals. Student evaluations of this assignment repeatedly recommend it as a way to encourage students' involvement in the policy arena. Community advocates have repeatedly signed on to this project year after year. The best feedback comes from students who report that when other students on campus learn what they are doing in the community, they are envious.

Conclusion

There is upfront work in developing the relationships with advocates; but in the end, both the students and advocates benefit. Students have reported being inspired by the advocates. Students "find their voice" in the policy arena through this project. Students are often frank about being turned off by politics, but have gotten hooked on working with committed and passionate advocates.

NOTES FROM THE FIELD(S): FROM PULLING UP WEEDS TO PUTTING DOWN ROOTS IN THE COMMUNITY

MONIQUE MIRONESCO
UNIVERSITY OF HAWAI'I, WEST O'AHU

Keywords: agricultural activities, food politics, farming, food production, food consumption

Introduction

Among other things, food can both be our sustenance, necessary to our survival, and our downfall at the same time, with alarmingly high rates of obesity and diabetes related to overeating, and for women specifically, high rates of eating disorders. The politics of the food industry have started to become more transparent through the efforts of academics and consumer advocates, as well as public health and environmental advocacy groups. This article explores the pedagogical results of teaching a class entitled Politics of Food, and assesses the student learning outcomes for the course over two semesters through the lens of several service-learning projects.

Project Description

At three farms (Ka'ala Farm, Hoa 'Aina O Makaha, and Ma'o Organic Farms), the class engages in agricultural activities that benefit the respective farms. At Ka'ala Farm, the students and I pull weeds in the lo'i kalo (taro patch), getting muddy in the process. At Hoa 'Aina, we are given a tour of the farm and pull lettuce plants gone to flower, replanting beans in their place. At Ma'o Farms, we help clear a new field of rocks for planting soon thereafter. We also spend some time weeding a field and mulching around the rows of Swiss chard and red Russian kale. At Sunset Beach Elementary, we clear garden beds and prepare them for planting for the kids involved in Kokua Hawai'i Foundation's 'AINA IS program intended to teach kids about the connection between sustainability, environmental awareness, nutrition, and their daily lives. By far, the most anticipated and difficult service-learning trip is to Ma'ililand Transitional Housing Shelter, where the students, some residents and I build garden boxes (modeled after those at Sunset Beach Elementary) and plant vegetables for recently homeless residents trying to make positive changes in their lives. The garden beds provide the residents access to healthy food, which is sorely lacking in their community, and the students become teachers of sustainable agriculture and wholesome nutrition.

Project Timeline

The Politics of Food course is taught on a "Part of Term" basis which entails six, three-hour Friday night classes and five, five-hour Saturday morning classes for a six week period. This time slot is a bonus for the course's success because it allows great flexibility for lectures, discussions and guest speakers as well as feature length documentaries on Friday nights, in addition to plenty of time on Saturday mornings for service-learning field trips, which take us all over the island of O'ahu.

Steps for Implementation

Contacting farms and other community partners is done three weeks prior to the start of the semester to organize Saturday field trips according to everyone's schedules. Each Friday night lecture prior to the next day's service-learning experience is geared toward understanding the particular challenges faced by the farms we visit the next day. For example, we discuss the challenges facing organic farms in terms of meeting USDA standards; the relationship between farm to school programs and constant cost cutting measures in school lunch budgets, and federal guidelines on what is considered an appropriate lunch; or access to healthy food by lower income, or recently homeless people in minority neighborhoods.

Outcomes/Assessment

Every day we make political decisions about what kind of food to eat, where and when to eat it, and why. In this course, students learn about the processes of food production and how government and corporate involvement have changed the way society eats. This course provides students with skills for everyday life through experiential learning. It also impacts how students regard their daily sustenance. Furthermore, students become more critical food consumers and are able to make informed political choices about the kinds of food they buy and eat. This class serves as a space to questions students' assumptions about political issues surrounding food production and consumption, the links between agribusiness and the food we put on our respective tables, as well as a new way of understanding food issues through a political perspective.

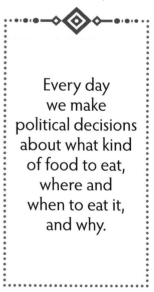

Every day we make political decisions about what kind of food to eat, where and when to eat it, and why.

Each student is asked to keep a journal of his or her field trip experiences. After the field trip experiences, they are asked to integrate the previous evening's assigned reading and lecture and/or guest speaker and/or film with the field trip. At the end of the course, I ask the students to turn in a final snowball paper, which uses all of the journal material and reflects on the various components of the course. The process of thinking through each of their course experiences provides some very rich material for the final snowball papers, as well as productive reflections on the process of the course itself. The course evaluations for the students in the second year's class included comments like: "This class was a great learning experience for me. Not only [did] we read about the politics of food, we got to experience firsthand what is great about fresh foods compared to ... processed foods. The [service-learning] field trips were really a good part of the class" and "The class is an eye opener ... The weekly service-learning projects make you appreciate how food is produced [through] the land and people. Every student is given the opportunity to shape their thoughts by journals and class discussions."

Conclusion

While the class seems to be an overall success, there are limitations to this model, which need to be addressed. With regard to Ma'ililand, the lack of follow-up is a serious shortcoming in the design of the service-learning project. While the project is community generated and rewarding for both parties, and the students and the residents do work together, the project timeline does not allow for a follow-up visit to the site by the student cohort. This seems to be a general design flaw in many service-learning models, but it seems particularly acute given the schedule required by this class, which I had originally identified as a positive aspect of the course.

This service-learning class has been a wonderful teacher to me as a teacher. I continue to learn how to use service-learning as pedagogy. Service-learning has the potential to be a vehicle for that effort combining content knowledge and experiential learning. This mixed plate (traditional Hawaii food with a variety of different ethnic foods on one plate) is our version of that endeavor.

LEARNING FROM THE UNINTENTIONAL OUTCOMES

GRETCHEN WEHRLE
NOTRE DAME DE NAMUR UNIVERSITY

Keywords: political engagement, course design, unintentional course outcomes, psychology, Carnegie Faculty Fellows Program

Introduction

One of the most exciting parts of a faculty member's job is to develop courses which are innovative and engaging. This is particularly true for service-learning classes. As a Carnegie Faculty Fellow, I was asked to "design and implement in one of my courses a service-learning project geared toward increasing students' understanding, skills, and motivation for political engagement."[2] To meet these objectives, my Community Psychology class was modified so that it included meaningful service-learning experiences and

integrated political engagement. In assessing the success of the course, both the anticipated and unintentional outcomes stood out as equally important.

Project Description

Before Community Psychology was modified, it included a review of the field of community psychology and its underlying concepts/assumptions and required students to participate in community service. The revised course (Community Psychology-PE)[3] had a similar focus on community psychology and service-learning, yet it specifically emphasized youth, including homeless/runaway youth, immigrant youth, positive/asset development, and policy development. Political engagement acted as the "umbrella" for the course. This concept was fully integrated into the readings, class discussions, and reflection activities.

Project Timeline

The three phases involved in designing and implementing

---

2. The California Campus Compact-Carnegie Foundation Faculty Fellow Service-Learning for Political Engagement Program is a two-year program funded by the Corporation for National and Community Service: Learn and Serve Higher Education. To address the challenge of political disengagement among young people and advance the field of service-learning by focusing on dilemmas inherent in teaching for political participation, California Campus Compact partnered with the Carnegie Foundation for the Advancement of Teaching to bring together 23 outstanding tenured and tenure-track California faculty members from academic disciplines as diverse as engineering, political science, English and agriculture as Faculty Fellows in our Service-Learning for Political Engagement Program.

3. Community Psychology-PE was the name of the modified course, indicating that political engagement (PE) was the primary focus of the class.

Community Psychology-PE—conceptualization, planning, and teaching/reflection—took place over a year-long period:

Conceptualization:
April 2007: Course was identified.

August 2007: A three-day summer institute was scheduled for Carnegie Faculty Fellows to discuss how to make political engagement the focus of a service-learning course.

Planning:
Sept.–Dec. 2007: Staff from Peninsula Conflict Resolution Center (PCRC) and a psychology faculty member collaborated on modifying Community Psychology so the course followed the recommendations of the Carnegie Faculty Fellows Program.

Teaching and Reflection:
Jan.–May 2008: A faculty member and PCRC staff were co-educators of Community Psychology-PE.

May–June 2008: Course evaluation data were gathered and analyzed.

Implementation Phases

Conceptualization:
The summer institute of the Carnegie Faculty Fellows Program provided faculty the opportunity to come together at Stanford University to discuss how political engagement could be integrated into service-learning classes from different disciplines. This faculty group became a resource and support network after the institute.

Planning:
Planning for Community Psychology-PE involved the co-educators of the class: a psychology faculty member, PCRC's manager of community engagement, and PCRC's public participation specialist. Since Community Psychology-PE was going to remain a service-learning class, "best practice" strategies were implemented: high quality community service opportunities for students; a syllabus that specifically indicated the relationship between service and learning; readings and discussions that focused on civic responsibility and public action; and reflection activities that were integrated into the curriculum.[4]

---

4. "Best practice" strategies for effective service-learning courses are discussed in a number of sources, including the American Association for Higher Education's Series on Service-Learning in the Disciplines, Christine Cress's Learning Through Service, Andrew Furco's "Service-Learning: A Balanced Approach to Experiential Education," Kerrisa Heffernan's Fundamentals of Service-Learning Course Construction, Cathryn Berger Kaye's The Complete Guide to Service Learning, Ellen Porter and Susan Poulsen's "Principles of Good Practice for Combining Service and Learning: A Wingspread Special Report," and Edward Zlotkowski's "Pedagogy and Engagement."

The co-educators selected one particular focus, "youth," believing that students would be more motivated if they could gain a deep understanding of an issue and the policies/legislation related to this issue. Community Psychology-PE provided students with opportunities to learn how being politically engaged can impact a specific issue in a community.

Teaching and Reflection:
Much effort was involved in the conceptualization and planning of Community Psychology-PE. As a result, the modified course was better focused and included components which were well-integrated:

- Readings and class discussions on policies related to youth (McKinney-Veto Homeless Assistance Act, California Assembly Bill 540, The DREAM Act);
- Expert speakers on specific issues affecting youth (educating homeless children, immigrant youth, positive youth development, giving youth a voice);
- Community service opportunities in youth organizations (youth commissions, county office of education, center for youth development, office of immigration);
- Training in facilitation and dialogue skills;
- A "political action"—a community dialogue focusing on undocumented high school students and their lack of access to higher education—was planned/facilitated by the students and was attended by 100 people; and
- A final reflection/evaluation activity involving students, faculty member, and PCRC staff.

Outcomes/Assessment

In reviewing the notes from the reflection/evaluation activity, it became evident that not only had the identified course outcomes been addressed, but that there were additional "unintentional" outcomes that had not been anticipated.

Intentional Outcomes:
The three outcomes that had been identified in the designing of Community Psychology-PE were "for the most part" met:

- *Students acquiring an understanding of youth development and policy development issues.*
  Students indicated that they learned the significance of focusing on young people's strengths, skills, and possibilities rather than looking exclusively at the negative.

- *Students acquiring leadership skills and planning/facilitating skills.*
  Students participated in nine hours of training in civic engagement and the planning and facilitating of community dialogues.

- *Students achieving a better understanding of their role as a politically engaged citizen and how youth in particular can have a stronger voice in their communities.*

Students indicated that the readings and class discussions provided them with a solid basis for understanding their role as an active citizen/young adult. What was missing for some of them was how they would actually do this—how could they make this a reality in their own lives.

Unintentional Outcomes:

The information gathered at the final group reflection activity also showed there were two "unintentional" outcomes that had a significant impact on a number of students:

■ *Community partners and guest speakers need to reflect the diverse backgrounds of students.*

Because a focus of the course was immigrant youth, many of the community partners/invited speakers were Latino. One third of the students enrolled in Community Psychology-PE were also Latino, first-generation students attending college. These students were some of the most engaged students in the class—they participated more, they were more eager to discuss the readings, and their bilingual skills were a great asset during the community dialogue. In addition, these students were very interested in the careers of the speakers/partners and the career paths they had taken. Unintentionally, Community Psychology-PE had integrated career development activities into the course and made it a more inclusive classroom experience.

■ *Students need to have opportunities to make choices within the curriculum.*

Even though the curriculum focusing on political engagement had been designed before the first class, students found a way to "have a voice" and make the course uniquely theirs. A group of students was successful in raising money ($500.00) for a scholarship fund for undocumented high school students attending college in the fall.

Conclusion

As a Carnegie Faculty Fellow, my project was to design a service-learning course whose primary focus was political engagement. Community Psychology-PE was such a course and, based on a review of both intentional and unintentional outcomes, proved to be successful in increasing students' understanding, awareness, and needed skills for political engagement. In order to continue to develop innovative and engaging service-learning courses, it is important that faculty build on the anticipated and unintentional outcomes of a course.

SERVICE-LEARNING COURSE IN PHILOSOPHY

ALAN PENCZEK
STEVENSON UNIVERSITY

Keywords: Philosophy, self-directed/one-time projects

Empty is the argument of the philosopher which does not relieve any human suffering.   ~ Epicurus (341–270 BCE)

Introduction

Philosophy may seem the academic discipline least amenable to service-learning. Yet hands-on service to the community nicely complements the abstract thought typical of philosophic study. Philosophy informs our perception of the world, our interactions with one another, and our understanding of the community. The 200-level course "Applied Philosophy and Community Service" requires students to make connections between the ideas presented in their reading assignments and their actual service work. The course is one facet of a campus-wide initiative designed to increase students' awareness of the local community and promote civic engagement.

Project Description

The course was developed as part of a sabbatical project to increase the number of service-learning opportunities across campus. The goal of this particular course is for students to combine theory and practice in a particular area of philosophy of their own choosing. Once each student has chosen a type of service, a customized reading list is provided by the instructor. The premise of any such course is that the integration of academic study with direct experience is synergistic: the value to the student is greater than if the two components were completed separately (traditional classroom learning in and of itself; volunteerism in and of itself).

Some examples: A student with an interest in environmental ethics may volunteer at a nearby state park or conservatory, providing such services as trail maintenance or the removal of invasive species. In conjunction with this work, the student reads selected philosophical writings on environmental and conservation issues. A student with an interest in animal welfare may care for animals at local shelters or rescue agencies, or help in their placement, while studying issues in animal rights. A student who wishes to work with the impoverished may provide services at a shelter or community center, and read on social justice or community empowerment. A student with an interest in child development may tutor or mentor at a public school or recreation center, and read on the philosophy of education.

A minimum of 30 hours of service is required, as well as written assignments (journal and papers) and a presentation. As a way of providing a common reading, all students are asked to read *Better Together: Restoring the American Community*, by Robert Putnam and Lewis Feldstein (2003). Because of the significant amount of individual attention given to students, the course has a student cap of 12. The class meets as a whole once a week for one hour, to free up time for the service activity.

Project Timeline

The course is geared to a traditional 15-week semester. See Steps for Implementation below for details.

Prior to First Class: Introductory e-mail sent.

First Class: Introductions are made. The syllabus and the mechanics of the course are discussed. A schedule is set up for each student to meet with the instructor individually over the next two weeks. The common reading is introduced.

First Two Weeks: Students choose a service location of interest to them. Students are responsible for contacting the organization and making all arrangements.

Weeks Three–Twelve: Students share their service experiences with their classmates. Problems are addressed. The common reading is discussed. Two or three short papers are assigned on the students' individualized readings. Additional one-on-one meetings with the instructor are scheduled.

Final Weeks: Students or teams make formal presentations to the class, where each student or team is asked to do their best to synthesize their assigned readings with their service experience. Time is allowed for discussion. Final comments and questions are addressed.

Steps for Implementation

Two or three weeks prior to the start of classes, an e-mail message is sent to all students enrolled in the course, informing them as to what to expect in the course, and asking them to begin thinking about the areas of philosophy and service in which they would like to work. Resources and tools to help with this decision, such as volunteer search engines found on the internet, are provided.

At the start of the course, each student, with my help, chooses a service location of particular interest to them (students are allowed to work in pairs at the same location). A customized reading list of relevant philosophical writings is then assigned to each person or team, along with a reading timetable. In some cases, the instructor may provide photocopied material; in other cases, the student may be asked to purchase a book. In still other cases, the material may be available on the web.

With readings in general, I prefer a mix of classical and contemporary sources. With regard to education, for example, I might ask students to read selections from Rousseau or Dewey, together with recent work by Nel Noddings. With regard to environmental ethics, students might read Thoreau or Leopold, together with articles from recent journals or anthologies.

In following weeks, each class begins with each student describing and reflecting on his or her service experience from the week before. Students are able to share both rewards and challenges, and may receive helpful feedback from fellow students on dealing with possible frustrations. Chapters from the common reading are assigned and discussed.

At least two other times during the semester, each student is required to meet with the instructor individually. These meetings serve to check on how the service work is going, and to monitor the student's understanding of the readings.

Each student writes two or three short papers in which they are asked to integrate their experience with the ideas encountered in their readings. A final presentation shares these results with the rest of the class. Students working in teams still write their own papers, but may present together.

Outcomes/Assessment

By the end of the course, each student submits a "Record of Service Hours" form provided by the instructor. The purpose of this form is to obtain signatures verifying the student's hours from the contact person(s) at the service location. Some locations may have their own forms for students to use. Because the total number of hours (30) is relatively small (compared, say, to a typical internship), asking for qualitative feedback on the student's performance is probably not necessary, and may be an inconvenience to the supervisor. Actual site visits by the instructor are desirable but might not be feasible for reasons of time.

Each student maintains a journal with separate entries for each visit to their service location. The entries briefly describe the types of activity engaged in, as well as reflections on that experience. Entries are collected weekly.

The short papers together with the final presentation allow

the instructor to assess the student's understanding of the reading material and their success at integrating this with their work.

Service-learning awakens students' interest in a way that is most refreshing. The feedback received from three semesters of teaching this course has been quite positive. More than one student indicated that the course has been the most rewarding of their college career thus far.

Conclusions

I found advantages and disadvantages in allowing students to choose their own service locations. The primary advantage is one of empowerment: the student is taking responsibility for the logistical and contractual arrangements with the organization, which is both a learning experience and one that develops maturity. In addition, I suspect such students are more likely to seek out volunteer opportunities on their own after the course is over. However, the disadvantages to this strategy are also significant. As instructor, it is unlikely you will have rapport with all of their chosen agencies, and there may be little assurance as to the quality of the student's experience. From an organization's point of view, having one or two students spending 15-odd weeks as volunteers may do little to advance its own long-term objectives, and may not be worth the investment in terms of training and other formalities. Then again, several students were offered paid positions at their service locations at the completion of this course.

I have since learned that public schools and community organizations generally prefer more formal partnerships with colleges and universities, so as to provide a greater number and more continuous supply of volunteers, and for increased communication and familiarity among all parties involved. In the case of this particular course, I believe the optimum strategy may be to allow students to choose a location from a relatively small, preapproved list, as a way of combining the best of both worlds.

References

Putnam, R. D. & Feldstein, L. M. (2003). *Better Together: Restoring the American Community.* New York: Simon and Schuster.

SERVICE-LEARNING FOR MATHEMATICS EDUCATION IN THE PUBLIC INTEREST

LAURA JACOBSEN SPIELMAN AND JEAN MISTELE
RADFORD UNIVERSITY

Keywords: mathematics, teacher education, after-school programs, pre-service teachers

Introduction

The service-learning opportunity described in this essay is a component of a new mathematics course at Radford University, *Math for Social Analysis* [Math 312], designed for elementary and middle grades students in the teacher education program [pre-service teachers]. We implemented a service-learning component beginning fall 2007 to help pre-service teachers learn about children and their communities, while also becoming more civic-minded and gaining valuable knowledge and skills needed for teaching mathematics. Our community-based organization [CBO] partner indicated children in after-school programs needed more, and better, mathematics learning opportunities and capable mathematics volunteer support.

Project Description

The CBO recommended providing students an option to complete either the service-learning semester project or an alternate project, to ensure service-learners are all interested and committed. We agreed with this recommendation, offering a second option, which involved writing a research paper and creating and teaching related mathematics lesson plans at elementary or middle grades levels. The alternate project takes approximately the same amount of time as service-learning. These projects each represent 30 percent of the overall grade in the course. The other 70 percent focuses on students' learning of mathematics, taught in interdisciplinary contexts or in connection with social issues.

The service-learning project involved three components: (a) service-learning training sessions and service in an after-school program, (b) service-learning portfolio and written reflections, and (c) class presentation.

Service-Learning
Training Sessions. CBO staff visit Math 312 in the first week of the semester to introduce service-learning opportunities and invite interested students to three required training sessions. Students then have one week to choose between the service-learning and alternate option. CBO staff provides training to service-learners to communicate goals and requirements. One session provides an orientation to the after-school programs, program locations (three sites), and

program structures. A second session addresses guidelines for working with children in dealing with discipline. A third session provides tips and suggested tutoring strategies.

35 to 40 Hours of Service. Pre-service teachers work closely with children filling roles and responsibilities in mentoring, tutoring, mediation, discipline, activity planning and implementation (both mathematics-related and otherwise), and program evaluation. Service-learners also have opportunities to ride the bus or walk home with children to learn more about them as individuals, to see where they live, and to become more familiar with the surrounding community. The CBO organizes the schedule. We meet with CBO staff before each semester, at least once during the semester (preferably more), and after the semester is over to communicate ongoing needs and current success levels.

Portfolio and Reflections

We require service-learners to create mathematics activities or games for children, typically lasting 20 minutes each. Over the semester, pre-service teachers submit mathematics mini-lessons and reflections, some of which relate to children's out-of-school interests or to relevant social issues. Write-ups include the goal or objective and Virginia Mathematics Standard of Learning (related to the No Child Left Behind Act), a description of the activity, and reflections on who participated, how they participated, what worked well, and what needs to change to improve the activity. Further, they summarize their thoughts and feelings about the service-learning experience, describe how effective they have been in the program, provide a record of their experiences, and document what they have done and learned. These reflections update instructors while also helping preservice teachers assess their own growth and development. Time is provided regularly in class for service-learners to share reflections. Students submit one final reflection at the end of the semester.

Class Presentation

All service-learners give a 10 to 15 minute presentation of their portfolios at the end of the semester. Having follow-up panel presentations for several service-learners at a time has also initiated positive learning experiences.

Project Timeline[5]

- **Prior to Week 1:** Instructors meet with CBO staff to set goals and objectives.
- **Week 1:** CBO staff visit course to introduce service-learning option.
- **Week 2:** Students select either service-learning or alternative project option.
- **Weeks 2–4:** CBO training sessions for service-learners.

- **Weeks 4–15:** Service-learning.
- **Week 15:** Final presentations.

Steps for Implementation

Several tips for successful implementation are below:
- Establish working connections addressing CBO needs and interests. The course and service-learning project must be complementary.
- Offer an alternate project, so uninterested students do not disrupt the service-learning site.
- Training sessions are helpful.
- Require regular reflections and have students share reflections.
- Involve service-learning site in student assessment.

Outcomes/Assessment

Evaluation of service-learning is divided into: (a) quantitative and qualitative student evaluations on students' attendance, initiative, participation, and attitude, (b) service-learning portfolio and written reflections, and (c) class presentation of service-learning experiences.

Student Evaluations

Evaluations by CBO staff represent 15 percent of the course grade. The quantitative evaluation includes 10 items, each rated on a scale of 1 (lowest) to 10 (highest). Ratings are based on punctuality and self-presentation, attendance, training attendance, program skills, discipline and conflict resolution, activity planning, attitude, initiative, reflection and listening, and overall. The qualitative evaluation explains why the student received various high and low ratings. CBO staff provides concrete examples to explain numerical ratings.

Portfolio and Written Reflections & Class Presentation

The service-learning portfolio and written reflections represent 10 percent of the course grade and the class presentation represents 5 percent. Course instructors evaluate these assignments in similar ways as for other types of submitted course materials.

Conclusion

The service-learning project has been very successful overall. We have learned the importance of meeting and talking regularly with CBO staff and of doing much advance work to coordinate planning and make sure everyone's needs are met. We find it essential to make sure CBO staff understand course requirements and also help to shape these requirements. We seek to create a win-win situation for all: students, course instructors, and the service-learning organization. We look forward to continuing and strengthening our service-learning project in future semesters.

---

5. Radford University switched from 15 to 14-week semesters in spring 2008. Schedule below is for 15 weeks.

SERVICE-LEARNING FOR CRIMINAL JUSTICE MAJORS WITH A MINOR IN AFRICANA STUDIES

NANCY J. NELSON
EASTERN WASHINGTON UNIVERSITY

Keywords: Africana Studies, Criminal Justice, juvenile detention, mentoring, teaching

Introduction

The Africana Education Program (AEP) at Eastern Washington University (EWU) implemented a service-learning opportunity for students majoring in Criminal Justice with an interest in juveniles and earning a minor in Africana Studies. The project provided hands-on experience in leadership roles. The work with juvenile detention involved being active members of the Juvenile Racial Disproportionality Board and youth mentors. The project lasted one quarter for each participating student.

Project Description

The Juvenile Detention Racial Disproportionality Board was formed in Spokane, Washington to address the disproportionate treatment and sentencing of youth of color throughout the juvenile justice system. Statistics developed by the detention center demonstrated African American youth in particular are more likely to be charged and processed through the system, to serve time, to be prosecuted as adults, and to be placed outside the home. The board examines reasons for this occurrence and what may be done to correct it. This includes educating police who charge youth, intake methods, the manner in which prosecutors present the youth in court, as well as providing adequate representation for the youth. The board also assesses the needs of each population housed in detention. An example of this is providing hair grease or lotion for African American youth or an appropriate place for Islamic youth to pray on Fridays.

Service-learning students who participated in the juvenile system were active board members along with judges, commissioners, prosecutors, guards, and community representatives. Service-learning students raised questions and provided input, such as possible reasons for the high truancy rate for students of color and the need to implement mentoring and after-school programs.

Service-learning students also served as mentors for incarcerated youth, which included sometimes having dinner with the youth. Youth were given the opportunity to speak with people who were closer to the youths' age and were part of various cultural groups. Service-learning students also served as one-on-one mentors, each meeting with a youth once a week. In addition, students attended the Saturday class providing input, guidance, and one-on-one tutoring. The Saturday class, a mandatory class for incarcerated youth, taught the meaning and acceptance of diversity, day-to-day concerns, and provided guidance on making appropriate choices. As the detention population changes often, service-learning students were required to present repeated topics and answer repeated questions, which was an excellent lesson in patience and how youth are sharing the same concerns.

Steps for Implementation

The first step for service-learning students to participate in the project was to gain permission from the juvenile detention to work with the youth. Juvenile Detention required background checks of all participants to be screened for any previous child abuse charges. Once clearance was granted, service-learning students scheduled meeting times with the Juvenile Detention mentor coordinator and the guard who led the Saturday class to receive training in working with the youth in detention and warning signs to be aware of, such as depression or aggressiveness. They were also taught methods youth may use to be manipulative, particularly repeat offenders or those who lived on the streets. Further, service-learning students were informed of privacy rights of the youth.

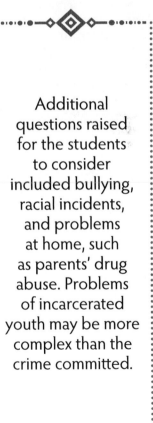

Additional questions raised for the students to consider included bullying, racial incidents, and problems at home, such as parents' drug abuse. Problems of incarcerated youth may be more complex than the crime committed.

The service-learning students were welcomed onto the board without the background clearance. They were required to attend all monthly board meetings.

Service-learning students met with the EWU faculty each week to access meetings with the youth and to discuss the strengths and weaknesses of the Juvenile Detention Racial Disproportionality Board meetings. During class sessions, students reported experiences and problems to their peers for the feedback.

Outcomes/Assessment

The service-learning students spent several hours with their mentees. They felt dining with the youth was a comfortable setting for the youth to open up. Service-learning students also learned many of the youth enjoyed reading and learning, which led the students to wonder if the youth acted out at school from boredom. Additional questions raised for the students to consider included bullying, racial incidents, and problems at home, such as parents' drug abuse. Service-learning students gained insight that problems of incarcerated youth may be more complex than the crime committed.

Students felt empowered by participating on the Juvenile Racial Disproportionality Board, as they had a voice in the process. The experience taught service-learning students about the disproportionate treatment of youth in the detention system, speculation of why this might be, and what is being done to correct the problem. Further, they gained an understanding of the many steps youth must go through in the detention process, as well as the difficulties in correcting the disproportionate treatment of youth of color in the system.

The small sampling of students participating in the service-learning made an evaluation of success difficult; however, based on student course evaluations and anecdotal sources such as student conversations and class discussions, those who participated felt the experience was worthwhile. A larger sample may have demonstrated different findings.

Conclusion

Active participation in the juvenile criminal justice field may be important for students intending to work in the juvenile criminal justice field. This may be particularly important when desiring to work with a specific culture. As some service-learning students want to help youth, they need to learn a high percentage of those in juvenile detention return upon release. Service-learning students need to know they themselves are not responsible for this; that the student does what he/she can and the rest in up to the inmate.

The faculty head of the service-learning should be educated about the juvenile justice system and aware of any subtle problems that may develop for service-learning students. The safety of the student is paramount. Much may be learned by working with incarcerated youth that may influence service-learning students' career choices.

COMMUNITY SOCIAL SERVICE PROJECTS: A SERVICE-LEARNING MODEL FOR COMMUNITY ACTION

MARILYN D. FRANK
MINNESOTA STATE UNIVERSITY, MANKATO

Keywords: task groups, community service, reflection, social service, social work

Introduction

Hunger, homelessness, need for opportunities for cross cultural interaction, alcohol abuse, and teen pregnancy are all issues which concern social work students. In an undergraduate service-learning course, student task groups choose a social problem or issue, and implement activities to provide education and/or support for people or community agencies affected by this issue. While this is an introductory course for social work majors, it is open to any student in the university. Students contribute to their communities, learn project management skills, enhance their skills for working in task groups, and reflect on these experiences.

Project Description

In a 15-week sophomore level course, 25 students actively participate in task groups to complete a 4-step service-learning

Through reflective assignments and class presentations, students illustrate an increased sensitivity to the challenges faced by people.

project which consists of: (a) choosing a social problem, (b) conducting library and web research, (c) designing and implementing a detailed project plan to include at least two community activities, and (d) formally presenting project results to their colleagues. The activities students implement are designed to lessen the impact or increase understanding of a social problem or issue for an identified target group. As a part of a community social service project (CSSP), a task group might raise awareness of a social problem through an educational session and activities, raise money, or create new opportunities for interaction between two groups. In other words, task groups will do more than help out with an ongoing service activity. A manual, developed by faculty, guides task groups through a process for the successful completion of a

CSSP. Students also learn about group dynamics and have many opportunities for reflection.

Project Timeline

Pre-course preparation: Three weeks prior to beginning of semester:

- Review syllabus, manual and current assignments to make any updates or changes.
- Update information regarding previous course projects for student use.
- Check with campus and community organizations to identify possible areas for student involvement.

Table 2.1. Project Timeline.

	Course Content	Task Group Activity
Week 1	Social problem, need, target group, action system and CSSP activities to modify conditions related to social problem.	Form task groups. Groups begin attendance record; choose out of class meeting times.
Week 2	Communication skills, group decision making, leadership, task and maintenance roles.	Discuss individual ideas and choose a social problem.
Week 3	Professionalism, making community contacts, Social Work values and ethics.	Make community contacts.
Week 4	Conducting library and web research. Stages in task group development.	Submit Step 1: Problem identification and potential CSSP activities and self-reflections.
Week 5	Writing a literature review to better understand problem, populations affected, and potential interventions. Conflict and styles of conflict management	Oral progress reports. Prepare for visit to library.
Week 6–7	Problem solving. Making community connections, working together in task groups.	Find relevant books, articles and websites. Continue to make contacts for CSSP. Submit Step 2: Literature Review and individual reference assignments.
Week 8–9	Project plan and implementation. Writing goals, timelines, and evaluation plans. Determining activities and ways to measure effectiveness of activities in addressing problem.	Submit Step 3 Project Plan and individual self-evaluations. Finalize arrangements for CSSP activities.
Week 10–13	Evaluation of results. Problem solving. Alternative plans. Making professional presentation of results of CSSP	Implementation of CSSP activities.
Week 14–15		Step 4: Analysis and presentation of project results and lessons learned about task group dynamics. Submit project statistics report and final individual reflections.

Steps for Implementation

Pre-Course Preparation. While the content of the course stays primarily the same, students are becoming more technologically savvy and dependent. For some, Facebook and e-mail have become the preferred mode of communication over meeting together as a group. Since an important aspect of this class is working in groups, course materials are reviewed to assure assignments will maximize opportunities for task group interaction. The importance of face-to-face interaction is also discussed in class.

A table of information regarding selected course projects is updated and made available to students. Arrangements are made for additional meeting space since five groups meeting together in a small classroom does not provide an atmosphere for students to get to know each other and work through challenging situations which often arise such as finding a site, agreeing on different aspects of the CSSP, or effectively working together.

The instructor maintains contact with university offices, social service agencies and community groups to become aware of current issues that might be of interest to students or sites where a service-learning project might be completed. Since many elementary and high schools now require background checks before anyone can interact with students, the instructor renews an agreement with the University's Department of Education to complete background checks for students doing projects in local schools.

Week 1: Forming task groups. The first day of class, the instructor discusses various ways task groups can be formed such as random assignment, social problem or target group populations, or available meetings times. Generally students do not know each other, and random assignment by counting into 5 task groups seems to provide the greatest learning opportunities.

Week 2–9: Preparing for CSSP implementation. While there is a clear structure of steps from the beginning to the end of the project, a lot of flexibility is built into this course. Class time begins with an overview of a step and the accompanying report, a group process concept, and/or time for class problem solving such as needing additional time to complete a step. The instructor serves as a mentor, consultant, and resource person, meeting with task groups throughout the semester. This role varies depending on the needs of each group. Some groups are very organized and make efficient use of class time. Some groups complete much of the work outside of class and use class time to check in and organize upcoming assignments. Some groups procrastinate and have made little effort prior to the middle of the semester. Sometimes this is due to personality conflicts, issues around leadership, or different ideas about the problem to address or methods of task completion. Around the 7–8th week, the instructor meets with each task group specifically to discuss group process with a focus on what is working and what is challenging about working together in this task group.

Week 10–13: Project Completion. Implementation dates depend upon task groups finding a site, getting approval for group activities and arranging dates to accommodate schedules of task group members and sites.

Week 14–15: Analysis and presentation of results. Task groups give a professional-level presentation and submit project statistics that indicate the number of people served and the specific outcomes of the service-learning project. Outcomes might include the amount of money raised, differences in target group knowledge as measured on pre and post-tests, task completion and/or participant observation.

Outcomes/Assessment

Each year, approximately 100 students complete a community service-learning project which impacts the work of 20-30 social service agencies, schools, church groups, homeless shelters, group homes, battered women's shelters and community centers. Through reflective assignments and class presentations, students illustrate an increased sensitivity to the challenges faced by people. By the end of the semester students report an increased confidence in working in task groups and an understanding of what it takes to design and implement a community project.

Conclusion

Students work in a task group and complete a community service-learning project. This provides students with real life opportunities to make a difference in their community. Both students and the communities have benefited. Students have gained knowledge, skills and confidence in their abilities to create change.

Service-learning provided students with real life opportunities to make a difference in their community.

LANGUAGE, LITERATURE, AND COMMUNICATION

INTRODUCTION

BARBARA JACOBY
SENIOR SCHOLAR, ADELE H. STAMP STUDENT UNION
UNIVERSITY OF MARYLAND

As an avid advocate of service-learning both on my campus and nationally, I spend a fair amount of time expounding service-learning's benefits, principles, and challenges. I get excited when I talk about service-learning because I have seen students who participated in high-quality service-learning act on the problems communities and individuals face, engage in dialogue and problem solving with the people most affected, and observe firsthand the effects of racism, sexism, poverty, and oppression. When we lead students through reflection designed to achieve our desired learning outcomes, they begin to see the relevance of course content to real-world issues, the interdisciplinary nature of problems and solutions, the complexity of the social fabric, and how they can choose to be part of the solution rather than part of the problem. A student once told me that service-learning enabled her to test out theories in real time, in real places, with real people, and with real consequences.

In the spirit of reciprocity, community benefits of service-learning include new energy and assistance to broaden delivery of existing services or to begin new ones, fresh approaches to problem solving, and opportunities to participate in teaching and learning. Colleges and universities enjoy improved town-gown relationships, additional experiential learning settings for students, and new opportunities for faculty to orient their research and teaching in community contexts.

That said, my academic discipline is French language and literature. Over the nearly 20 years that I have been laboring in the vineyards of service-learning, I have worked with many of my colleagues in the college of arts and humanities at my university who just could not see service-learning as appropriate or relevant to their courses. A kindred spirit, Barbara T. Bontempo, in her introduction to the first example in this chapter offers a quotation that addresses this issue head-on: "Service-learning is a wonderful idea; I wish I could get my students involved in the community, but I teach [introduction to Theater, Journalism 101, Philosophy & Ethics…]. Field work is for social science or education majors; besides; my course is so crammed with content now…" (p. 51).

However, over time, we have made headway, both on my campus and across the nation, in integrating service-learning into the humanities. More faculty members have embraced service-learning if and when it can enable students to achieve desired learning outcomes more effectively than other pedagogies. In the Intermediate French course I taught for many years, the students found conversation to be more difficult than reading or writing. When I integrated service-learning into my course, conversation came more easily to them because they were speaking about something that mattered to them. Instead of using only the readings and dialogues in the traditional textbook, I asked my students to read about a social issue of concern to them in French newspapers and engaged them in service activities at a local community site related to that issue. As a result, students' classroom conversations became more clear, convincing, and grammatically correct.

It's not hard for faculty members to understand service-learning's potential benefits and to grasp its basic principles of reflection and reciprocity. However, they are often stymied, and understandably so, by the challenges: How do I find and work with community partners? What does it really look like to combine service experience with academic content? How much service is enough? What is critical reflection, and how do I make it happen? How do I grade service-learning? The courses described in this chapter provide compelling reasons why service-learning benefits students and communities, answers to all of these challenging questions, and much more.

The first example from Barbara T. Bontempo's Ethnic American Literature course at Buffalo State College makes the case that service-learning provides students with a lived experience that enriches the study of literature in ways that traditional methods like reading, discussing, writing papers, watching videos, and even role-playing cannot. She then provides a detailed description of the service-learning projects, a timeline, and steps for implementation that will enable others to replicate aspects of this course across the humanities.

In the following two examples, Corinna McLeod of Grand Valley State University and Veronica House of the University of Colorado at Boulder offer two different approaches to first-year writing courses. McLeod worked with colleagues to construct environmentally themed service-learning classes, while House's rhetoric-based course took the tack of moving "students from classroom readings and discussions about a subject into the community, the place where subjects come to life" (p. 54).

Chris Liska Carger of Northern Illinois University clearly demonstrates how service-learning is a natural fit for an emergent teacher education program by engaging students in the hands-on practice of reflective teaching. Similarly, Paige Averett of East Carolina University engages senior social work students in service-learning projects that prepare them for their field placements.

Next, Scott Smithson of Purdue University North Central describes the service-learning component of his courses in business communication and advanced public speaking. The students research and deliver one-hour workshops for elementary school children, providing opportunities to place students in front of audiences outside the classroom as well as enrichment training that meets community needs.

The recently implemented General Education program at Malone University includes a required cross-cultural experience. Jane Hoyt-Oliver's course enables students who may not be able to spend time away from their home communities to engage in a cross-cultural experience in the communities surrounding the university.

Dina Mansour-Cole of Indiana University-Purdue University Fort Wayne recognizes that service-learning is "not without risk: the outreach program won't work if students do mediocre work" (p. 63). She describes the development of a course in the Division of Organizational Leadership and Supervision that engages a diverse group of girls in a theory-based and fun leadership experience, Girls Leading Others. In the final example of this chapter, Service-Learning and the First-Year Experience, a two-credit course, Karin de Jonge-Kannan of Utah State University uses a non-traditional format that includes three and one-half days before the beginning of the fall semester and four weekly one-hour sessions in the first month of the semester. Service-learning fits well into this format, which serves well as a model for service-learning courses in a variety of disciplines.

To close with another of the many reflections by the authors of the examples in this chapter, Veronica House notes that using service-learning as a pedagogical tool "requires a commitment to the belief that students need ways to process and then address the difficult issues they encounter in their course readings and research" (p. 54). For those of us who have made or are considering making this commitment, this chapter provides both philosophical and practical insights that will stand us in good stead.

ENRICHING ARTS & HUMANITIES THROUGH SERVICE-LEARNING

BARBARA T. BONTEMPO
BUFFALO STATE COLLEGE

Keywords: arts & humanities, diversity, literature

Introduction

"Service-learning is a wonderful idea; I wish I could get my students involved in the community, but I teach [Introduction to Theater, Journalism 101, Philosophy & Ethics...]. Field work is for social science or education majors; besides, my course is so crammed with content now..."

So goes the typical response from many instructors in Arts & Humanities. But are these perceived obstacles insurmountable? Can an American literature course, for example, be reworked to viably integrate service-learning without loss of valuable content? An Arts & Humanities course I regularly teach is Ethnic American Literature. Beyond the aesthetics of the literature, the course addresses issues of ethnicity, race, class, religion, and language in an historical context and as they relate to students' lives today. Through the literature, students come to know something of the struggles, hopes, and successes of people from diverse cultures who together make up the mosaic of America. However, reading/discussing, writing papers, watching videos, and even role-playing, can only go so far in allowing students to have a "lived through" experience of another culture. Adding a service-learning component was the next logical step in the development of this course; my experience convinces me that I will not teach it any other way in the future.

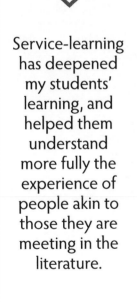

Service-learning has deepened my students' learning, and helped them understand more fully the experience of people akin to those they are meeting in the literature.

Service-learning has deepened my students' learning, and helped them understand more fully the experience of people akin to those they are meeting in the literature —refugees from war and terror, those still living with the legacy of slavery, those disinherited from their own native land, and those grappling with ethnic identity and language barriers. Just as important has been students' service to the community. They do not approach this experience as "outside observers" but as full participants working in tandem with established community agencies—offering their knowledge, experience and special talents, sharing their own values and cultural backgrounds.

Project Description

While the study of 20th and 21st century ethnic American literature remains the primary focus, time has been carved out to enable students to become service-learners:

- The course has been revised to include 15 hours of community experience, taking care to integrate course content and concepts with the field experience both in the course outline and in the classroom interaction (15% of grade).
- Placements are selected from a list of community partners currently collaborating with the College and chosen by the instructor as a "best fit" for the course, one that takes place in a diverse setting. Experiences have included after-school homework help/tutoring; Saturday morning literacy training for Somali mothers; work with recent refugees on negotiating an unfamiliar environment (shopping, banking, schools); serving at a city mission; or design of drama, art, poetry activities for evening youth programs. Students chose to work alone, in pairs, or in groups of three.
- Scheduling, observations and evaluation are coordinated by the Service-Learning Center, but the instructor maintains close ongoing communication with all community partners. Though on-site visits by faculty are optional, I have found them to be extremely useful for authenticating the dialogue in the classroom.
- Students discuss/share their service-learning experiences in small groups throughout the semester, and keep a reflective journal which is turned in twice.

Project Timeline

Week 1: community partners present their programs in a panel, giving students an opportunity to hear firsthand the purpose/scope of each and make an informed decision about which to choose.

Week 2: pre-assessment survey conducted by Service-Learning Center.

Week 3: schedules solidified and students attend orientation at their chosen placement.

Weeks 4–12: students participate weekly at the agencies, writing journal reflections on each visit. (I make one on-site visit to each community placement when several of my students will be there - highly recommended).

Mid-term: journals turned in for feedback and to give me a sense of the depth and quality of the experience students are having.

Weeks 5–12: students orally share experiences and discuss literary connections during several scheduled mini-sessions.

Week 15: one entire session devoted to debriefing the service-learning experience in terms of its impact personally, and academically; post-assessment conducted by the Service-Learning Center; reflection journal collected.

Steps for Implementation

1. If your campus has one, contact the volunteer or service-learning center and identify the point person(s) for an initial meeting. This was extremely helpful for me and led to brainstorming ways to reshape my course and align the major themes and concepts for community involvement.
2. Through the Internet, secure a list of recent resources on service-learning in higher education and do some reading research. There is a wealth of information on-line with many examples of successful programs.
3. Find others on campus doing service-learning and meet informally, or at least look at their course syllabi, even if they are not in Arts and Humanities, just to see how much time has been invested and how they integrate service-learning into their course description and classroom activities.
4. Sketch out your "proposal" if you need to formally sub-

mit to your Dean or other campus official. Be sure to emphasize the academic connections
5. Select/contact/meet the potential community partners/agencies to discuss the ways your students can best meet their needs while gaining insight into environments that complement your course.

Outcomes/Assessment

Students report that the course does involve a somewhat greater time commitment than other literature courses. Still, their journal reflections have overwhelmingly indicated that service-learning is well worth the extra effort:

> Analye came to America in 2000 from Africa with her family (except her father). She works hard but is getting discouraged trying to care for her son, go to school all the time missing her father so far away...I have never interacted with many people from cultures very different from mine. I have a lot of respect for people like Analye who is trying so desperately to adapt and excel in a new culture with a new language...   —Tim

Formal assessment reflects positive pre-post results, especially in terms of student knowledge and understanding of the daily issues faced by newer Americans. Students also comment on their increased sense of how privileged they are to live so freely.

Conclusion

Today, perhaps more than ever before, students need a college experience that is relevant to a world both increasingly diverse, and immediately connected. And, although social sciences and education may seem to provide a more "natural" fit for service-learning, it is the Arts & Humanities that offers students a reflective context for examining the full range of community life. As one student wrote: "Now I see the literature with new eyes." All of Arts & Humanities may benefit from seeing itself "with new eyes" through service-learning.

Today, perhaps more than ever before, students need a college experience that is relevant to a world both increasingly diverse, and immediately connected.

ECOCRITICAL SERVICE-LEARNING IN THE FIRST YEAR COMPOSITION CLASSROOM

CORINNA MCLEOD
GRAND VALLEY STATE UNIVERSITY

Keywords: first-year composition, ecocriticism, first-year writing, environment

Introduction

This service-learning project developed out of my experiences teaching first-year composition at the University of South Carolina in fall 2000. After the success of an initial service-learning project, I was in contact with the Sustainable Universities Initiative (SUI), through USC's School of the Environment. With the help of Christy Friend, Ph.D., the then-Associate Director of First Year Writing and with an initial grant of $3000.00 from SUI that was divided up as a modest stipend to support instructor development in the weeks leading up to the fall 2001 semester, I invited fellow graduate teaching assistants to participate in this service-learning pilot project to begin in fall 2001. Friend and I selected five additional TAs. And, with the help of Friend, the six of us constructed environmentally-themed service-learning classes for First-Year Writing. The classes were: "Writing, the Environment and Citizenship" (two sections), "Writing about Urban Environments," "Writing about Humans and Nature," and "Writing and the Global Environment" and "Writing and Environmental Sustainability."

Project Description

Each instructor worked with the Office of Community Service to establish a list of contact organizations for his or her class. Many of the instructors also contacted those agencies themselves to introduce the pilot project and the instructor to the agency, and to ascertain how best the agency could use the students. This initial set-up was the most time-consuming for the instructors, as many agencies were leery of working with student groups, either preferring only one or two students per semester, or only having group projects (requiring groups of students) for an afternoon. Through phone and the occasional in-person meeting, however, the instructors were able to set up a selection of service opportunities with their students that would fulfill the theme of his or her section of the service. The instructors met to give each other moral support, plan their writing assignments, and exchange tips and contacts on working with local service organizations.

In my section, "Writing and the Global Environment," students were required to write five papers in addition to the community service. The first paper required students to identify a social concern connected to the Global Environment. They had to develop a purpose for their service-learning, identify an organization with which they wanted to work, and through their research of the organization argue why they wanted to work with the particular organization. The second paper was the "anticipation" essay in which students had their opportunity to explore their concerns about working for an agency and voice their complaints about the process of finding a placement. This essay was pivotal in helping the class become a community through their shared concerns, excitement and fears. The third essay for the course was an observation essay. Students documented their experience with the service-learning organization with which they worked, recording what they saw and what they experienced. At that point, it was helpful to remind students that because they had a bad experience, as some of them inevitably will, it does not mean they will have a bad culminating essay. In fact, the bad experiences were important in helping us, as a class, to reflect on the nature of service-learning and to identify what is constructive, helpful service. The fourth essay, the reflection paper, required the students to focus on the overall idea of service-learning. Representatives from the Office of Community Service came to my classroom again to run "Reflection Workshops" where students reflected on their role as volunteers, the role and function of the organizations, and the nature of community service in the undergraduate classroom. The final paper was the research-intensive paper that required students to merge their hands-on experience with the organization to their library research. Students returned to their first essay, and from there would write about the social issue of interest blending their "life research" and "book research."

Project Timeline

This project took place over the course of one semester. The class schedule was three days a week (Monday, Wednesdays and Fridays) for 50-minute increments.

Steps for Implementation

1. The semester before the service-learning class is to take place, contact different agencies and cultivate a relationship with them. The Office of Community Service will be helpful, but if you are targeting a particular issue you might need to develop more contacts.
2. Discuss the project goals with the volunteer coordinators from the agencies. Giving them a better sense of the assignment is helpful for the students and for the agency. Planning ahead increases the likelihood that the agency is able to use the student volunteers effectively.

3. Have the registrar indicate the course has a service-learning component. As students sign up for the course, send emails explaining the service-learning intent and the theme (if there is one) for the course.

4. If you are working with a cohort, make arrangements for you and your colleagues (and possibly your students and their students) to meet and discuss the progress of your different service-learning sections. You and your students will benefit from the relationships that occur within the university and between the university and its community.

Outcomes/Assessment

Students who participated in these service-learning programs reported caring more about the environment after their service-learning project than they did before. They also reported a greater awareness of their "environmental footprint" and their role as environmental citizens. Students demonstrated greater engagement with their writing, and also showed a greater understanding of rhetorical strategies of arguments as they studied environmental debates in comparison to their volunteer experiences. Students also discovered and wrote about the economic, social, political, and educational "aftershocks" of their experiences—for instance, male students who worked with groups cleaning up the sides of highways reported being asked why they were being punished, while female students in the class reported being praised for their volunteerisim.

Conclusion

Not only did students become better writers, better arguers and more informed citizens, they also developed greater independence as learners and critical thinkers. Some students were reluctant to engage in the service-learning projects and/or were concerned that they would be forced to subscribe to a particular political agenda, but by the end of the class realized that service-learning was a tool to promote investment in their own work as scholars as well as encourage them to apply their work from class in the "real world." The "So What? Now What?" reflection workshops were particularly important in helping students move from seeing service-learning as homework to thinking critically about the service the different agencies asked them to perform, and to reflect on the efficacy of the agency and their own role within the agency. Students also left the class with a greater realization that issues, in this case the environment, don't exist in a vacuum; whether English major or Business major, Hospitality, Tourism and Management major or Physical Education major, we have to think of ourselves as active participants in our society and see how these social issues influence the fabric of our own lives.

‖‖‖

STEPPING OUT: CROSSING THE CLASSROOM/COMMUNITY THRESHOLD

VERONICA HOUSE
UNIVERSITY OF COLORADO AT BOULDER

Keywords: composition, freshman, reflection, first-year writing, rhetoric, citizenship

Introduction

This article explains the design and implementation of The University of Colorado at Boulder's first service-learning based First-Year Writing and Rhetoric course in the Program for Writing and Rhetoric. The course attempts to move students from classroom readings and discussions about a subject into the community, the place where subjects come to life. Through this process, students gain an understanding of a social issue, community dynamics, problem-solving, and written advocacy.

Project Description

The course consists of three units: (a) a research-based cause/effect paper, (b) a proposal letter, and (c) an oral presentation. Students volunteer at least 15 hours at a local non-profit of their choice while researching their causal paper that studies either three causes of the social issue their organization addresses or three effects of the issue. In the first version of this paper, students do strictly library research. At the end of the semester, they revise the paper based on their experiences with the non-profit. Students conduct interviews with volunteers, activists, and the people the organizations aim to help, which constitute research that expands and shapes the ways in which they will conceive of the social issue they are investigating in their writing. These end-of-semester revisions of the causal paper allow students to articulate how their understanding has deepened over the semester as they integrate the cultural and political forces that have led to the problem with which they are working.

Project Timeline

After writing the initial version of the causal paper, and about a month in, students have spent an average of 4–6 hours at their non-profit. During the next month they propose and then enact a project that they determine with their organization's volunteer coordinator. One student, Lauren, volunteered with an animal rescue organization.

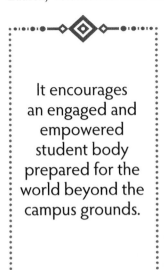

It encourages an engaged and empowered student body prepared for the world beyond the campus grounds.

Her proposal letter urged the head of programming at a local news station to include a "Pet of the Week" segment in the 5:00 news featuring an animal from the rescue site to help encourage adoption. Another student, Evan, volunteered at a homeless shelter. He noted how difficult many of the homeless found it to eat the food provided because of their need for dental care. He sent out letters to twenty-four dentists in Boulder County proposing that they partner with the shelter and provide one day of free dental care each year. Students could put their projects together because they were in the field and saw firsthand what the non-profits needed.

In the last month of the semester, after they have completed an average of 10–15 hours, students make PowerPoint presentations to the class about their work, concerns, and ways in which their peers can become involved through volunteering, letter writing, and petitioning.

Steps for Implementation

You may consider several questions as you plan your course: What do you want students to learn (course objectives)? Will your assignments showcase both traditional classroom and service-learning? How do you hope that this experience will relate to the students' future lives—do you want to help them to become more active and engaged citizens in the long-term, to build their résumés, to demystify career ideas? An instructor's motivations for teaching this kind of course are not always apparent to students, so the policy statement and syllabus should explain upfront what service-learning is and how it is different from charity work. Throughout the semester, reinforce and reflect with students about what they have been doing and learning. Service-learning's effectiveness comes with well-integrated work and reflection activities throughout the semester, as the reflections encourage students to connect theories from the classroom with fieldwork. You might begin with questions such as, "What does citizenship mean to you? Are you an active citizen?"

The questions can become increasingly detailed:
Are there not only personal reasons for why you are where you are in life (i.e., I work hard, so I'm successful), but also deeper social and political structures that support why or

how you get certain opportunities? As you write, think about the people you have encountered so far in your volunteer experience. Do you share opportunities and privileges or are there differences?

Discuss excerpts of their written responses in class. Ask them to reflect again, "What did you learn today about others' ideas concerning participation in civic life?" Assigning several written reflections throughout the semester helps students to challenge their engrained ideas. Determine when you will have students reflect and how reflections will build on one another and connect to readings and assignments?

In terms of logistics, you will need to consider questions such as the following:
Do students have cars, or are the non-profits on bus routes that students can access easily? What are the required training hours before a student can start volunteering? What are the weekly hour requirements, and do these fit with the student's schedule? You might compile a list of non-profits from which students may choose and contact the agencies to explain your course objectives, to find out all of their orientation and work requirements, and to make sure that what they need is appropriate and doable.

Consider your exit strategy. Be clear with the non-profits about course dates, and when students will have to begin and end work. Students should not make false promises to the non-profits. If the project must go beyond the semester, think about creating multi-semester projects. You can plan ahead with the organizations and students about what happens to the proposed project when the course ends.

Outcomes/ Assessment

At the end of the semester, contact agency representatives to verify students' work and hours, to ask what worked, and how to improve for the following semester. This is the time to take stock of what happened and assess with community partners and students: What do you need to change/add? How can you better communicate with your partners/students? Which partners worked well/did not work? You will begin to gather a list for future students.

Conclusion

Using service-learning as a pedagogical tool requires a commitment to the belief that students need ways to process and then address the difficult issues they encounter in their course readings and research. When students form relationships with community members and learn how to create localized change for a specific issue, and when they share their successes with their peers, it encourages an engaged and empowered student body prepared for the world beyond the campus grounds.

CREATING AND MAINTAINING A SERVICE-LEARNING PROGRAM: ROARING FOR A DECADE

CHRIS LISKA CARGER
NORTHERN ILLINOIS UNIVERSITY

Keywords: literacy English Language Learners, tutoring, multicultural/bilingual education, mentoring, methods course

Introduction

Service-learning provides a natural fit for an emergent teacher education program of studies, for service is an integral part of the teaching profession. The Reaching Out Through Art and Reading (ROAR) project that I designed and have directed for over 10 years enables me to guide my education students in the hands-on practice of thoughtful, reflective teaching. In doing so, it provides service to children who participate in a bilingual education program by providing them with instruction aimed at developing their English language comprehension and literacy enjoyment. It gives my students the opportunity to work with ethnically diverse English Language Learners rather than merely reading about multicultural or bilingual education in a textbook or journal study. The classrooms that host the ROAR program are part of transitional bilingual (English/Spanish) programming in two school districts within the service region of my university.

Project Description

ROAR is offered through a 3-credit course that can be repeated; experienced students receive differentiated assignments and take on mentoring responsibilities. ROAR coaches (a term I prefer to tutors) work two hours per week in school sites, and meet for two hours in a weekly on-campus seminar. Their assignments revolve around their coaching/tutoring responsibilities and include lesson planning, journaling, curriculum projects, and readings related to early literacy and English Language Learners. This program serves over 120 primary grade aged students each semester.

ROAR follows an apprenticeship literacy teaching model. College students are not just thrown into a teaching situation. In addition to weekly seminars preparing the curriculum they will facilitate, they are observed in the field and given feedback on their teaching. I also read every structured journal entry ROAR students submit, and interactively journal back to them. ROAR students learn how to design engaging lessons, and to collect assessment data throughout the semester. ROAR requires far more than showing up to do volunteer work.

Project Timeline

The initiation of the ROAR program was expedited at my large state university due to the existence of a course for elective credits in our college entitled Techniques of Tutoring. Because that course was already in place, my timeline was reduced to a semester-length of work recruiting school principals and classroom teachers interested in participating in the ROAR program. With a succinct description of the program in an attractive flyer, replete with our own logo, I personally visited teachers and administrators I knew in our college community and several past graduates teaching in nearby urban areas. I also wrote several small grants to our university's partnership office and our community's Altrusa Society and gained quick funding for the children's literature in which ROAR is based.

Steps for Implementation

The basic steps for implementing a service-learning program similar to ROAR include selecting populations of interest both at the university and in the host community or communities. Obviously, your target population should be related to your professional expertise. I have taught bilingual education courses and multicultural children's literature for years, concentrating on K-5 ages, and ROAR blended these areas perfectly for me. Several communities in our university service region are grappling with their bilingual students' needs, particularly in literacy, and they welcomed input from our faculty and teacher education students. The need for service existed and so did the means to do it.

Once an appropriate course vehicle was identified, my course syllabus became an integral part of the program's implementation, reflecting its design in detail. Readings, projects, rubrics, teaching activities, and assessment plans for participants were all woven into the ROAR syllabus.

Next, I designed a ROAR Handbook so that graduate assistants and work-study students could clearly see the goals and structure of the program. All of the forms used in the program with college students and host schools were included in the handbook. Lists of books and art and science activities were added, with pictures of our most successful projects.

An electronic class Blackboard© was posted with handbook information, the syllabus, as well as maps and directions to the various ROAR host schools. E-mail groups were set up for each coaching team. These were very helpful when emergency situations such as weather-related school closings occurred.

Next, a budget needed to be planned. In my experience, a combination of financial sources was needed. My university, our coaches, and the districts we served all contributed either through monetary grants or by providing consumable materials. Finances for ROAR books, art and science related supplies, photocopying, student assistants, and university cars for off-campus transportation is pieced together each academic year. Financially maintaining a project like ROAR is challenging, as many grants fund only for one initial time period. Searching for grant monies is an integral part of a program like ROAR.

Outcomes/Assessment

There are two prongs to an assessment of the ROAR service-learning program. The first deals with assessing the program's success with the school children it serves. This assessment is built into ROAR's teaching structure with pre- and post-vocabulary assessments, Likert scale literature response data, and anecdotal records. ROAR coaches assist in compiling these data which I put into graphs and reports.

The second prong of the assessment of ROAR deals with outcomes for college coaches. A pre- and post-survey in Likert scale format is given to the coaches, which attempts to garner their perceptions about teaching minor-ity language learners and their assessment of their own instructional development. Interviews and questionnaires are also conducted with the coaches. These data, as well as anecdotal reports, reveal that ROAR coaches often develop new understandings and higher comfort levels in working with diverse language learners. They also report an increased appreciation for the necessity of good organization and planning and the realization that books that are culturally related to their students' backgrounds engender much more response even when language is a struggle.

Conclusion

Many students leave ROAR saying that it should be a required course, and that they learned more through ROAR than through traditional required methods courses. They report that they would consider working in a school that serves linguistic minority children, which is a change from how they previously felt about this group of students. To me, that is ROAR's strongest outcome: the dissolution of stereotypes of what minority language learners are actually like in a classroom setting. We have been ROARing for a decade now, and I have seen guided service-learning bring out the best in our young adults which has been one of the greatest perks in my career.

PROFESSIONAL READINESS: SERVICE-LEARNING PROJECTS AS PREPARATION FOR THE FIELD EXPERIENCE

PAIGE AVERETT
EAST CAROLINA UNIVERSITY

Keywords: professional readiness, program development, senior projects, field placement, social work

Introduction

Undergraduate social work students are required for graduation to spend an entire semester in field placements, which serve as an internship-style learning experience. The field experience provides students with the opportunity to take textbook and theoretical knowledge and apply it to professional and practical experience. Service-learning projects can provide both educational and professional steppingstones for students to prepare them for the transition into their field placements.

The following describes four consecutive cohorts of social work seniors that have engaged in service-learning projects the semester prior to entering their field placements. In the service-learning projects, seniors have engaged in small group projects that include program development and are in the area of social service delivery.

Project Description

As preparation for field placements the student groups were highly independent in connecting with agencies, securing placements, negotiating tasks, implementing programs, and evaluating the services they provided. The students were given a great deal of freedom as they could form their own group memberships, choose the agency and population served based on their interests, and design projects of their own making. Each group had to secure a professional agency contact person who evaluated them and was their management and support at the agency. They had to negotiate and coordinate with each agency for the project(s) they would create.

Each Service-learning group was required to complete:
1. An Introductory proposal and project description that included all contact information for the agency and described in detail the project plan of the group.

2. Active and ongoing involvement in the project with each student completing a minimum of 15 hours of service to the agency.

3. A journal kept by each student, over the course of the project. Journal topics included the basics of who, what, where, when, and why. Students were encouraged to express feelings about the project and to use the journal to describe the group interactions, reflections on the agency, issues in the field of social work, and theory in action.

4. A final professional group presentation that shared the experience and outcomes of the project.

5. A final professionally written summary of the project that connected the project to class content.

The majority of the service-learning projects focused heavily on issues of fundraising, program development, education and outreach, and service delivery. The projects demanded a great deal of group teamwork and incorporated many of the practice, policy, theory, and research skills that they had learned in their course work.

Project Timeline

The service-learning projects were the duration of the entire semester. They were begun the first day of class and continued until the last week of the semester. The following schedule was implemented:

> The main aspect of implementation on the part of the instructor was in creation of a classroom atmosphere where the service-learning projects were a part of the ongoing conversation and used as examples in the lectures.

Week 1: Requirements were outlined for the students on the first day of class. During the second class, a representative from the service-learning center would present the students with paperwork and information to help them begin. They were given a list of potential agencies to work with but ultimately were allowed to work with agencies of their choosing. At the end of the class, students were asked to form their project groups and discuss their areas of interest. Students were required to begin their journals.

Week 2: Student groups were expected to have contacted agencies of interest.

Week 3: Students were expected to have begun their hours at their chosen agency.

Week 4: Each group turned in a project proposal to the instructor and agency.

Weeks 5–7: Students completed half of the required 15 hours. Students were reminded to maintain journals.

Week 8: The instructor contacted each agency to check on the status of each group.

Weeks 9–11: Groups were to have the majority of their hours completed and planning termination.

Week 12: Groups were required to have their supervisor complete evaluations on them, and to complete termination activities if direct service was performed.

Weeks 13–14: Group presentations were completed during class time. Final reports, journals, supervisor evaluations, and grading of group members were all turned in for final grading by the instructor.

Steps for Implementation

Through the experience of requiring the service-learning projects in four consecutive semesters for senior level students, the instructor found that once the basic requirements and expectations of the project are transparent for students, it is best to then step back and let them take responsibility for their projects. As long as students were given a general structure (hours required, group size, assignments and due dates), the freedom of designing their own projects created an investment in and ownership of the project, which lead to a great deal of commitment and creativity on the part of the students. The main aspect of implementation on the part of the instructor was in creation of a classroom atmosphere where the service-learning projects were a part of the ongoing conversation and used as examples in the lectures.

Outcomes/Assessment

As a result of the four semesters of students engaging in service-learning at the same point in their educational program there have been several consistently demonstrated outcomes.

- **Student readiness**—Strengths and weakness displayed in the service-learning project have been strong indicators for students' success in field placements.
- **Student preparation**—Students valued the increased hands-on experience and began to develop professional identities sooner.
- **Enhanced learning**—Students began to apply course material sooner and in smaller steps, making the synthesis smoother.
- **Community engagement**—Community partners were assisted in service delivery and program evaluation efforts.

Conclusion

Utilizing service-learning projects in preparation for field placements has assisted both social work faculty and students in easing the transition from "student" to "professional." Faculty has found that the students' performance in service-learning is a strong indicator of performance in field placements and can prepare students accordingly. As well, students begin the transition to a professional identity sooner and in smaller steps. They begin to apply theory to practice sooner. In addition to being engaged in creative and unique projects, students are afforded more variety in their professional experience through the service-learning projects. Service-learning projects that allowed students to create new programs and assist agencies in their specific needs also enhanced the university's relationship with the local community.

CONNECTING TO COMMUNITY IN A PUBLIC SPEAKING COURSE

SCOTT SMITHSON
PURDUE UNIVERSITY NORTH CENTRAL

Keywords: public speaking, group work, teams, enrichment training, interpersonal communication, team building, community partners, after-school programs

Introduction

This article describes the development of a service-learning component for courses in business communication and advanced public speaking. In such classes, a student typically faces the same audience of classmates while making various presentations throughout the semester. In looking for opportunities to place students in front of audiences outside the classroom, a community need for enrichment training was discovered. Students are challenged to use their creativity, imagination and presentation skills.

Project Description

This public speaking assignment requires teams of students to research and deliver one-hour enrichment workshops for elementary school-aged children attending Safe Harbor, a large local after-school program. The topic options include the life skills that Safe Harbor promotes, including effort, courtesy, integrity, pride, patience, courage, common sense, responsibility, cooperation, and perseverance, among others. In order to successfully design and conduct these workshops, students utilize a wide array of communication concepts and skills, including those related to public speaking, team building, and interpersonal communication.

Learning outcomes driving this service-learning effort include:
- Students should be able to identify and implement important oral and written strategies for organizing and presenting effective workshops to varying audiences.
- Students should be able to identify major obstacles to effective teamwork and understand the methods available to manage such problems.

- Students should become more aware of local community needs and opportunities for service as well as the value of such service.

Project Timeline

An instructor using such projects should plan to be vigilant and accessible. At a minimum, bi-weekly checks on group progress are recommended, as well as occasional group time in class to monitor group progress and the state of team development. Instructors must also make certain that students follow through on projects in a timely manner, and that time is provided at the end of the term for students to reflect on the challenges and rewards of the experience.

Steps for Implementation

Prior to the Course
1. Confer with campus administration regarding the policies and procedures in place to manage the risks and liabilities that may naturally be associated with such an initiative.
2. Develop an alliance with one or more community partners. After-school programs are recommended, as program directors often seek enrichment training to enhance the after-school experience for their young charges. Local Youth Service Bureaus and campus development offices can provide important networking suggestions for those interested in forging such alliances.
3. Structure the course in such a way as to complement the design of the service-learning project. Course study units should be timed so as to coordinate with the likely stages of the project. For example, topics related to interpersonal communication and/or team-

building can be placed early in the semester, with course discussion of oral presentations scheduled a bit later. The grading and weighting of the project must also be carefully considered and discussed in the course syllabus. As this project demands a significant amount of time and energy, a clear statement of grading criteria will be expected by students.

4. Create a general timeline for implementation and preparation of course materials.

5. Design the key materials needed for the project. Handouts summarizing all key requirements are absolutely essential, and should include a project description as well as all important deadlines.

During the Course

1. Distribute and discuss the project overview very early in the term. Underscore the importance of student participation and the potential worth of the project in the community. Consider inviting the community partner into the class to make a presentation and field questions related to the project. This will enhance project credibility, student knowledge, and networking opportunities needed to make the project successful.

2. A special session on organizing enrichment workshops is usually helpful. Locate and refer students to outside resources such as websites that contain free exercises for use. Emphasize the value of targeting materials to children and detail approaches to managing relationships with children.

3. Student work teams can be organized. Students may rank the three topics of most interest before placing them in teams with others who share those same interests. At this stage, some attention also must be given to the safety screening procedures for those participating. In some instances, organizations may require students to submit to a screening process that can take one to three weeks. Ordinarily the community partner will handle screening chores; but required information must be given to them in a very timely fashion.

4. Teams should select a leader and liaison to the community partner. This person should be responsible for handling scheduling issues and establishing a team link to the sponsoring agency.

5. Students should be encouraged to design and provide feedback forms for the children participating in their workshops, and for the site supervisors and program

directors that may be on hand. As it seems unlikely that most instructors will be able to attend student presentations outside of class, this feedback is absolutely essential in determining the grade for the project.

Outcomes/Assessment

Each student should engage in a considerable amount of individual and team reflection. Students might be encouraged to maintain individual logs of experiences working with others in workshop development. These logs can then be used as the basis for a final reflection effort.

Evaluation forms for the site supervisors, the children involved, and the students participating have also been valuable and help to provide a broad-based assessment of the service-learning effort.

Oral presentations are recommended as assessment tools and can be designed to bring the project full circle. Such presentations require teams to incorporate key skills in the areas of teaming, training, presentation organization, presentation delivery, and visual aid development. Questions addressed here challenge students to think about the strengths and weaknesses of their preparation, the application of course concepts and skills in real-world settings, and the value of community engagement. This final presentation can be taped, reviewed, and critiqued by each member of the group, thus intensifying the learning associated with the effort. Consider inviting members of the community agency as well. This adds motivation for the students, offers opportunity for program improvement, and allows the community partners to personally thank students for their efforts.

Conclusion

While challenges do exist, the project has succeeded on many levels and seems to provide a win-win outcome. Community partners report that the children identify with student presenters and look to them as role models. The college students involved report greater understanding of course topics and an increased commitment to serve their communities as a result of participation in the project. As one team reported, "We feel that this is not only a worthwhile project, but a responsibility that we have to our community."

College students involved report greater understanding
of course topics and an increased commitment to serve their communities
as a result of participation in the project.

IMPLEMENTING THE MISSION: SERVICE-LEARNING IN THE COMMUNITY

JANE HOYT-OLIVER
MALONE UNIVERSITY

Keywords: mission, cross-cultural, general education, town and gown, non-traditional student

Introduction

In 2007, Malone University, a sectarian university in Northeast Ohio, implemented a new General Education (GE) program. The program requires students to take courses from nine component menus that prepare all students for the 21st century.

As part the new GE, all students engage in a cross-cultural experience. Prior to the implementation of GE, this was often fulfilled through a "traditional" three-credit course entitled "Cross Cultural Studies." Those who taught the course were concerned that students might be gaining "head knowledge" but were not actively engaging in the community. The professors saw the implementation of the new GE program as an opportune time to implement curricular structures that would increase the chance that students would strengthen their understanding of others through hands-on service experiences.

Project Description

Two primary courses are provided in the GE which fulfill the cross cultural requirement. One course mentors students through various overseas work projects. Almost one third of Malone students elect this option. This essay will focus on the second option, a cross-cultural experience that is based in the communities surrounding the university.

Project Timeline

In an ideal world, all students might be able to spend three weeks away from their home communities, but that is not always possible. Many of Malone's students are the first in their families to attend college. Most students work at least one outside job while attending Malone. An increasing percentage are "non-traditional" students with responsibilities to children and families, or have commitments that preclude a lengthy stay outside the country. All students are making significant sacrifices to obtain a university education.

To this end, faculty within the Social Work Program developed a class called the Community-Based Cross Cultural Experience (CBCCE). Students combine both classroom discussion and a 30-hour field requirement in which they work for a non-profit organization servicing the needs of individuals who the students have identified as outside their area of cultural expertise.

Prior to the class, students meet individually with the faculty member in charge of the CBCCE. Each completes a short form, which outlines the student's availability, contact information, transportation needs and other basic information. In addition, students are asked to give a brief summary of the community in which they grew up, and racial, ethnic, or economic groups with which the student has had [self-defined] "significant contact." Students discuss their information with the professor. Each is informed that although accommodation to student schedule is considered, the cross-cultural component mandates that student comfort level with a particular population group is not.

Steps to Implementation

In advance of the semester, letters are sent to area agencies inquiring about available placements for student interns. Agency participation varies from semester to semester. Each semester offers a variety of opportunities, (e.g., a faith-based homeless shelter for men in the city, a therapeutic riding center in the rural areas of the county, community-run grassroots outreach in a transitional neighborhood). Students from urban areas are placed in rural settings whenever possible; those from suburban or rural settings are placed in city placements. If a student's experiences cannot be *geographically* cross-cultural (e.g., a student who has lived for significant periods in both urban and rural settings), faculty elect a placement that is *culturally* or *sociologically* cross-cultural (e.g., working with a prison re-entry program or with the elderly in a nursing home setting).

Two weeks prior to each semester, the Director of Service-learning meets with the faculty member in charge of CBCCE. Agency needs and available times are matched with student need for a truly cross-cultural experience.

On the first day of class, students are provided with the name of their agency match and who to contact to set up an interview. (Agencies are always given the "last word' as to whether the student will be placed at the site). Students are also provided with a copy of a memorandum of agreement, which is filled out by the agency field supervisor. This must be brought back and signed by the CBCC professor within the first two weeks of class.

Early in the semester, students take a 3-hour "cross-cultural tour" of the county, which is led by the professor, the Director of Multicultural Services and/or by a local community Organizer. Each leader provides an impression of the history of the community. These impressions reflect the perspectives of those who have traditionally had less power and influence. This is often the first time that students have been formally introduced to the rivers of power and politics that undergird community service provision in the area. In addition, statistics gathered for the local United Way provide broad-based understandings of the challenges and strengths of the county.

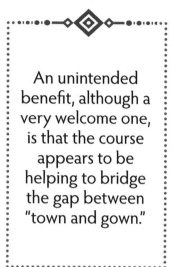

An unintended benefit, although a very welcome one, is that the course appears to be helping to bridge the gap between "town and gown."

In addition to community hours, the class meets for 10 sessions during the 15 weeks of the semester. Each class is designed to assist students to broaden their definition of community. Lectures on such topics as eco-systems theory, oppression, discrimination, and privilege, build a framework in which students learn about themselves and their agency's approach to service provision. The course also contains an online component in which students listen to a variety of podcasts of leaders speaking about community and social action. Students react by threaded discussion to the content of the podcasts. Thus, when students are not in the classroom, they remain connected as a class and broaden their understanding of community with each other online.

Initial assignments utilized Kretzman and McKnight's *Building Communities from the Inside Out*, which outlined a strengths-based approach to community building. The educational focus is on assisting students to comprehend the strengths that are found in connectedness. Additional readings from Claiborne's *The Irresistible Revolution* and G. Smith's Radical *Compassion: Finding Christ in the Heart of the Poor* demonstrate how groups of individuals with a commitment to community live out that commitment in inner city Philadelphia.

Outcomes/Assessment

A variety of assessment tools are used. Students complete an assessment of their experience, and have field liaisons sign off on the hours completed. Community liaisons are asked to complete evaluations of each student's work based upon the memorandum of agreement. Both qualitative and quantitative measures indicate students were assisted to expand their idea of which groups to include when thinking about "their community" and it also strengthened their desire to serve the community even after the course was completed.

An unintended benefit, although a very welcome one, is that the course appears to be helping to bridge the gap between "town and gown." Agencies are delighted to meet students from a wide variety of majors. Students, who often had previously given little thought to the community that surrounds the university, come away with a greater sense of being anchored in a living, breathing place with a history, a present and most importantly, a future. Through service, learning becomes mutually educational. As one student noted in his evaluation of the course, "My understanding as to who is included in the community has really changed. I realize now that there were whole categories of people that I simply overlooked when I thought about "my community." I think this is a permanent change."

Conclusion

General Education at Malone University is clearly connected to the University's student learning outcomes. Two of those learning outcomes indicate that students should "understand, appreciate and engage diverse views and cultures..." (MU Learning Outcome A-1) and "develop relationships characterized by love, compassion and service to others" (MU Learning Outcome E-4). The Community Based Cross Cultural experience provides an entry-level experience foundation upon which students can build as they progress through their education. Through service, a student's understanding of the diversity of communities is broadened is and the community is introduced to the compassion and service of Malone's student body.

Students, who often had previously given little thought to the community that surrounds the university, come away with a greater sense of being anchored in a living, breathing place with a history, a present and most importantly, a future.

CREATING A COMPANION COURSE FOR A UNIVERSITY-BASED YOUTH OUTREACH PROGRAM

DINA MANSOUR-COLE
INDIANA UNIVERSITY - PURDUE UNIVERSITY FORT WAYNE

Keywords: campus outreach programming, leadership, Significant Learning Model, social responsibility

Introduction

This submission chronicles activities used to develop an entire course that would serve as a platform for an outreach program developed by our academic department and serving middle/high school girls. *Creating & Assessing a Leadership Development Program* was first offered in the summer of 2007, but the GLO: Girls Leading Others outreach program that served as a learning laboratory for the course was developed in 2004.

Consistent with the mission of the Division of Organizational Leadership and Supervision (OLS) to integrate theory and practical application in developing leaders for roles in the dynamic organizational environment of the 21st century, undergraduate and graduate students study the skills associated with power, influence tactics, communication, facilitation, creativity, decision making, planning, leading change, and collaboration efforts. Recognizing that OLS was in a unique position to provide an economically, racially, and ethnically diverse group of girls a theory-based and fun leadership experience, OLS faculty and students developed GLO: Girls Leading Others. Three years later, we created a companion course where OLS students review their discipline's knowledge base (leadership and creativity), learn general program development principles, and then practice their skills in the GLO service-learning laboratory.

Project Description

By designing the course to maximize the inclusion of the elements in Dee Fink's (2003) *Significant Learning Model (SL)*, the course included most service-learning best practices. Fink's model requires attention to: (1) foundational knowledge (2) application learning (3) integration (4) the human dimension of learning (5) caring and (6) learning how to learn. Course goals said students should:

- Be able to understand/reproduce steps for developing leadership programming.
- Choose appropriate topics/training activities for youth leadership training.
- Demonstrate use of creative decision-making tools.
- Communicate with young leaders about how to lead others.
- Assess an actual program.

This highlights two SL best practices: students control important aspects of the learning program, while testing new roles in an environment that encourages risk taking/rewards competence (Erickson & Anderson, 1997). There is a great deal of reciprocity inherent in this program: students learn from and about community members, professors learn from students, and community participants learn from students. This approach is not without risk: the outreach program won't work if students do mediocre work, so an early and genuine commitment to the course goals by all students is needed. On the other hand, we don't have to leave campus to serve—our lab comes to us!

Project Timeline

Because the outreach program requires a full week of exercises, food, assessment, breaks, etc., it was key that the outreach program was somewhat established so that all of the tasks associated with the program were not the responsibility of any one class of students. Assessment information from 2007 influenced 2008 course planning. A theme, funding targets, and publicity for the next year are completed by the first class. Exercises/ideas not used become back-ups for the next class to use. A meeting three weeks *in advance* of the semester to discuss course expectations and concerns helps minimize students withdrawing from the course once it was started. Depending on the dates of the outreach program, the semester beginning/end dates are adjusted in order for students to "use" the learning laboratory and have time to reflect after the week is over.

Steps for Implementation

Since the outreach program and course were sponsored by the same division, the first (and one time only) step was to convince our curriculum committee to accept this new course as equivalent to a course previously taught: Creativity and Innovation for Business. This insured that the course "counted" for their program of study. I developed readings and materials to teach in a shorter summer semester, while showing course rigor. Next was to recruit students for the course, emphasizing content that they would learn and the service aspects of working with these youth. And finally, I prepared to make this a hybrid course, since reading and discussion could be done online (Blackboard©) and precious in-class time could be spent developing and practicing material with each other before presenting it at the outreach program.

Since an important principle of good service-learning is to familiarize students with the target organization, I arranged for a previous participant/high-schooler to address the class, armed with engaging photos and stories. A field trip to hear about the new program design activity at another girl-serving organization was held in week three. Weeks four and five completed a "killer" comprehensive exam. This scenario-based exam included eight questions that took students through all of the design elements of a program, and helped them refine at least one activity that they would eventually present to the girls. After the implementation week, all students prepared a reflective portfolio. A final wrap-up and assessment class meeting was held.

Outcomes/Assessment

Middle/high school girls learned how to work together in teams to reinforce concepts such as respect, trust, power, and communication. Girls also presented artistic technological projects about themselves and their teams in a closing community ceremony. Assessments of girls and parents showed high levels of satisfaction, learning, and intention to recommend the program to others.

Since this was a credit course, grading criteria was established in the syllabus. While there was a reflection requirement, it was also possible to grade items linked to other course objectives. Grading their pre-work is important for assessment and to adjust material prior to implementation with the participants. Grading did not damage enthusiasm or passion for the program, but was welcomed as feedback before "the real test" with youth.

Students also provided evidence of both the quality and quantity of their learning. In qualitative course assessments, students reported "never having worked as hard in something so fulfilling," making them "think in new ways" and "benefiting emotionally as well as educationally." They thanked us for giving them a place to practice their own leadership since "the key to leadership is action- and action takes practice."

> "But above all else, it is making leadership personal to you... You have to be confident in yourself and rely on what you know, your theories. After you understand that, you can incorporate those lessons into any activity."

Four students came back as volunteers for a second year (and brought friends!), showing that they had developed social responsibility.

Conclusion

This type of course could be replicated by many different disciplines that can access outreach programs that showcase their discipline-specific skills. On our campus this includes outreach programs in math, engineering, computer science, theater, visual arts and others. It is key that the course have real content, provided in a theoretically grounded way. By translating and teaching the material to audiences other than classmates in their own major, students must engage in a higher level of critical thinking and make their discipline's material simple, vivid, and relevant.

References

Erickson, J. A. & Anderson J. B. (Eds.). (1997). *Learning with the community: Concepts and models for service learning in teacher education.* Washington, DC: American Association for Higher Education.

There is a great deal of reciprocity inherent in this program: students learn from and about community members, professors learn from students, and community participants learn from students.

SERVICE-LEARNING AND THE FIRST-YEAR EXPERIENCE

KARIN DE JONGE-KANNAN
UTAH STATE UNIVERSITY

Keywords: first-year experience, high school to college programs, early start programs, freshman orientation programs

Introduction

The first few weeks after students arrive on the college campus is a critical time to engage them in new approaches to studying and learning. Recognizing the importance of sound beginnings, most American universities offer First-Year experiences of some kind. At Utah State University, the First-Year experience program is called "Connections" and takes the form of a 2-credit course held for three and a half days before the beginning of fall semester, plus four weekly one-hour sessions in the first month of the semester. While I had implemented service-learning (SL) in other courses, 2007 was the first time I used SL in my section of "Connections."

When implementing SL, one must be mindful of course goals when designing instruction that combines class readings and discussions with community involvement and reflection. The course goal for "Connections" is stated as follows:

> Connections is an academic course designed to ease students' transition to Utah State University and to prepare them for their college experience. The course covers academic expectations, study strategies, and time management skills, as well as providing an atmosphere to meet friends, faculty, and staff.

As the course title emphasizes, the purpose of "Connections" is to put students in touch with the resources and the people that can support them on the road to success, connecting them to campus and the community as they practice the skills they will need to be successful.

Project Description

To help my students better connect with the campus and the larger community, and to provide them an opportunity to practice skills that would help them be successful in college, I partnered with the university's Anthropology Museum for an SL project. The museum's mission is to introduce visitors to the field of anthropology through student-designed exhibits focusing on ideas—such as how human lives change over time, how people share knowledge, produce art, and practice religion. The museum, therefore, plays an important educational role not only for our university but also for K-12 students and adult community members from the entire region. Invariably, those who discover the museum say they wish they had found out about it sooner.

Because of its limited budget, the museum is always looking for economical and effective ways to promote its mission and programs.

Project Timeline

The museum coordinator and I worked together to design an SL project that could be accomplished by my 25 Connections students in the first two weeks of the semester.

Steps for Implementation

During the pre-semester session of the course, class time was provided for students to tour the museum, make themselves familiar with its exhibits, and ask questions. They became knowledgeable about the museum and its role on campus and in the wider community. With this knowledge, the students were able to design a booth, flyers, and presentations that were featured at the museum's booth on "Day on the Quad," which is an outdoor event in the heart of campus, held in the first week of classes of fall semester. During "Day on the Quad," many campus and community organizations promote their missions and raise awareness about their programs.

Outcomes / Assessment

A well-designed SL project must relate the service project to the course readings. The "Connections" program selects a book assigned to all first-year students for a Common Book Experience. In 2007, the featured book was *Complications* by Atul Gawande, a surgeon who writes about the art and science of medical practice. For their written reflections, students related selected quotes from the book to what they were learning in the museum and their expectations about college. For example, in a chapter on obesity, Gawande writes "We are a species that has evolved to survive starvation, not to resist abundance" (p. 170). Students were asked to reflect on this statement, and connect it with evidence in the museum. For other writing assignments, students reflected on their views of college in connection with quotes from the book. For example, in a chapter on medical errors, Gawande writes, "There are surgeons who will see faults everywhere except in themselves. They have no questions and no fears about their abilities. As a result, they learn nothing from their mistakes and know nothing of their limitations" (p. 61). Students connected this to their own perceptions of success and failure and the roots thereof. These writing assignments were shared in group discussions. They were also collected and responded to, but not graded.

Conclusion

This SL project was successful not only because students enjoyed it and commented positively on it, but more importantly because the objectives of effective SL were met: (1) The course goal was to connect students to the campus and surrounding community and help them practice skills for success in college. As the students learned about the museum and what it offers, they were able to recast and pass on that knowledge through cooperation and time management, using the variety of skills and strengths found among team members; (2) The museum benefited from the energy and enthusiasm of the students to accomplish a task (promoting the organization at a campus event) that the sole staff person could not have accomplished on her own; and (3) The students connected course readings (the text used in the Common Book Experience) with reflection on their involvement with the museum.

The museum benefited from the energy and enthusiasm of the students to accomplish a task.

Working with the university's anthropology museum was a rewarding experience, and I look forward to continued cooperative efforts with service-learning in the future. For 2008, the selected text for the common book experience is *A Long Way Gone*, by Ishmael Beah, which chronicles the experiences of a boy soldier in the civil war in Sierra Leone. I am currently in the process of drawing quotes from this book to assign as reflection pieces for the students as we partner with the anthropology museum again. I remain excited about the possibilities of introducing SL to students who are just beginning their college education.

References

Beah, Ishmael. (2007). *A Long way gone: memoirs of a boy soldier*. New York, NY: Sarah Crichton Books.

Gawande, Atul. (2002). *Complications: a surgeon's notes on an imperfect science*. New York, NY: Harry Holt & Company.

Global Studies and Local Outreach to Exceptional Populations

Introduction

Melisa K. Orozco and Robert W. Franco
Kapi'olani Community College

There's no better time than the present to explore educational opportunities that expose students to our increasingly interconnected and complex world. Globalization, for instance, has decomposed barriers to movement such that current migration trends have dramatically altered local demographics, hence the need for bilingual and culturally sensitive professionals and service providers. The Internet liberates knowledge and idea sharing in an unprecedented way; when an issue like environmental sustainability is at the forefront of political and economic agendas, we look to indigenous groups from across the planet for lessons on sustainable living. Mother Nature demonstrates vividly (and oftentimes alarmingly) interconnectedness: tsunamis, hurricanes, flooding, oil spills, and the like and their global repercussions clearly demonstrate the urgent need for cross-cultural collaboration and understanding of their causes and potential solutions.

This chapter, "Global Studies and Local Outreach to Exceptional Populations," illustrates the important role that indigenous, intercultural, and international service experiences—as "global" as Malawi or Belize, and as "local" as New Orleans or North Manchester—can play in the formation of globally competent students. Through the use of service-learning pedagogies, students from disciplines such as social work, foreign language, and education gain new perspectives and an enriched academic experience by directly engaging with individuals and communities representing diverse cultural, linguistic, and geographic backgrounds. The array of course and project models provided within will surely motivate you to consider what your unique indigenous, intercultural or international service-learning course or program might look like, and inventory the resources or support systems disposable for implementation. The following articles are quite complementary and provide valuable program examples. From them we created a list of hints to developing indigenous, intercultural, and international programs based on the valuable program examples.

Advance work and preparation is critical, as is a balance between the service experiences and opportunities to explore the community beyond the service site.
- For international service-learning, a long-term faculty connection to the host country assures quicker course and learning goal development and program implementation and helps to keep costs down (Luciani, Sylvia; Barber, Jones, Kelly). Where there is no prior connection, much more time and front-end work are required to assure a smooth program (Richards);
- Pre-departure orientation, prepares students for their service, learning, interactions, protocol, culture, geography, history, and language. The Internet can help facilitate this process (Barber, Jones, Kelly). In-country orientation should be delivered by local hosts and educators;
- Cultural excursions are a must; they solidify and add depth to the student's experience through informal interactions with nature, food, music, art, dance, etc. (Anderson; Luciani, Sylvia; Barber, Jones, Kelly; Richards);

Service-learning can engage language students with immigrant communities, and encourage them to envision using the language in their future careers (Rogers; Becerra, Espenschied-Reilly).

- Even at the beginner level, language students who serve start to breakdown cultural barriers and connect to the native community (Simon);
- Students gain a deeper appreciation for and understanding of the immigrants that live in their communities, by spending time in one of the sending countries (Bender, Huq);

Indigenous, intercultural, and international service programs can provide a multitude of benefits for the students and communities involved.

- Students in global programs serve with non-governmental organizations (NGOs), indigenous groups, and direct-service providers, engaging in tasks directly related to their academic majors or careers (Richards; Luciani, Sylvia; Barber, Jones, Kelly);
- Intercultural programs based on urgent needs, as a result of current events/initiatives or natural disasters, can be very effective and rewarding (Anderson; Maccio; Gustad-Leiker);
- Service-learning in courses fully dedicated to service and community engagement benefit students and service providers. The energy of an entire class can accomplish daunting tasks such as empirical data-collecting surveys (Maccio; Anstadt, Gustad-Leiker);

Outcomes, and their assessment, should be specific to the project, include students, service providers, and service recipients. They may include essays, portfolios, oral presentations, posters, etc.

- Daily reflection and journals are essential for the student to capture daily lessons, experiences, and should be monitored daily. Deep reflection can be accomplished post-international experience, especially when the experience prepared students for their local service; a seminar dedicated entirely to service (Connections Seminar) provides a forum where students can exchange ideas between 'there' and 'here' (Bender, Huq);
- For language students, portfolios, rather than a single reflection component, capture a greater picture of students' experiences (Becerra, Espenschied-Reilly; Abbott, Lear). Experiences can be further enhanced when the oral presentation is not a monologue read off a paper, but an elaborate poster that begs for discussion and impromptu use of the target language (Abbott, Lear);

And remember, no matter what happens, as the instructor, you should be flexible and always rise to the occasion. The students will follow!

As you peruse the chapter, keep outcomes in mind. Large amounts of time, effort, emotion, and money are invested in these often short-lived, but life-changing, experiences. It is imperative that their value is translated into common goals other global, intercultural or indigenous service-learning courses or projects also are trying to achieve. The American Council on Education (ACE, www.acenet.edu) and the Fund for the Improvement of Secondary Education (FIPSE) developed a tool to help create or strengthen international learning outcomes for courses and programs. Through its Center for International Initiatives, ACE has assisted colleges and universities in their pursuit to internationalize[1] their campuses. The following outline of international learning outcomes is a synthesis of knowledge, skills and attitudes, and serves as the foundation for many programs.

A globally competent student graduating from our institution gains... (www.acenet.edu)

Knowledge
- Understands his culture within a global and comparative context.
- Demonstrates knowledge of global issues, processes, trends, and systems.
- Demonstrates knowledge of other cultures.

---

1. According to ACE website, "internationalization" is defined by Knight (1999) 'as the process of infusing an international or intercultural dimension into the teaching, learning, research, and service functions of higher education'.

Skills

- Uses knowledge, diverse cultural frames of reference, and alternate perspectives to think critically and solve problems.
- Communicates and connects with people in other language communities in a range of settings for a variety of purposes, developing skills in each of the four modalities: speaking (productive), listening (receptive), reading (receptive), and writing (productive).
- Uses foreign language skills and/or knowledge of other cultures to extend his access to information, experiences, and understanding.

Attitudes

- Appreciates the language, art, religion, philosophy, and material culture of different cultures.
- Accepts cultural differences and tolerates cultural ambiguity.
- Demonstrates an ongoing willingness to seek out international or intercultural opportunities.

Opportunities in global service-learning and local outreach to exceptional populations offer students of all disciplines an invaluable experience in knowing their place in the world and how they can be of service to those in their local community and the global community. Purposeful travel and outreach provide education for the head, hands and heart. Every student and faculty member presented with the opportunity should rise to the occasion and seize the moment. With the entire process laid out before you, there are no excuses!

References

Knight, J. cited in Olson, C. L., Green, M. F., and Hill, B. A (2005). *Building a Strategic Framework for Comprehensive Internationalization.* Washington, DC: American Council on Education.

American Council on Education and Fund for the Improvement of Secondary Education. (2008) *International Learning Outcomes.* Retrieved June 12, 2010 from http://www.acenet.edu/Content/NavigationMenu/ProgramsServices/ cii/res/assess/intl_learn_Outcomes.htm.

INTERNATIONAL SERVICE-LEARNING (ISL): CREATING AN INTERSESSION SOCIAL WORK COURSE IN INDIA

JULIE RICHARDS
UNIVERSITY OF VERMONT

Keywords: international, global curriculum, social work, non-government organization (NGO)

Introduction

In an effort to build global citizenship into the curriculum and further internationalize students' experiences both on and off campus, this winter intersession course was created to provide an affordable alternative to a semester abroad, while also emphasizing human rights, social justice, and the strengths perspective.

Project Description

Social Work Practice in India provides students with an opportunity to engage with community social service providers in the delivery of volunteer services to children and families in Mumbai, India. This course enables students to have an international social work experience while also expanding their understanding of power and privilege, human rights, social justice, and the strengths perspective from a more global perspective.

Students were paired with one of three different non-government organizations (NGOs). Two of the projects included teaching English and other subjects to children within and from impoverished communities. The third project assisted with developing a database to monitor students with developmental disabilities' progress with acquisition of daily living skills as well as interviewing parents about their satisfaction with the school and presenting a report of the aggregated data.

Project Timeline

This course took approximately three years to develop. Because this faculty member had no previous connections to any NGOs or people in India, she needed to use networking skills through the World Wide Web to develop connections. Once she received a response from someone (about half a year after sending multiple e-mails and letters to various organizations, professors, and others in India or with Indian connections), she applied for a university grant to develop the course. Course development, from that point, to implementation took an additional year.

Steps for Implementation

Course development:
- Establish a connection/contact person in the host country
- Meet with faculty who have led study abroad and/or international service-learning trips with students to learn from their experiences
- Work closely throughout the process with the university's international education office and service-learning offices to access their resources as well as keep them abreast of your work
- Travel to the host country to meet with your contact person, network with others, develop service-learning projects with various NGOs, discuss training needs for students, explore and secure lodging and meal arrangements, in-country travel arrangements, field trips
- Develop the course syllabus (including pre- and post-trip assignments)
- Work with appropriate university offices to develop a budget
- Work closely with a travel agent as early as possible to secure a group flight so that everyone travels together
- Develop an application and screening process for enrollment in the class. This faculty member brings a maximum of ten students, but due to attrition for various reasons, encourages as many applications as possible and develops a waiting list
- Constantly maintain communication with service-learning partners in host country regarding both pre-trip training needs, planning in-country orientations and activities, confirming travel and lodging arrangements (ideally, with faculty and students all staying in one location), costs, and project development

Pre-departure:
- Develop a class list-serve to post communications pre- and post- trip
- Host at least three pre-departure meetings with the whole class. Included in these meetings:

  - review course assignments
  - service-learning projects
  - packing lists
  - confirm that passports are updated and travel visas are secured
  - perhaps plan a group trip to the travel clinic for vaccinations
  - invite someone who is from the host country (and hopefully the specific locale to which you are traveling) to come speak about cultural "do's and don'ts," and to answer student questions about the host country and cultures
  - view some clips from films that take place in the host country to offer students visual and auditory impressions
  - offer some basic host country language lessons
- With a service-learning partner, plan an in-country orientation to be held during part, or all, of the first full day in the country
- Ask the service-learning partners to plan an orientation to the NGO and project for their specific students

Once in the host country:
- Along with the service-learning partner(s), host the orientation
- Introduce students to their service-learning partners and projects
- Assist the students with navigating the transportation to/from the project on the first day
- Plan daily debriefing sessions as a whole group, while also allowing flexibility for the students to occasionally not attend a session if they are invited to participate in a cultural or educational event that conflicts with the session
- Check-in regularly with the service-learning partners to monitor the progress being made on the projects and any concerns
- Mid-trip, meet privately with each individual student to check in about:
  - What is working for him/her with this course
  - Any concerns/questions/issues
  - Anything more s/he needs for support from the faculty member
- Plan a mid-trip fun group outing (i.e., a dinner at a restaurant) to rejuvenate
- Do a field trip to another location and/or organization to give students exposure to another part of the country or another organization to compare and contrast their previous in-country experiences
- Plan and host an in-country debriefing/closure session for the whole class prior to departure, as well as encourage service-learning partners to plan a closure activity and feedback process for and with their project students

Re-entry:
- Host at least one re-entry/integration class one month after return to discuss assignments, reintegration,

how the ISL experience impacts students' daily lives, professional development, global responsibility and citizenship, and their next steps with processing this transformative experience.

Outcomes/Assessment

Students' and ISL partners' feedback highlighted the positive contribution through service-learning work. Students noted that the course did enhance their commitment to social justice and human rights, while community partners reported that the projects exceeded expectations and significantly improved not only direct services, but also encouraged NGOs to think about systems' enhancement.

Conclusion

Developing and implementing an ISL course is a profoundly rewarding experience. Not only can it enhance one's scholarship, but it also enriches personal and professional relationships with students and colleagues in a context outside of the home campus.

Internship/service-learning experience in Belize

Johnelle Luciani and Barbara A. Sylvia
Salve Regina University

Keywords: Belize, Central America, social work, internship, multicultural

Introduction

The past decade has witnessed a growing interest among social work educators in ensuring that baccalaureate level programs prepare students for the realities of globalization. One aspect of that response has been the design of curricula that are not only inclusive of current international issues, but help provide students with the knowledge, skills and values necessary to function cross-culturally. The development of cross-cultural competence is both a process of personal growth and professional development, best realized in a context that Tesoriero (2006) has referred to as a reflective practice process.

The call to develop skills in international social work brings with it both challenges and opportunities, but as Mathiesen and Lager (2007) remind us, mutual respect and reciprocity are essential program elements. Engstrom and Jones (2007) further recommend that educational programs not only address an understanding of global problems, but country-specific interventions to address transnational problems. Immersing students in the culture of a developing country affords them an opportunity to gain such a perspective. This entry describes such a program, which also builds on the recommendations of Abram and Cruce (2007) who emphasized learning from indigenous people in host countries.

Project Description

This two-week interim service-learning internship provides students an opportunity to explore the history and culture of Belize (Central America) while learning through direct service in health and human service settings. Through interdisciplinary exchange and a blend of classroom and field encounters, students are challenged to think critically about global issues in healthcare, education and social welfare. A group of 12–15 students spend 10 days with two faculty members, working in health, education and human service settings in Belize (assisting in the building of homes for low-income families; working in a soup kitchen, clinic and nursing home; participating in outreach services to frail elderly in the community and working with children in an orphanage and in various school settings). Four days of the fourteen are devoted to travel within the country, where Mayan ruins, rainforests and the largest barrier reef in the western hemisphere sit juxtaposed to areas in which small over-crowded shanties provide the only shelter from the elements.

Prior to departure, students gain a familiarity with the country through readings and three two-hour class meetings. Upon arrival in Belize, students are oriented to the country (its history, culture, peoples and present day realities) by Belizeans. This is an important element in the process of establishing and maintaining mutual respect. Classes are held each evening, lasting from one to two hours as needs dictate. These sessions are designed to be both content- and process-oriented, with instruction and organizational details often giving rise to discussions concerning student perceptions, acculturation issues, and responses to the many emotionally draining experiences they encounter. The skills of seasoned social work faculty become essential in the process of helping students as they process their experiences. So too, the faculty draw upon their skills as clinicians in helping students to design and deliver programs that are developmentally and culturally appropriate to the population with whom they are working (elders, young children, school aged youth, or families).

Project Timeline

One year prior to the scheduled start date of the program, the instructors visited the country, spending a full week re-establishing contacts, determining the viability of various internship placements, seeking counsel on areas in which the needs of the community could best be met, and making arrangements for the following year. Respect for cultural norms demanded that careful attention be paid to ensuring that there would be reciprocity between the students and those with whom they would be working. Three months later a postcard announcing the program offering was distributed to students, complete with course description, dates of travel, cost, and the names of the faculty with contact information useful should students or parents have questions. The program was also posted on the University's website as a study-abroad option. The deadline for submitting an application and deposit was three months prior to departure, after which flights, side trips, and hotel accommodations were arranged. Students were screened by the program faculty. Two months prior to departure, the first class meeting was held to review the full course syllabus, provide an overview of the country, review behavioral and academic expectations, gather medical and other (e.g., t-shirt size) information. Students also became familiar with their traveling companions, and were provided a link to access a series of articles and other information placed online for students in the program. The final meeting prior to departure provided an opportunity to distribute t-shirts (used to build a team spirit as well as to ensure that student attire was culturally respectful). Questions from parents and students were usually fielded via email or phone.

Steps for Implementation

The program leaders must have some basic knowledge of the country, its people and their customs. It is helpful if one or more have lived and worked in the community or if at least one group leader has several contacts in the region who are willing to serve as key informants in researching how to best approach the planning process. It cannot be over-emphasized that each and every step in the process of planning and executing the program serves as a means of teaching students, by example, how to be culturally sensitive to diverse populations. It is, after all, the example provided by the program leaders that establishes the context for students' own personal and professional growth. Likewise, the rules governing student behavior in the host country must be set in advance, in writing, and also clearly communicated verbally to the group. It is helpful if there are only a few rules, focused specifically on safety, respect for others, and personal responsibility. Students must be encouraged to act like adults; therefore they must be treated as such.

Since one of the program leaders had lived and worked in Belize as an educator and human service worker for five years, she had an established history with several key

contacts and a relationship of mutual respect, shared values and trust with several professionals from the country. Those contacts provided entry into various agencies and settings often inaccessible to most visitors. To provide students equal access to all available experiential learning opportunities, a matrix was created to record scheduled assignments and to facilitate rotations across agencies. Special care was taken to ensure that group members and assignments varied, discouraging the establishment of subgroups.

Outcomes/Assessment

Students were required to be fully engaged in all activities. During the program, they were required to complete an individual journal that was reflective in nature. The completed journal was due within 10 days of returning to the U.S., although it was collected and reviewed several times while in the host country as a means of monitoring student progress in attaining stated objectives. One month after returning, students were also required to submit a final paper consisting of a cross-cultural analysis/comparison of the United States and Belize on issues pertinent to the student's major area of study. Students' final grades were based on the quality of participation in class discussions on readings/experiences (15%), the final paper (20%), field placement evaluations while in Belize (40%), and the quality of the reflective journal (25%).

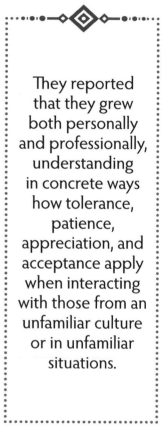

They reported that they grew both personally and professionally, understanding in concrete ways how tolerance, patience, appreciation, and acceptance apply when interacting with those from an unfamiliar culture or in unfamiliar situations.

One debriefing was held upon return to the U.S. and after the required reflective journal and final paper were received. Feedback suggested that students gained a great deal from the 80+ hours of direct service at health and human service agencies. Their journal and final papers demonstrated a critical understanding of the processes by which culture and globalization impact life in a developing country. They developed an understanding of the way public policy is developed in Belize; how the healthcare and social service systems of the United States and Belize differ. The students were generally able to utilize available resources to reflect on the service-learning experience in completing individual journals. They reported that they grew both personally and professionally, understanding in concrete ways how tolerance, patience, appreciation, and acceptance apply when interacting with those from an unfamiliar culture or in unfamiliar situations. This was evident in both their written work and their behavior of appreciation for the diverse cultural mix of the country and the lived experience of those being served.

Conclusion

The goals of the program were achieved and, after just two years of offering the program, inquiries about the next session suggest that the demand will exceed available spaces. The use of key informants from the local culture, with guided class discussion encouraging analysis of what has been observed, informed reflection, and mutual support seem to be essential ingredients in helping students to move toward a greater understanding and appreciation for not only the value of their learning opportunities, but of their

unique gifts. Students report that they broadened their scope of understanding within their own discipline through this cross-cultural, international experience.

References

Abram, F. & Cruce, A. (2007). A re-conceptualization of 'reverse mission' for international social work education and practice. *Social Work Education*, 26(1), 3-19.

Engstrom, D. & Jones, L. (2007). A broadened horizon: The value of international social work internships. *Social Work Education*, 26(2), 136-150.

Mathiesen, S. & Lager, P. (2007). A model for developing international student exchanges. *Social Work Education*, 26(3), 280-291.

Tesoriero, F. (2006). Personal growth towards inter-cultural competence through an international field education programme. *Australian Social Work*, 59(2), 126-140.

LEARNING THROUGH SERVICE IN A GLOBAL CONTEXT: THE MALAWI STUDY ABROAD

ELIZABETH ANNE BARBER
NORTH CAROLINA AGRICULTURAL AND TECHNICAL STATE UNIVERSITY

JENNIFER JONES
RADFORD UNIVERSITY

PATRICIA PROUDFOOT KELLY
VIRGINIA POLYTECHNIC INSTITUTE AND STATE UNIVERSITY

Keywords: Malawi, global, collaboration, international, HIV/AIDS, multicultural

Introduction

At no time has there been a greater need to envision sustainable change for the many, instead of just the few. But what contexts provide the seeding ground for envisioning better futures in a globally-intertwined world? It is difficult for students to envision what they have not experienced. This chapter examines service-learning within the context of a study abroad in Malawi, Sub-Saharan Africa.

Project Description

For approximately four weeks in the past five summers, faculty and students from Virginia Tech, Radford University, and North Carolina A&T learn about education and life in a global context as they join forces with teachers in three Malawian schools. Students spend the year prior to travel investigating needs and preparing projects to support Malawi's universal public education initiative, begun in 1994. Upon arrival, faculty and students become participatory action researchers as they build and maintain school libraries, support classroom instruction, assist

teachers in creating HIV or career instructional materials, and complete tasks such as painting worn blackboards or re-instituting a feeding program for hungry children at a village school. Each year students read at least one text in common (*A Democracy of Chameleons*, 2002), share reflections, and anchor those reflections in journals and field notes. Peppered among days in the schools are excursions that deepen student understanding of Malawian culture.

Project Timeline

Collaboration and diversity define the program. Two majority institutions and a Historic Black University populate the study abroad with undergraduate education majors, as well as masters and doctoral students from a range of disciplines. Faculty coordinate to provide meaningful opportunities for all participants, while meeting the needs of each unique student group. Collaboration facilitates student participation in cross-university projects.

Getting Started. Selection of a service-learning study abroad site involves negotiating the learning goals of the experience, the needs of the in-country partners, and most importantly, faculty background experience. Our study abroad takes place in Malawi, but developing country sites south of the U.S. border and in the Caribbean involve less expensive travel, less exotic language requirements, and provide easier faculty access prior to planning a project with students.

Within the target country, a specific site should be thoroughly researched, and working relationships established with in-country collaborators. At least one faculty member should be known and trusted in the site prior to implementation. Returning with study abroad students to the same site over time provides opportunities for deep working relationships, and greater sustainability of innovations co-constructed there.

Recruitment. Flyers and posters vivid with photographs, and multimedia events such as study abroad fairs, advertise the program to the campus community. Brief presentations given to meetings of deans, department chairs, and their faculties encourage interdisciplinary participation. Student newspapers, the campus radio station, and posters in central locations such as the bookstore and student center, provide further opportunities to disseminate information.

When there has been sufficient time to spread the word about the study abroad project (a month from the beginning of the school year), student information sessions are offered at different times of the day and week to provide ample opportunities for attendance. At these sessions information about the purpose and nature of the study abroad, the country, cost, and application process are shared. Once it is clear that this study abroad involves service-learning (not a "tour"), the project tends to attract the students who want to serve. Offering CDs with PowerPoint presentations about the experience, and financial aid information, eases family concerns and illuminates the value of service-learning in an international setting. After the first year of the project, former student participants become the most powerful recruiting tool, as they tell others about their experiences in Malawi.

As early as possible after the student information sessions, applicants are screened and notified of acceptance. The screening process differs slightly across our three partner institutions, but students should apply through their college or university's office of international education (if one exists), undergo any background checks required, and submit letters of application in which they explain why they want to participate, what they hope to offer to the service-learning team, and hope to accomplish and learn in the experience.

Final acceptance comes when students pay their first deposit, in November, which should be a sufficient amount to cover the full cost their plane ticket, which is the most expensive item in the study abroad budget. Students are cautioned that once tickets are purchased in January or so, money cannot be refunded.

Two more installments paid in January and February or March complete the payment process in time for pre-payment for lodging and other in-country expenses, as required in advance for groups. Costs for the study abroad budget should be estimated high in cases in which student funds that remain unspent can be returned to them. If college or university policies require that no funds can be returned to students, budgeting must be much tighter, and it is recommended that the institution provide the faculty member(s) with an "emergency fund" to cover unexpected expenses.

Factors that influence the number of students who can participate in a given year include the number of faculty participants, and the type of safe and affordable in-country transportation available. In our case, rental of a van and driver from a college in Malawi limits participation to the total number of seats in the van.

Pre-Departure Orientation Sessions. Pre-departure orientation generates excitement, provides needed information and a forum for sharing expectations. Meetings are scheduled once to twice a month during fall and spring semesters, following selection of student participants.

Student-reported fears about international service-learning include health and safety issues, the success of their service-learning projects (making a difference), and communication. To address "basic needs" issues, students receive a packing list and the required inoculations for travel abroad. Local health departments often provide travel health and safety orientations, sometimes at discount prices to student groups.

Next, a number of sessions focus on the Malawian culture, history, politics, and education system in an effort to develop cultural sensitivity among the students. Language CDs are also provided early on, and it is helpful for all students to read some texts in common. Students are connected with Malawian educators via e-mail and the postal service, so that their work plans can be constructed collaboratively to make sense in the study abroad setting, and time is allowed for students to prepare the materials they will need for their work in the schools.

Service-Learning and Cultural Experiences. Service-learning projects are conducted with the utmost respect for and involvement of Malawian teachers, their pupils, and local communities. While in-country, students spend time each morning assisting a teacher; afternoons are spent as needed on their service-learning projects and in classes conducted by faculty members. Classes include time for debriefing, a critical component of service-learning experiences that involve cross-cultural engagement. Students need structured time in which to share and reflect upon experiences in order to develop cultural competence.

Cultural excursions broaden student understandings of the study abroad context, and in our case include an overnight trip to Mvuu Preservation Camp (with three safaris in a 24-hour period), trips to a sustainable farm, a traditional village, an orphanage, a cultural museum, a church that has incorporated traditional music and dance into its services, and hiking on the third largest mountain in Africa.

Steps for Implementation

Having prior, in-depth experiences within the target country is imperative to establish the connections needed to facilitate travel and lodging within a developing country. In our case, Patricia worked with two different U.S. sponsored projects in Malawi for more than five years prior to the current collaboration. She had developed working relationships with schools and colleges that wanted to become part of the study abroad program. A local college rents us transportation. Lodging is negotiated for less-than-tourist rates, due to the service-learning activities, which benefit the community and the schools.

Pricing for the trip is established before recruiting begins. Because the single largest portion of the budget is the flight from the U.S., the first step each year is to find the best airline rate. Hotels, lodges, and supplementary excursions are booked at the same time. Deadlines for money deposits are determined, and a general itinerary is constructed. School-specific service-learning projects are determined via collaborative efforts across the universities and the schools served in Malawi.

Outcomes/Assessment

Grade assessments vary from journaling to conducting, presenting and/or publishing formal research projects. Student outcomes depend upon maturity level, but include:

1. Global awareness & cross-cultural competencies.
2. Understanding of global colonialism.
3. Leadership skills.
4. Critical thinking & problem-solving in diverse settings.
5. Ability to learn from diverse others.
6. Understanding of sustainability.

All participants report that the experiences in Malawi personalize how they understand themselves in terms of globally situated others.

University communities have also become involved. One faculty has begun a "Malawi Initiative," striving to strengthen its relationship with the schools in Malawi. Funds at each university have been established to pay for the education of three Malawian sponsored teachers-in-training. Local school children donate books and supplies for our partner schools.

Conclusion

The Malawi service-learning program serves as seeding ground for envisioning better futures. Students depart, suitcases full and eager to serve, but return with much more than they took:

It wasn't until I saw that moon, the same moon that I see very night back home, but with the crescent on the bottom, that I realized ... how even the familiar can be different.

References

Englund, H. (Ed.). (2002). *Democracy of Chameleons.* Kachere Books No. 14. Malawi: Nordic Africa Institute.

||||||||||||||||||||||||||||||||||||||||||||||||||||||||||||||||||||||||||||||||||||||||||||||||||||||||||||||||||||||||||||||||||||||||||||||||||

CONNECTIONS: LINKING GLOBAL SERVICE-LEARNING TO LOCAL COMMUNITIES THROUGH ACADEMIC COURSEWORK

DEBORAH E. BENDER AND JENNY HUQ
THE UNIVERSITY OF NORTH CAROLINA

Keywords: global, international, study abroad, home-stays, team-building, multicultural

Introduction

Traditionally, students who choose to study internationally as undergraduates select from among semester or year-long programs offered by the study abroad office. Many times students participating in international study experiences stay in dormitories with others similar to themselves. Some offer home-stays or internships in addition to classes, opening a window for understanding social, economic and cultural frameworks. Few programs offer students opportunities to reflect on ways to integrate the global experience into professional and personal plans after their return.

The traditional study abroad program lacks a structured, meaningful way of integrating the student's global experience. Too often, the start of the next semester forces the global experience to become a memory. Within a short time, story-telling and showing of photographs becomes less frequent. The message is clear: it's time to move on. The experience becomes frozen in time and place.

Program Description

The APPLES Global Service-Learning Initiative places students in countries that are "sending communities" for immigrants settling in North Carolina. Currently, students spend 9 weeks in Mexico during the summer or 14 weeks in Namibia and South Africa, Mexico or Vietnam during the fall semester. The Program has affiliated with a variety of third-party providers, taking advantage of established linkages and logistic support. The goals of the Global Service-Learning Initiative are to provide students with a global learning experience; to promote language skills; and to facilitate the integration of the global experience into their career through reflection and application.

During the global component of the Initiative, students live with a host family, leaving the "outside world" of a visitor and entering into the "inner world" of host-country families and communities. They also engage in service-learning in host-country agencies to better understand the agency's role in meeting local social needs. When appropriate, students also polish foreign language skills through intensive coursework. The goal is for students to develop both respect for cultural differences and an appreciation of commonalities among people.

Project Timeline

In the fall or spring semester following return, students enroll in the Connections Seminar and participate in parallel local service-learning. The focus of the seminar is on the migration transitions faced by new immigrants to the United States, and to North Carolina, in particular. Three challenges facing new immigrants—health, education and social justice—are central to the Seminar. Local service-learning links students with immigrants in local area schools, through ESL (English as a Second Language) classes.

Through related focused readings and class discussion, the connections between "there" and "here" are brought to life. Students consider ways in which health practices and beliefs "there" influence patterns of use of health services by recent immigrants "here." This usually includes lively discussion of overuse of emergency services and, conversely, underutilization of preventive services. Comparisons of levels of education "there" and "here" are also striking. Students realize the risks that immigrating parents take to provide their children formal education. Discussion of social justice, the third theme, introduces broader issues of global migration, equity, and distribution of resources.

In the local service application, students interact with immigrant students, using their newly acquired language and cross-cultural skills. Each is challenged to apply their global experience through mentoring roles with the high school students. The seminar linked with local service-learning facilitates students' understanding of global and local immigration trends and its impact on families and the community.

The one-credit seminar meets weekly for 75 minutes, with a minimum of 30 hours of service required during the semester.

Steps for Implementation

Students are introduced to the APPLES Global Service-Learning Initiative early in the academic year through a campus-wide study abroad fair. Applications are due in mid-February for both upcoming summer and fall semesters. Applications are reviewed by student leaders of APPLES and selected applicants are invited for interviews. One important component of the process is a review of requirements of the Global Service-Learning Initiative, including participation in a Pre-Departure Orientation, enrollment in the Connections Seminar and engagement in local service in the semester following their return.

The Connections seminar challenges students to reflect and synthesize their own global experience and to make connections with local immigrants.

Selected students participate in a two-day workshop. The workshop introduces social, cross-cultural communication and logistical information about the host country visit and previews the reflections seminar and local service-learning. Role plays based on realistic scenarios and panels led by returned students lay a firm foundation for students going abroad. An additional half-day low ropes course experience is held to strengthen team skills.

Outcomes/Assessment

Through the linking of academic course work with global cross-cultural experiences, students actually have the time to reflect on how the global experience might serve as a beacon to guide future personal and professional choices. Assessment is done through questionnaires and narrative reflections on the value of the Initiative. Selections from two assessments are presented below as exemplars:

Now that I have live in and worked in Mexico, the United States looks quite a bit different. It is now common for me to compare the way things were done in Mexico to the way they occur here. For example, although I am aware of poverty here in the United States, it became much more real to me while in Mexico. In addition, I am aware of the differences in racial issues between Mexico and the United States. —SJ

I recall my first interactions with Latino immigrants in the United States four years ago. I was wandering in circles in the Pediatrics Department at a local hospital. I was contemplating whether or not I should talk to the precious Latina girl and her family in the room nearby. According to the nurses, the family had just recently moved from Vera Cruz; spoke little English; and 5-year-old Isabela had been in the hospital for weeks.

…Although my conversation skills were strong, I never took the chance to converse with the family and offer my comfort. Why? Looking back I realize that I was terrified that I would say something offensive or rude. With the exception of learning about Cinco de Mayo, I had no solid background in their traditions or values!

…I tell this story to emphasize how important my experience in Mexico was in familiarizing me with the everyday life and customs of Latin Americans. [On return], I was comfortable and open with the Latina students. When they described the intimacy of their families or their value of respect, I could relate to them on a new level. —PC

Conclusion

Designing global service-learning experiences should include a post semester-long reflection course in an innovation in global service-learning. The Connections Seminar challenges students to reflect and synthesize their own global experience and to make connections with local immigrants. The seminar also eases the impact of reverse culture shock and provides an opportunity to consider ways of integrating the transformational global experience into professional and personal life goals.

DEVELOPING A RESOURCE MANUAL FOR NEW IMMIGRANTS

INGRID ROGERS
MANCHESTER COLLEGE

Keywords: Spanish language guide, bilingual incentives, university/community partnerships

Introduction

The small town of North Manchester currently has about 100 Hispanic immigrants among its population of 6000. Much larger groups live in the nearby towns of Akron and Mentone. In the summer of 2007, a faculty/student team produced a resource guide for the Hispanic residents in town and in the surrounding counties of Wabash, Fulton, and Kosciusko.

Project Description

The bulk of the information included in the resource guide is general enough that it can serve in many communities. For instance, a chapter on health issues, in addition to listing local medical clinics includes basic information on alcohol abuse, diabetes, depression, and other illnesses that frequently affect immigrants. A chapter on family and adult resources mentions WIC, ESL classes, survival strategies in a foreign environment, and explanations about social services. The section on schools provides a sample in English and Spanish of how to write an excuse when a child is ill. The final section of the book includes maps and addresses for local clinics, help centers, adult education facilities, schools and colleges, churches, legal services, town government offices, and license branch locations. The guide also lists important phone numbers, including emergency numbers.

Because a model for the guide is already available, a similar project in a different location is easy to implement. The manual assembled for the North Manchester area is available free of charge as long as credit is given. Its graphics and attractive layout make it a useful template for other communities. Manchester College made access to an electronic version of the manual available via its website: http://www.manchester.edu/Academics/Departments/ModLang/resource_guide.pdf

To get started in your own county, you may want to follow these steps:

Project Timeline

Week One: Introduce project
Weeks Two–Four: Explore community assets and resources

Weeks Five–Seven: Gather materials for guide
Weeks Eight–Thirteen: Compile and translate materials
Weeks Fourteen–Sixteen: Complete and distribute guides

Steps for Implementation

Step 1: Assessing community needs

■ Collect information about available local resources for the growing Hispanic population.

■ Consult with employees from the county community foundation, Chamber of Commerce, banks, schools, police departments, and social service agencies. Contact them by phone or in person both to assess their wishes and needs regarding outreach to Spanish-speaking clients. Assess, based on these consultations, whether a manual would be a useful tool for new immigrants in your area.

■ Talk to immigrants with the help of interpreters, to get an idea of what information would be most helpful to include in the guide. The manual composed in North Manchester, written in Spanish with bilingual index and content pages, contained sections on schools, health clinics, medical information, family resources, children's services, adult education, churches, legal services, and social agencies.

Step 2: Involving the college

At Manchester College, a faculty/student team produced the guide as an internship project over the course of ten weeks during the summer. Other formats, such as a service-learning component of an existing course or collaboration with partners from different disciplines, are also feasible.

■ Look for a student intern or a group of students who can help assemble a guidebook. Each individual will need skills in at least one for the following areas: a) Composition, b) Spanish language at the advanced level, c) Interview & PR skills, and d) Computer skills for formatting, layout, and graphic design

■ Contact the office of volunteer services about funding of summer internships

■ Talk with colleagues about incorporating the project as part of a college course

Step 3: Research and writing

■ Look online for documents relevant to new immigrants, such as brochures and resource lists in English or Spanish.

■ Locate already existing guides and secure permission to use parts of their material. The easiest would be to update the Manchester manual, "Bienvenidos," since permission is already granted.

■ Select relevant materials from already existing sources and write new sections in consultation with local agencies.

■ Translate the text into Spanish.

■ Finalize the resource book after editing, formatting, and proofreading the manuscript.

Step 4: Disseminating the information

■ Seek funding through community partners to print the guide.

■ Print enough copies for each local immigrant family and each agency that regularly works with them.

■ Provide access to an electronic version on a local website.

■ Allow other communities to use the material for further adaptation, to create manuals for their own immigrant communities.

Conclusion

The production and dissemination of the resource manual can lead to fruitful dialogues and interactions between Anglos and Hispanics, thereby contributing to cooperation, tolerance, and greater cross-cultural understanding in the community. By engaging college students in the creation and translation of the guide, they gain valuable experience, not only in Spanish speaking and translation, but in mapping and networking community needs and resources.

By engaging college students in the creation and translation of the guide,
they gain valuable experience, not only in Spanish speaking and translation,
but in mapping and networking community needs and resources.

LEARNING BEYOND THE CLASSROOM: A SPANISH FOR THE PROFESSIONS COURSE

CLARA H. BECERRA AND AMANDA ESPENSCHIED-REILLY
MOUNT UNION COLLEGE

Keywords: Spanish, profession, career development, multicultural, language proficiency

Introduction

Spanish for the Professions is a one-semester language course that is required for Spanish majors. In this course, students are given the opportunity to review and expand on areas of vocabulary and language skills aimed at their professional interests. This class is conducted in Spanish and is supplemented with examples and in-class internet activities to reinforce learning, and to provide examples of opportunities in different professional fields. The idea is to empower students to utilize their language skills in their future careers. Teaching them to be bicultural is essential in building a successful career. Complementing the course with required service-learning opportunities is an excellent way of adding practical experiences to enhance the course that meets needs in the community.

Project Description

The service-learning project in this course is included in the syllabus as part of the learning outcomes. Students are expected to incorporate this project in the assembling of a portfolio (described below) with the theme: *El español en mi trabajo futuro* (Spanish and my future career). Early in the semester, students think about what their career goals are and how those goals can be directly related to the service-learning opportunity they will experience outside the classroom. This is challenging for both the instructor and the students because some of the students don't know about the applicability of their college preparation in the job market. That is why this course not only focuses on mastering language skills, but also on showing students a variety of job opportunities they could explore in the future. The added real-life experience that service-learning provides often aids students in making career decisions.

While the first sections of the portfolio constitute preparatory steps for the student, the remaining parts focus more on the field experience. They perform a minimum of 10–15 hours of service-learning, and conduct an interview with a professional in their field. Ideally, these two facets are done in Spanish.

An essay and an oral presentation are additional opportunities for the student to demonstrate mastery of language skills while reflecting on the service-learning experience. The essay reveals benefits, accomplishments or failures, results, and ways in which this experience could affect the student's future. We also reflect orally in class about the stu-

dents' service-learning projects at least three times during the semester. These oral sessions are key to connecting the service-learning to the course objectives and for monitoring the progress of each project.

Project Timeline

The Director of Service-Learning provides assistance by contacting community partners for the service-learning project in the fall semester after students enroll for the spring. Partners and projects are selected based on individual student majors and future career goals. The Director contacts all students prior to the first day of class with their project site, supervisor, and description. She visits the class early in the semester, and introduces the paperwork for the project (service agreement, time sheets, waiver and evaluations) and the project goals and expectations. Afterwards, the students contact their sites and initiate their projects. The service must be completed prior to the final portfolio due date. Collaboration and regular communication between the Director and the instructor are essential for project and course success.

Steps for Implementation

1. **Nov.**—Instructor gives Director of Service-Learning the course syllabus and a list of enrolled students and their majors/minors after registration for Spring semester
2. **Nov./Dec.**—Director arranges for individual or small group service-learning projects based on student majors/minors and career goals
3. **Jan.**—Director contacts students via email with project and supervisor information and makes any needed changes; Director and instructor present project assignment and go over paperwork procedures during the first 2-3 weeks of class
4. **Late Jan–Apr.**—Students implement service-learning projects
5. **Apr/May**—Students complete final portfolio assignments and give presentations last 2 weeks of class

Outcomes/Assessment

Assembling a portfolio is a motivational reflective task for the student that allows for practical application of classroom content and language skills, and facilitates assessment. Some of the portfolios centered on teaching basic Spanish in an after-school program, volunteering in a center for rural migrants, individual ESL tutoring, and helping with translation for Spanish speaking patients at the local hospital. These students want to become teachers, lawyers, consultants for non-profit organizations, nurses, etc. They found their experience informative and positive because they were faced with the task of finding possible places of employment, learning about job responsibilities through interviewing, and practicing problem-solving skills while developing personal relationships with community members. The outcome is an enriching service-learning experience that prepares them for a responsible job search after graduation.

Each student's portfolio includes the following items: (1) an introduction describing three specific career oriented goals according to the student's field of expertise; (2) a brief survey of three prospective companies/institutions to which the student would send applications for a job, with an illustration (a company logo, or a picture of the facility, or a company/institution's flyer or pamphlet); (3) a letter addressed to the company/institution of the student's choice expressing his/her intent to apply for a particular position; (4) student's curriculum vitae; (5) an interview with a professional in the student's field: five questions to find out

about the job responsibilities and benefits; and (6) an essay (600–700 words) synthesizing the process and results/benefits of this independent project, accomplishments. In the essay the student reflects mainly on his/her service-learning experience, including a paragraph noting whether or not the interview was beneficial to him/her. The interview can be conducted in English or Spanish, with the list of questions (also the name, job position, and institution for the interviewee) included in the portfolio. All remaining components of the project and the class presentation will be done in the target language. This portfolio represents 25% of the final grade in the course, and each student is responsible for completing each section of the portfolio throughout the semester.

Conclusion

We believe this course empowers students to utilize their language skills in their future careers. Teaching them to be bicultural is essential in building a successful career. Complementing the course with required service-learning opportunities is an excellent way of adding practical experiences to enhance the course that meets needs in the community.

MATCHING STUDENT PRESENTATIONS TO THE NATURE OF SERVICE-LEARNING WORK

ANNIE ABBOTT
UNIVERSITY OF ILLINOIS AT URBANA-CHAMPAIGN

DARCY LEAR
UNIVERSITY OF NORTH CAROLINA – CHAPEL HILL

Keywords: alternative presentations, poster sessions, portfolio assessment, assessment techniques

Introduction

Each semester, our Spanish service-learning students engage in meaningful community-based projects, yet the typical end-of-the-semester oral presentation is the opposite: boring and delivered to a passive audience. Without extensive training, most PowerPoint presentations simply recreate the pitfalls of oral presentations with students reading each slide's text. Instead, we have found that a poster session modeled on the professional conference format allows students to present their projects in succinct yet eye-catching posters that necessitate active dialogue with their audience.

Project Description

Clearly, student projects vary according to the academic discipline of the service-learning course. In our Spanish

courses, students work on any project that is of service to the community partner organization and its clients in linguistically and culturally appropriate ways. Projects have included publishing a Spanish-language version of an after-school program's flyer with testimonials from Latino tutors, raising money in the community for Spanish-language books for a bilingual school's literacy program, and even creating a public service announcement in Spanish for Univision.

At each poster session, 6–8 students display their posters around the classroom. The audience consists of the other classmates, the instructor, and invited guests. Like any professional poster session, the presenter stands by the poster and audience members respond to posters' noteworthy text and images with follow-up questions. Therefore, the students' presentations align more closely to the projects themselves: they are dynamic and build students' linguistic, cultural, and professional skills.

Project Timeline

The poster project can seem daunting precisely because the work is extended throughout the semester, not allowing for the kind of procrastination that results in last-minute presentations prepared in an "all-nighter." Working with multiple community partners creates a wide range of possibilities for the final project, and this can be disconcerting for those accustomed to traditional academic projects such as term papers and traditional presentations on topics assigned by the instructor.

In order to reduce the stress associated with the novel approach of a poster presentation, it is useful to provide students with tasks and deadlines throughout the semester. For example, a brainstorming activity might start with students jotting down some topics, themes, problems, or ideas they have experienced in the community. From that list, they identify all the ideas that are actually feasible within the community partner's organizational structure and then determine which remaining idea best fits the course content. Students read each other's results and write down two things they like and two potential problems.

Near the end of the semester, students can prepare for the poster sessions by delivering an "elevator pitch." Can they describe their project in a compelling manner in the time it takes to ride an elevator? There are three parts to the elevator pitch:

■ Define the problem or unresolved issue
■ Acknowledge what already exists to address the problem/issue
■ Present your new idea (which offers something innovative/better)

Students take turns presenting their ideas, reacting to others' ideas, and revising their presentations. It works best if students are arranged in two rows facing each other, with one row moving over one seat every 3–5 minutes, like a speed dating activity.

Steps for Implementation

A clear, concise description of the project and poster presentation must be part of the course syllabus so that all parties have a framework to follow. Students prepare a cumulative portfolio that leads to the final poster presentation. The project is worth 25% of students' grade for the course, with each portfolio assignment (including multiple drafts in some cases) worth 4%–5% and the final poster presentation worth 5%. While this puts a lot of weight on the project, it also spreads the assignment of the project grade across the entire semester and ensures that the final project is built step-by-step.

While each discipline will have specific parameters to follow, general guidelines for poster presentations that we have used across various courses taught in English and Spanish include:

■ Although based on portfolio assignments, the posters must identify the broader theme addressed and describe the community need that the project meets or could meet.
■ Each poster represents a deeper dimension of selected content from the course that the students presenting know more about than anyone else.
■ Posters synthesize all elements of the course: academic content, community partner organizations, community needs, and structured reflection.
■ The posters speak for themselves and the students are prepared to answer general questions ("Tell me about your project." or "How did you get the idea?") as well as specific questions about the poster ("What does 'ECIRMAC' stand for?"); under no circumstances can they speak from a prepared script.

Outcomes/Assessment

The semester-long development of a portfolio that culminates in a professional conference style poster session is conducive to showcasing scholarship, reflection, and practical applications of both. Student projects must benefit community partner organizations in some way so that the real-world applications of their work are evident. This means that the formal assessment of student projects must also reflect this convergence of academic course content, community service-learning and critical reflection.

Ideally, community partner assessment figures into the poster presentation grade. However, if community partners are not available, the rubric used to assess the poster presentations must hold students accountable to their partner organizations. We integrate this part of assessment into the preparation grade on a rubric that includes a possible 20 points in each of the following categories: quality of interaction, preparation, and organization. While every discipline has different criteria for grading, a clear rubric for grading of portfolio assignments and poster presentations is an essential part of the core materials to include in the course syllabus.

Conclusion

In foreign language teaching, traditional oral presentations serve a dual purpose—to assess the content as well as the students' foreign language abilities—but lack a meaningful context. However, Spanish service-learning courses require students to use their language, culture and professional skills in real-time and for a real purpose. As in any discipline, a poster session in place of traditional oral presentations more accurately reflects the nature of students' service-learning work, allowing instructors to test both what and how they teach.

PARTNERING WITH THE COMMUNITY TO BRIDGE THE LANGUAGE CLASSROOM TO THE LATINO POPULATION

JULIEN SIMON
INDIANA UNIVERSITY EAST

Keywords: ELL, ESL, Spanish, Latino, Hispanic, Five C's, community involvement

Introduction

Learning a foreign language is the first step toward understanding the culture of the "other." At our institution located in the rural Midwest, students have rarely been in contact with the Latino population alongside which they live. A service-learning component designed to bring together language and culture from the start was developed and implemented in our introductory Spanish courses. In this program, Spanish learners engage in 12 hours of service-learning in which they tutor Hispanic migrant workers who want to become more proficient in English.

Project Description

The Spanish class is, for most students, a required course which helps them to develop the skills to understand, accept and relate to people of different backgrounds and beliefs as well as be more "fluent" in a pluralistic world. To help accomplish this, a service-learning component was developed. Along with the time spent in class studying Spanish language and culture, students participate in tutoring sessions that take place throughout the semester. They join the program of a community organization (AMIGOS) that provides tutoring in English to the local Latino population. The tutoring sessions occur twice weekly for two hours each time.

During each session, one Hispanic tutee is paired with one or two student-tutors. Novice student-tutors work with a more experienced one for the first few times. Depending on the level of proficiency of the tutee, the tutoring session can concentrate more on basic linguistic skills, on reading and analyzing newspaper articles, or on whatever the tutor feels appropriate to bring to the session.

Project Timeline

At the beginning of the semester, a member of the organization is invited to present the program to the students. At the meeting, this person informs them about what they will be asked to do. For the first couple of weeks, the instructor is present during the tutoring sessions in order to alleviate the fears students may feel at the beginning.

Throughout the semester, student-tutors keep a log of their hours on a timesheet that includes a brief description of the work done during each session. Students don't need to sign up ahead of the session and can participate whenever they have time. About eight to ten weeks into the semester during a regular class meeting, they are asked to share their experiences. At the end of the semester, students submit a reflective essay.

Steps for Implementation

The first step is to find a community partner offering English classes to the Latino population. If such a group does not exist, public schools may need Spanish speakers, even with limited language skills, to interpret at Parent-Teacher conferences or help in English as Second Language classes[1].

Once an organization has been identified, the next step is to discuss each other's needs. For instance, the fact that this program is designed for first-year Spanish students rules out any tasks that necessitate being even minimally fluent in the language. Additionally, this program was piloted in one or two classes before being deployed to the entire Spanish language program.

Outcomes/Assessment

Students are asked to keep a diary of what they do each time they work with tutees. This information is to be submitted along with the reflective essay. About a month before the end of the semester, a special session is organized in which students share their experiences with the rest of the class. The

---

1. This type of classes is also being called ELL: English Language Learners.

...became more confident with their speaking abilities, as they went from a "constrained" environment (conversing in the classroom) to an "unconstrained" environment (communicating with native speakers).

enthusiasm of the students for whom the experience has been "eye-opening" becomes a catalyst for the remainder of the semester. It encourages the "skeptics" to complete their hours and the "convinced" to exceed the required number of hours.

At this session, they are reminded about the reflective essay. Listed below is a sample of guiding questions that are used to orient the students:

- What did you expect before the start of your service-learning program?
- What did you gain from the experience?
- What was your most memorable experience? Explain why.

Students participating in our program have reported gaining linguistic fluency. They became more confident with their speaking abilities, as they went from a "constrained" environment (conversing in the classroom) to an "unconstrained" environment (communicating with native speakers).

Their sense of purpose was heightened, too. Academically speaking, they understood why learning Spanish was important to them. And on a personal level, they realized that they had the ability to make a difference in somebody else's life.

Although they felt a little anxious at first, unsure about what to expect and if they would be able to really help, they all reported having learned and grown a lot thanks to this experience, and viewed the program at the end more as an opportunity that was given to them rather than as a requirement for a class. Some of the participants even planned on continuing to volunteer after the end of the program.

Conclusion

Culture and community involvement have become a central aspect of the language classroom since the implementation of the five C's (Communication, Connections, Cultures, Comparisons, Communities)[2] as a standard for the design of foreign language programs. The ever-growing Latino population in urban as well as in rural areas of the United States provides Spanish instructors with a great opportunity to have their students discover and better understand the Hispanic culture and communities near them.

Through this program, students become role-models for a group of people whose immediate environment does not always see higher education as achievable. At the same time, they are helping this population get more integrated into their community, both culturally and linguistically.

2. These are the National Standards for Foreign Language Education. American Council on the Teaching of Foreign Languages. http://actfl.org/i4a/pages/index.cfm?pageid=3392

SERVICE-LEARNING IN POST-KATRINA NEW ORLEANS

SEAN ANDERSON
CALIFORNIA STATE UNIVERSITY CHANNEL ISLANDS

Keywords: restoration ecology, hurricanes, wetlands, disaster recovery, natural disaster

Introduction

Hurricane Katrina made landfall in Buras, Louisiana on August 29, 2005, ushering in a wave of destruction in excess of $125 billion, ultimately killing more than 2,000 people, and inducing the second greatest mass migration of people in the history of the United States. As fate would have it, August 29 was also my first day of teaching at California's newest public university, California State University Channel Islands (CSUCI). Students at our then three-year old campus immediately responded to the devastating news from the Gulf Coast by raising over $10,000 for the Red Cross. Still, once these funds were donated, many students immediately asked, "What's next?" I responded by designing a service-learning course wherein undergraduates would travel to the Gulf Coast to participate in the recovery of both the human and natural communities in southern Louisiana.

Project Description

CSUCI's Service-learning in New Orleans course allows students from any major the opportunity to participate in an intense ten-day field experience in and around New Orleans, Louisiana for upper division credit. A series of four to five pre-trip seminars and an array of background readings and music prepare students for our trip. We then travel to New Orleans, Louisiana to examine firsthand the ongoing disruptions to daily life and the lingering impacts of poor coastal resource management.

We spend the first two days touring the greater New Orleans region, familiarizing ourselves with the local culture, geography, and the current state of affairs. These travels initially focus on the drivers of wetland loss and historic mismanagement of the Mississippi

River delta by the Army Corps of Engineers, local levee boards, etc.

The next three days find us conducting environmental impact assessments and wetland restoration projects in Belle Chase's Woodlands Trail and Park, one of the few remnant bottomland hardwood forest tracts surrounding Greater New Orleans.

Next, we transition into an examination of the cultural landscape of southern Louisiana, including introductions to the literary, musical, and culinary traditions of the region. Guest speakers and guides hail from Tulane University, Louisiana State University, the United States Geological Survey, Basin Street Records, The New Orleans Times-Picayune, the Army Corps of Engineers, and the New Orleans Mayor Office. Of particular note are our meetings with and performances from numerous musicians and chefs. Our final four days are devoted to helping demolish and reconstruct housing units and community buildings in Orleans, St. Bernard's, and/or Plaquemines Parish. The emphasis on this last phase of the trip is on the rapidly subsiding and widely ignored Mississippi peninsula that comprises the bulk of Plaquemines Parish.

Upon our return to California, students create individual and/or group presentations which explore a particular aspect of our trip or expand upon a given theme or topic of our course. Posters, slide shows, videos, levee failure models, found art, cooking demonstrations, and other presentations are unveiled at an open session for the campus community.

Project Timeline

Previous Spring—Apply to CSUCI Instructionally Related Activities Fund for monies to defray trip cost to students

Summer/Fall—Trip scheduling/travel arrangements/ speaker invitations

Late October—Information sessions to advertise the course and answer questions

Late November—Student course applications due

December 1st—Selection of 16 students and a short list of alternates announced

Early January—Confirm enrollment and collect course fees

Late January—Design and printing of course t-shirts (these serve as our trip uniforms and thank you gifts for our guest speakers & community partners)

February—Pre-trip orientation, seminars, and discussions (typically evenings)

March—Travel to New Orleans over Spring Break for the core of the class

April—Students submit and revise drafts of their presentations

Early May—Two-hour Poster/Video/Demonstration Session and Celebration

June 1st - Course assessments to CSUCI & reports to our community partners

Steps for Implementation

Design and implementation of a course of this nature requires strong and consistent institutional support, flexibility in scheduling, and faith that even when logistics become daunting, our students will understand any difficulties, rise to the occasion, and persevere. Before any specific plans were made, funding to defray approximately two-thirds of the trip costs was secured from a CSUCI fund supported by student fees. Without such funding (~$900 per student) virtually none of our students would be able to participate in this course (full cost ~$1,500 per student for the 10-day trip), even with airfare (government rates), hotel (discounts for volunteers), and other discounts.

Because this course is built around interpersonal engagement and directly assisting communities that are under extreme stress and at times day-to-day changes to infrastructure, planning can be quite difficult and requires multiple contingency plans. I made a pre-trip visit approximately six months prior to our first course trip to assist with planning and afford me material to better justify budgetary requests. An earlier trip would have better assisted with my course and budget justification, but a visit closer to the actual student trip would have been of much greater help to logistic planning (even by 2006 and 2007, on the ground conditions were sometimes changing radically week to week). Preliminary trips also help focus pre-trip logistic training such as equipment safety and natural hazard awareness (e.g., alligators and venomous snake safety).

An excellent working knowledge of the area and issues in question are essential to a successful course and provide the scaffolding over which local experts and the service activities themselves can readily build upon. Contacting numerous local experts early and often assures that when last minute changes crop up (as they definitely will), contingency arrangements can be made with relative ease. I have found that while local academics are fantastic additions to such a course, the most unique perspectives and most memorable learning experiences tend to come from non-academics and the service itself.

Lastly, it is key to make any such trip a celebration of the peoples, cultures, and places in question; we eat as much gumbo and hear as much jazz as possible! The spirit of this service-learning experience is "friends helping friends," rather than an exercise in disaster tourism.

Outcomes/Assessment

The primary learning outcomes of this service-learning experience are to:
1. intimately understand the environmental, policy, and social contexts that allowed the massive national disaster and disgrace that was Katrina to occur and that continues to hamper recovery efforts
2. gain an appreciation for the people and culture of New Orleans and the greater Gulf Coast region
3. materially help with the recovery of New Orleans and the Gulf Coast by giving of our time and labor

While this trip is organized around one region, many of the lessons and learning outcomes bear directly upon life back home in the Coastal Zone of California and beyond. Some of these more general learning outcomes include:
■ explaining the links between environmental quality and human well-being
■ articulating ecosystem services associated with intact coastal wetlands
■ understanding incompetent and corrupt leadership kills
■ appreciating the influence of New Orleans culture on American visual, musical, and culinary arts
■ being empowered through community service
■ fostering active citizenship

Student efforts are assessed throughout our time in New

Orleans and students are strongly encouraged to keep a video or written journal of their experiences. Upon our return, students prepare and present independent research project/community service documentation posters, videos, and/or demonstrations during the last week of classes in a session open to the campus community. These are evaluated by faculty and staff from various disciplines.

Several students have indicated that this course has changed their outlook upon the world and that it "just brought together everything we have been learning about for the past four years." Many have returned to New Orleans for additional volunteering stints, including one recent graduate who plans to take six months off from his engineering firm to move to New Orleans to assist with the ongoing recovery efforts fulltime.

Conclusion

My service-learning in New Orleans class has been exceedingly difficult to design and implement due do to the difficulties of working in a disaster zone, but has been the most rewarding course I have yet taught at any university. More importantly, it has often served as a transformative and empowering experience for my students by giving them a chance to witness, grapple with, and in some small way help reverse challenges they may otherwise only know from texts or lectures. Service-learning courses such as this should have an integral place in the spectrum of curricula offered, but particularly so in applied disciplines wherein it is easy for students to become despondent about the problems facing our society or planet. In such settings, the opportunity to make a tangible difference translates into our students benefiting at least as much as the communities they are striving to serve.

SERVICE-LEARNING PARTNERSHIPS WITH THE LESBIAN, GAY, BISEXUAL, AND TRANSGENDER COMMUNITY

ELAINE M. MACCIO
LOUISIANA STATE UNIVERSITY

Keywords: lesbian, gay, bisexual, transgender, community-based research, human subjects

Introduction

One of the many strengths of service-learning is its emphasis on improving the lives of vulnerable populations. Service-learning community partners commonly serve people of color, people with disabilities, people who are poor, and older persons. However, very few service-learning projects involve partners serving the lesbian, gay, bisexual, and

transgender (LGBT) population. The paucity of LGBT service-learning projects may be the result of any number of factors, not the least of which may be service-learning administrators' and instructors' simply not knowing how to find, engage, and serve the LGBT community. This entry seeks to remedy this knowledge gap and encourage partnerships with the local LGBT community by describing a community-based research project implemented in five stages: partnership, collaboration, set-up, implementation, and dissemination.

Project Description

Seventeen graduate students enrolled in "Social Work with Lesbian, Gay, Bisexual, and Transgender People," a graduate social work course, partnered with Capital City Alliance (CCA), a local grassroots organization that advocates for the Baton Rouge LGBT community. Together, we designed and implemented a study entitled "Assessing Quality of Life among Lesbian, Gay, Bisexual, Transgender, and Queer (LGBTQ) Residents of the Greater Baton Rouge Area." A 53-item survey captured participant demographics and five quality-of-life domains. Three hundred forty-nine study participants were recruited from Baton Rouge and surrounding areas.

Project Timeline

The five stages of implementation discussed in the previous section are presented here in a visual timeline (Table 4.1). It must be noted that stages may not be completely linear or discrete, with some steps being repeated or carried over into subsequent stages, nor are the stages fixed, as glitches and setbacks must be accounted for and time to recover expected. Therefore, this table is intended as an estimate of stage progression.

Steps for Implementation

Partnership
The partnership began prior to the semester, when I met with Kevin Serrin, CCA chair, whom I learned of through a local news story. Finding him was no easy feat, as CCA had not yet established a Web site or publicized their contact information. I was finally put in touch with Mr. Serrin through CCA's original founder.

Mr. Serrin and I were excited about CCA partnering with the university, and saw the service-learning project as an opportunity to help his organization meet the needs of the local LGBT community. To do that, the students would collaborate with the CCA board to develop and implement the survey. We agreed on a quality of life study as the service-learning project and solidified the collaboration by signing a service-learning partnership agreement.

Collaboration
On the first day of the semester, I introduced the service-learning project idea and partner to the students, who were invited to ask questions about service-learning, the proposed project, and their participation. To kick off the collaboration, Mr. Serrin and the other CCA board members invited some of the students and me to the next board meeting, which occurred two weeks after the start of the semester. Board members brainstormed dozens of survey items, which the students took back to the classroom.

The partnership gave students the opportunity to work with and for LGBT people, implement a real-life research project, and be involved in community change.

Set-up
Students spent class time refining the wording of survey items submitted by the CCA board, adding items the students felt were missing, and arranging all items according to themes. Following revisions, students were invited to assist with publishing the survey to the Web using commercially available online survey software from QuestionPro (www.questionpro.com).

Recognizing the time needed for approval by the university's institutional review board (IRB), the students began brainstorming recruitment methods, such as fliers, outreach, e-mail, and audiovisual media. The class was divided into three small groups, each of which devised wording for the study announcements and for the consent form that would accompany the IRB application and proposal.

Table 4.1. The Five Stages of Project Timeline.

	Pre-semester	Weeks 1–3	Weeks 4–6	Weeks 7–9	Weeks 10–12	Weeks 13–15
Partnership						
Collaboration						
Set-up						
Implementation						
Dissemination						

While awaiting IRB approval, students delegated the tasks necessary to publicize the study and identified outlets for each of their recruiting methods.

Implementation

Upon receiving IRB approval, students employed their recruitment strategies by hanging fliers, contacting local radio and print media outlets, sending e-mail, and coordinating outreach events at local LGBT-friendly churches and business establishments. Thus began the waiting period, during which the students eagerly anticipated their study sample.

Dissemination

Since the final data from the 6-month study would not be ready by the end of their semester, students presented preliminary outcome data. In addition to a class presentation to which the community partner, service-learning office staff, and school of social work faculty and staff were invited, three other events were planned, as well: (a) a campus-wide showcase, where the students presented a full-color poster of their service-learning project, (b) a monthly luncheon of LGBT business professionals, at which students presented the preliminary study results, and (c) a regional service-learning conference, for which their abstract was accepted as a poster presentation.

Outcomes/Assessment

Collaborating with the university provided CCA with the resources necessary to better understand through empirical research the community they serve. CCA has already shared the results with members of the local government in an effort to advocate and to demonstrate their LGBT constituents' needs and concerns regarding, for example, LGBT resources, anti-gay discrimination and violence, and partner recognition.

The partnership gave students the opportunity to work with and for LGBT people, implement a real-life research project, and be involved in community change. One student recognized the link the students helped establish between the LGBT community and CCA. "I believe [thus] far the LGBT community has been positively impacted just by becoming aware of CCA and that there are steps being taken to make them more visible and give them a voice." Another student recognized the larger impact of the students' collaborative efforts. "We are giving the LGBT community the chance to let the city know who they are, [and] that they are here and no longer an unspoken, invisible part of the larger community."

Conclusion

The LGBT community may well be a willing collaborator with institutions of higher learning. LGBT organizations serve an often invisible population and might value, as CCA did, research that identifies their constituents' needs as well as other community-serving efforts. Involving students in the process via service-learning provides an invaluable learning experience that students appreciate. "As a student, I often feel useless and not active within the community. I often sit and listen to all of the misfortunes in our society and wonder what I can do. This class has offered me the chance to actively learn, which is something I feel more classes should offer."

COMMUNITY CONNECTIONS: A COMMUNITY OUTREACH INTERGENERATIONAL AND MULTICULTURAL OPPORTUNITY FOR SERVICE-LEARNING

SCOTT P. ANSTADT
FORT HAYS STATE UNIVERSITY

ANN GUSTAD-LEIKER
CENTER FOR LIFE EXPERIENCES

Keywords: multicultural, intergenerational, outreach, groups, social work, community partnership, aged population, elderly

Introduction

Students of a baccalaureate Social Work Group Interventions class attended at least two meetings of the Community Connections (CC), an intergenerational community outreach group which represents a partnership between the local community and university. CC invites people from a variety of age groups and cultural backgrounds to experience together a sense of community centered around presentations, activi-ties, and narrative storytelling and sharing. Participants are invited consumers of local public and private community group services such as schools, faith based organizations, family oriented retirement communities, and civic organizations. Events are organized by a representative Taskforce to celebrate universal themes and traditions. Benefits include mutual assistance, affective giving and receiving, and communicated kindness, kinship, and discovery of a common universal legacy of shared expressions.

Project Description

CC as a format for service-learning meets several simultaneous needs of a university and local community. CC is a twice-a-month event in which local adults, their caregivers, and university students and faculty, including multicultural and international students, gather for cultural exchange through presentations, meals, and small group sharing. This is an opportunity for students to view a community partnership in action. International students get a chance to practice their English conversational skills. Universal themes are developed as a format for the activities. These themes allow for the diverse sharing that comes from the participants as they engage in structured activities. Examples of themes would include: holiday celebrations, food preparation, importance of family, and forms of artistic expression, among others. Examples of activities include: crafts, presentations, dancing, and small group focused discussion among others.

Project Timeline

1/06: CC Taskforce convenes and plans for monthly events conceived
4/07: Application for university service-learning grant
6/07: Acceptance of grant application
11/07: Expansion of CC to include a service-learning component
1/08–5/08: CC service-learning component infused in social work group interventions course
1/08: First CC event attended by service-learning students. First reflective paper
4/08: Second CC event attended by service-learning students. Second reflective paper
5/08: Task force conducts focus group of the students and report prepared for future service-learning projects

Steps for Implementation

CC originated in January 2006 with a Taskforce group representing various community agencies and university student groups. This group served as the planning committee for the bi-monthly events and included enthusiastic community leaders who could encourage attendance of their organization's constituents. With continual evaluation and feedback from this Taskforce and attendees, CC evolved in content and format of presentations. This has created emergence of a truly multicultural and intergenerational focus and a handing down of legacies through a narrative storytelling format while, sharing a community meal prepared by the participants.

The CC Taskforce added a service-learning component in an effort to infuse practical community based experience into a social work group interventions course. Modest funding was needed for additional educational resources in preparation for the student CC involvement and was secured through a service-learning grant through the university.

The service-learning project extended over the spring semester of 2008. The students' first attendance and participation occurred early in the semester, shortly after basic group theory was reviewed in class. Students observed the CC presentation and activities and experienced firsthand how the group setting helped to facilitate sharing. Later, students sat in on small facilitated storytelling discussion groups over a community dinner. Their experience was shared in class and served as a reflective teaching tool of the "narrative" approach to group process.

In the second participation, late in the semester, students participated in the CC Taskforce meetings and helped design the CC upcoming events. Since the class was well-represented by various ethnic and cultural groups, students were able to design a presentation on "Holiday Celebrations-Passing Down Our Family Legacy the World Over." They coordinated the community meal preparations and co-facilitated the small group narrative storytelling discussions regarding this theme.

Outcomes/Assessment

Students wrote a short paper on each CC meeting attended. These papers included student observations, analysis of group process, critical application of feedback forms from CC attendees, and personal reflections based upon their experience and class discussions. The professor gleaned themes from these papers and shared them with the class to stimulate further discussion including suggestions for CC improvements to be passed on to the CC Taskforce.

The CC Taskforce has been collecting consumer satisfaction data after each meeting through a simple quantitative survey handed out to the participants and qualitative impressions from volunteer focus groups. The class volunteered to be one such focus group and gave useful feedback on their experience directly to the CC Taskforce. All of the above has been used to improve future CC events in scope of activities and service toward developing a cohesive community. To date, several hundred students and community residents have attended CC. The above evaluations have yielded a picture of a very successful service in: creating a welcoming atmosphere, building lasting relationships beyond the CC events, and broadening cultural awareness amongst participants.

Conclusion

The intergenerational and multicultural group outreach process has been embraced by the community and university, and has served as a bridge between groups that heretofore have remained somewhat segregated. The CC service-learning component has helped bring group theory studied in the classroom to life and simultaneously provided a service to adults who may otherwise remain socially isolated and unappreciated.

Students' citizenship and civic engagement is enhanced as students maintain connections with various participants they

met during the CC events attended. For example, students have begun to visit elderly persons in the community, now more likely to receive them, having met them during the CC events. The CC Taskforce is working toward formalized arrangements where students can work in conjunction with a Foster Grandparent or Senior Companion on regular home visits to supply both companionship and simple services to the home bound.

STUDENTS EDUCATING THE COMMUNITY TO ADDRESS A PUBLIC HEALTH CONCERN: THE ALZHEIMER'S SAFE RETURN™ COLLABORATIVE

JACQUELYN FRANK
EASTERN ILLINOIS UNIVERSITY

Keywords: Alzheimer's, Safe Return™, public health, gerontology, aged population, elderly, public safety

Introduction

Alzheimer's Association program offices across the country are seeking to educate key community players on both the importance of the Safe Return™ program and how best to communicate with someone they suspect may have dementia. However, local Alzheimer's Association program offices do not have the manpower or flexible schedules to train groups such as police officers and fire/rescue personnel about wandering and the Safe Return program. For example, the Bloomington-Normal Alzheimer's Association program office is responsible for 15 counties in central Illinois and there are only two staff people working in this particular program office. Therefore, it would be impossible for them to train the 200+ police officers and firefighters in the Bloomington-Normal area.

Project Description

The service-learning partnership between Illinois State University and the Alzheimer's Association was created as part of the *Issues in Gerontology Seminar* (a combined graduate/undergraduate sociology course). The seminar is organized around a particular theme or topic related to aging and connects the readings, assignments, and service-learning with the issue being studied. For this project, the seminar focused on Alzheimer's disease as seen from the family, community, and societal perspectives.

The main academic goal for the service-learning project was to help students better understand civic engagement by tackling a major public health issue in their community. In the case of this service-learning project, social capital theory was applied to address the challenges of providing care and protection for people with

Alzheimer's and to reduce caregiver burden for their family members.

Project Timeline

A few months prior to the beginning of the semester, the professor learned from the local chapter of the Alzheimer's Association that Alzheimer's training for first responders was a key area that they needed assistance with. After learning of this need, the professor contacted the police and fire chiefs in Bloomington-Normal to discuss the idea of training their first responders and to work out logistics for the collaboration.

Students in the *Issues in Gerontology Seminar* studied all aspects of Alzheimer's disease and visited an Alzheimer's residential care center so that they would be equipped to instruct law enforcement and fire/rescue personnel (i.e., "first responders") in the Bloomington-Normal community. The students also spent time with Alzheimer's caregivers in their homes and learned the impact caring for someone with the disease has on their lives.

Prior to conducting the training sessions with the first responders, the students and professor developed a training module that focused on four major areas of concern to the Alzheimer's Association: wandering among people with Alzheimer's disease, communicating with someone with dementia, the Safe Return™ program, and statistics and data on people with dementia who become lost.

Students worked collaboratively and were responsible for educating every shift of the Bloomington and Normal police departments, and each shift of the fire and rescue workers. Students ended up conducting 22 separate training sessions for police officers and firefighters, at all hours of the day and night, Monday through Saturday.

Steps for Implementation

1. This type of service-learning project would work best with an upper-level undergraduate or graduate course because of potential confidence and maturity issues among the students. The reason is that standing in front of a group of uniformed police officers and fire fighters to conduct these training sessions can be intimidating for some students.

2. This service-learning project represents indirect service-learning because the population that will be served by this community engagement project is not the population that students are interacting with directly. Therefore, it is critical with an indirect service-learning project that students have the opportunity to read about, meet with, and reflect on the population that is intended to reap the benefits of the service-learning project in order for the students to understand the impact of their service.

3. In order to develop and administer the training sessions, the project requires strong teamwork and collaboration among the students and the faculty member. If students in the course are not "on board" with the project and do not fully understand the need to work in teams then administering the first responder training sessions will be very difficult. Students will also need to take initiative in coordinating responsibilities among themselves (including transportation to and from the training sites).

The faculty member will also find this type of project challenging for three main reasons: (a) the number of community partners involved; (b) coordinating student schedules with those of police and firefighters' shifts; and (c) the logistics of the number of locations that may be involved in

conducting 20+ training sessions. It might be advisable for a faculty member who is experienced with service-learning to integrate such a project into their course or try it in a course that is team taught so that the extra faculty responsibilities can be split.

An additional challenge for this type of project might be the cost. While this project was not expensive to run (about $900 total), it will require some money if the students take a field trip to an Alzheimer's residence and if they plan to produce CDs, etc., as part of their training materials.

Outcomes/Assessment

Student learning objectives were carefully articulated in the syllabus and assessed through on-going reflection (both journaling and group discussions). Student learning was also assessed through final group presentations that were given by the students at the end of the semester. Representatives from the Alzheimer's Association were invited to view the presentations and offer additional feedback.

For this particular service-learning partnership the faculty member and students also developed a training evaluation form for the fire fighters and police officers to complete after their training. The first responders' completed evaluations also helped offer feedback to the students and professor about the usefulness and success of the training sessions.

Conclusion

This service-learning project has great opportunity for replication in communities across the U.S. It also lends itself to being integrated in a variety of types of courses from health science courses to sociology courses to gerontology courses to nursing courses.

THE STUDY OF HISTORY, THE SOCIAL SCIENCES, AND THE ARTS

INTRODUCTION

JULIE ELKINS
DIRECTOR OF ACADEMIC INITIATIVES
CAMPUS COMPACT

*L*earning through service is an opportunity to expand beyond the confines of a specific discipline and merge the cognitive with the heart. While this is true for all disciplines, there are some, such as social work and the performing arts, where the connection to others and the expression of learning is part of the very fabric of the field.

In fact, the ability to connect, to feel, to empathize, and then to synthesize the interactions is at the core of these disciplines. What better way to learn these critical skills sets than to experience real life situations and provide service? At the heart lies the diversity of human realities, of the spirit, and the day-to-day challenges faced by individuals and communities in need. This collection of service-learning courses provides students and community's opportunities to participate in the art of reciprocal learning and service.

Growing up in an Irish/Cherokee family, all of my lessons were articulated through the art of doing, reflecting, honoring others' stories and engaging with the community. This enculturation imprinted a specific way of interacting with the world based on these early experiences. This chapter brings together a collection of courses that provide opportunities for students to learn about the world through individual stories. The significant reciprocal nature of these service-learning projects provides community members an opportunity to tell their story and to honor the past through oral histories and photos. At the end of each experience both the student and community member leave with a gift to mark their journey. This style of service-learning is revealed through the Hands of time project by Barbara Rich University of Southern Maine, Housing and quality of life: Student interviews with farm worker families by Elizabeth Hartung of CSU Channel Islands, the Photovoice Project by Barbara Rich University of Southern Maine and the importance of competencies to alumni of the Sociology/Anthropology department by Laura Khoury and Helen Rosenberg at University of Wisconsin-Parkside.

One of the core tenets of service-learning is the opportunity to lean outside of one's comfort zone and improve individual cultural competency. It is difficult to simply read about poverty, oppression, or imagine an identity other than your own. It is significantly more challenging to embrace an opportunity to learn by putting down a book and opening up your heart and mind to real individuals that you can interact with. There are several examples of this type of service-learning in this chapter such as Integrating Service-Learning into a Social Work Cultural Diversity Course by Emma T. Lucas-Darby at Carlow University, and Ruthanne Hackman at the University of Pittsburgh and Reinventing the Settlement House: Using a Social Work program to provide campus-wide service-learning opportunities by Melody Aye Loya and Mo Cevas at West Texas A&M University, and Service-learning: a sociological experience by Janice G. Rienerth.

Appalachian State University's Increasing cultural competency through refugee focused service-learning projects: bringing the world home by Caile E. Spear and Aileen Hale at Boise State University, and Confronting poverty's impact on the community by Judith I. Gray at Ball State University.

While there is a great deal we can learn from our peers there is something exceptional about intergenerational opportunities for mutual learning and service that is quite unique. During my time at the University of Connecticut I provided leadership for the development of a new community-campus partnership (CCP) to address on-going issues regarding noise, irresponsible behavior under the influence, and other off-campus concerns of undergraduate students and full-time residents. An unexpected outcome of this partnership was the relationship I developed with the Mayor who had retired from the University years before as the Bursar. I remember attending her 65th birthday party. I met her grown children, whom she had raised as a single parent while putting herself through school, as well as a vast array of the Mayor's political and personal friends. The Mayor's insights and sharing of her experiences with me surpassed any classroom lessons on politics, parenthood, feminism, and leadership. There were several examples of service-learning projects working with intergenerational relationships include several of listening/story projects. In addition, UGIVE: An Intergenerational Service-Learning Program by Sharon M. Ballard and Angela Lamson at East Carolina University, The Profession of Social Work through Service-learning by Connie M. Fossen of Viterbo University, and The healing power of music by Cynthia Green Libby at Missouri State University.

One of the challenges in life is deciding when to choose between the heart and head to best tackle the situation at hand. I would argue that it is not so binary. Some of my best learning has occurred when I was able to truly integrate the two with the right mixture of each depending on the situation. The following service-learning examples demonstrate a vast set of opportunities to stimulate learning on both cognitive and emotional levels. Service-learning pedagogy opens up possibilities to create a place where students and the community can also learn in ways that cannot be achieved alone.

Despite the non-hierarchical presentation of Kolb's learning styles, I have always placed experiential learning above the rest. As an academic, I can advance the research on service-learning to support this argument. As a learner, I know that it has reached me on a deeper level somewhere in the center of who I am as a person. As an experiential learner, I am constantly aware of the opportunities to connect learning and service in ways that really capture the spirit of service-learning.

This broad collection of programs illuminates service-learning courses across many disciplines in five main areas, oral histories, cultural competence, direct service, and resource development.

HANDS OF TIME PROJECT

BARBARA RICH
UNIVERSITY OF SOUTHERN MAINE

Keywords: elderly, photography, oral history, gerontology, aged population, social work, low-income, human subjects

Introduction

Maine is currently distinguished by having the oldest population in the country. In the next decade, 77 million people born between 1946 and 1964 will begin to move into their retirement years and by 2030, the number of persons older than 65 will have doubled.

It is estimated that 60,000–70,000 new gerontological social workers will be needed by 2020. Unfortunately, students have accepted our societal stereotypes of the elderly as passive, boring, sick, and dying. The social work profession is challenged to develop creative and exciting programs that confront those stereotypes and bring students into contact with healthy, active, elderly people who have rich lived experience. The Hands of Time Project is one answer to this challenge.

Project Description

This service-learning project matched University of Southern Maine Social Work students with residents of a congregate living facility for low-income elderly. Each student was matched with a volunteer resident and, together, they engaged in a modified oral history that answered the question, "What have these hands accomplished in your life?" This process elicited reminiscences about child rearing, work, leisure pursuits, community and religious activities, and other areas. The oral history was audiotaped and partially transcribed by the students.

The pictures and partial transcriptions were exhibited three times. The first was in the classroom when the students described their experiences to everyone in the class. Next, there was a colloquium where all university students could hear about the project and see the pictures. Finally, there was a reception and exhibit at the congregate living facility. There, the residents were presented with the framed pictures, tapes, and the transcriptions. These items are nice mementos for the residents, or they may choose to give them to family members as gifts or as part of the family history.

The aim of the Hands of Time Demonstration Project was three-fold:
1. to expose social work students to healthy, independent elderly who live in a congregate living facility and to engage them in a project that will highlight the rich lived experience and the enduring vibrancy of the elderly participants,

2. to demonstrate that a positive experience with healthy elderly people will contradict the stereotypes and encourage students to find gerontological social work more attractive as a field work placement and a career,
3. to allow students to practice the skills and knowledge they are learning in their course; and to create an enjoyable and rewarding experience for the elderly participants who will be able to reminisce about their past life roles to an interested and attentive student who will record the oral history.

Project Timeline

Months	Activity
Prior to semester	IRB approval sought and received
December	Planning, community partner negotiation
January	Class presentation by community partners
	All congregate living facility residents receive an invitation to participate
	Both students and residents sign consent forms
	Pretest of students
February	Students are matched with residents and receive orientation, training, and a tour of the facility
February–April	Students and residents work together
May	Exhibits of the photographs Posttest of students

Steps for Implementation

Because this is an oral history, an evaluation by the Institutional Review Board is required prior to the beginning of the project. Implementation begins with discussion between the teacher and the community partner to negotiate the learning needs of the students and the needs of the older residents. In January, the community partner representatives come to class to discuss the project, the client populations, and logistics. Since there are other community partners to choose from besides the Hands of Time project, students write an essay describing their first, second, and third choices of sites, what they want learn, what they have to offer, and what hours they have available. The teacher then makes matches based on these essays. The next week, typically the 4th week of the semester, the students who are assigned to each of the sites are given one class period so that all can go to their sites for a tour, introductions, orientation, and scheduling. Students then generally spend two hours a week in service-learning work. Following this, each Hands of Time student/resident pair complete the oral history and take the pictures. Then, the student transcribes parts of the audiotaped history and frames the photographs. The students who were assigned to each service-learning site present their learning and the photos in a formal class presentation at the end of the semester. A similar presentation is made at a university-wide colloquium. At the end of the project, the facility hosts a wine and cheese reception and exhibit for the students, all of the residents, and their families. After the exhibits, the framed photographs and the oral history are given to the residents.

Outcomes/Assessment

One of the tenets of service-learning is that there is reciprocity in the relationship between the educational institution and the community partner. This means that both parties benefit from the collaboration. This project gave a voice to elderly people who have been marginalized and stereotyped. The elder participants saw themselves in a new light, as unique and talented, and with a long and valued life story to share with their families and the community.

The social work students who took part in the project had a chance to see elderly people in a different light, free of the stereotypes of our culture. They were pre-and post-tested for knowledge and comfort level in working with elderly people, and for their interest in a placement or career in gerontological social work. There was a significant increase in both variables. Students also kept reflection journals that chronicled their thoughts, feelings, and learning from their service-learning experiences. A content analysis will be done of these writings.

Conclusion

The Hands of Time project was a successful in meeting all of the goals that had been set out. Service-learning projects are usually win-win-win situations. All parties benefit—the students and the university, the agency and the clients, and the community in general.

INTEGRATING SERVICE-LEARNING INTO A SOCIAL WORK CULTURAL DIVERSITY COURSE

EMMA T. LUCAS-DARBY
CARLOW UNIVERSITY

RUTHANNE HACKMAN
UNIVERSITY OF PITTSBURGH

Keywords: social work, cultural diversity, cultural sensitivity, pluralistic community, race, multicultural perspective, advocacy

Introduction

In an urban university committed to service and community partnerships, faculty are encouraged to integrate service-learning components into their courses. Service-learning (SL) is a component of *Cultural Awareness and Human Services,* a required undergraduate course for social work majors. The course content focuses on the far-reaching implications of racism, sexism, discrimination, bigotry, classism, poverty, and ethnic differences. One learning objective of this course is for students to develop an understanding of a culturally sensitive and practical social services process-stage approach to ethnic and cultural groups. Community partners and the course instructor identified a mutually agreed upon SL project that would meet a community's need and provide interactions that enhance students' learning related to this course's content.

Upon completion of the SL project, students gained knowledge of pluralistic racial and cultural communities, a multicultural perspective for human service delivery, and an introduction to the interplay of advocacy, community empowerment and social change.

Project Description

The community partners were after-school programs in economically and culturally diverse communities. They offer tutoring, computer literacy, self-awareness, and homework assistance to neighborhood children. The university students tutored children in math and reading, taught computer skills, developed and led self-awareness exercises, as well as coordinated and facilitated cultural awareness programming, such as word identification in several languages, African American history, and Kente cloth designs. While students provided 20 hours of service, they learned from the community regarding socio-economic experiences and traditions, as well as cultural diversity. Course content and orientation exercises emphasized community, individual strengths, and basic human needs that define one's quality of life. Orientation exercises included demographic information about the community (socioeconomic data, cultural patterns, availability of social services, community interactions) and educational characteristics of school-aged students.

Project Timeline

Extensive planning and collaboration is necessary prior to integrating a service-learning component into a course. A year in advance of implementation, faculty evaluated and adjusted the curriculum for the optimal integration of the service-learning component. Concurrently, the instructor negotiated with existing community partners to serve as service-learning placement sites. The instructor observed institutional guidelines for applying and receiving course approval as a new SL course. The SL project was designed to be completed within the semester that the course was offered.

Steps for Implementation

1. Redesign the course content to fully integrate the service-learning component.
2. Discuss SL component with department chairperson and colleagues for support.
3. Apply and receive university approval for integrating a service-learning component in the course.
4. Evaluate existing community partners as potential SL placement sites and identify an agency contact person.
5. Collaborate with community partners regarding a SL project that meets the community's needs and supports students' in-class learning experience.
6. Early in the course, provide pre-placement orientation.
7. Provide students with guidelines for completion of 20 hours of SL. Identify guidelines for the reflective journal of the SL activity, which is submitted bi-weekly. Allow time during class for reflections as this shared exchange assists to better understand the placement and its connection to course content.
8. Recognize the learning from the SL experience through celebration. This may include tangibles, such as food, special site observations that were meaningful and lasting, or a combined gathering of learners and community partners.
9. Evaluation the SL experience.

Early in the semester, students participate in three 75-minute SL pre-placement orientation sessions led by the course instructor, the staff of the university's Community Education Program, and community partners. Pre-placement orientation for students is critical to students' SL preparation. Components of the pre-placement orientation

included the after-school programs' goals and policies, skill building and expectations of tutors, community history and demographics, language usage including distinct and contemporary "slang" words, and the NASW's *Code of Ethics* (1999) and *Cultural Competence Standards in Social Work Practice* (2001). Speakers came from community partners and local organizations including the Race Relations Center to present and to lead discussions about racism, bias, white privilege, cultural diversity, community strengths, and cultural sensitivity. Dialogue guidelines were established to create safe and open environments and to respect all statements shared.

During one class session, students completed a cultural communications worksheet. This exercise encouraged students to reflect on their verbal responses, body language and reactions to interactions when communicating in a variety of settings and with racially and culturally diverse groups. During week four, students made on-site visits to the community partners to become familiar with the placement environment.

Outcomes and Assessment

To evaluate the SL experience, three pre-post questionnaires were administered: an attitude survey, Self-Assessment of Leadership Qualities, and the Social Problems Survey (from the America Reads Tutor Evaluation II Outcome Evaluation, the Minnesota Campus Compact).

Overall, students began with relatively positive attitudes toward SL that improved somewhat. The Leadership Survey indicated that the SL experience appears to have significantly enhanced students' beliefs about themselves as leaders.

In regards to social problems, the Social Problems Survey assessed students' opinions regarding causes

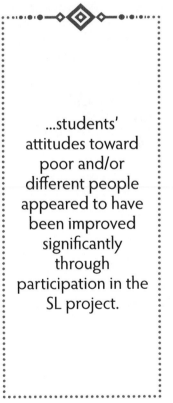

...students' attitudes toward poor and/or different people appeared to have been improved significantly through participation in the SL project.

and solutions of a variety of social problems that typically affect people in low-income communities. Students attributed the causes of social problems to circumstances beyond the control of the individual, and that with adequate resources and assistance, individuals and communities can be empowered to affect change, generally and specifically to the social problems represented in the survey.

The results of the pre-/post-assessment showed students' attitudes toward poor and/or different people appeared to have been improved significantly through participation in the SL project. Additional assessment tools may be found through the National Service-Learning Clearing House [http://www.servicelearning.org] and Campus Compact [http://www.compact.org].

Conclusion

Thoughtful planning for the SL component includes observing institutional policies and processes and collaborating with university colleagues and community partners. A comprehensive pre-placement orientation is an essential foundation to the service-learning experience. Prior to placement, advancing an understanding of differences and the recognition of social justice and social responsibility will result in reciprocal benefits for students (servers) and the community (served). The goal is to change students' perceptions of service from "do-gooders" or "charitable volunteers" to socially responsible citizens contributing to social change and advocacy.

References

National Association of Social Workers. (1999). *Code of Ethics*. Washington, D.C: Author. Downloadable at http://www.socialworkers.org/pubs/code/code.asp.

National Association of Social Workers. (2001). *Standards for Cultural Competence in Social Work Practice*. Washington, D.C: Author. Downloadable at http://www.socialworkers.org/pressroom/2001/090601.asp.

Reinventing the Settlement House: Using a social work program to provide campus-wide service-learning opportunities

Melody Aye Loya and Mo Cuevas
West Texas A&M University

Keywords: social work, community-based, service center, field experience, practicum

Introduction

As the education of future social workers moves toward a competency-based model, exposing students to as many experiential activities as possible becomes essential. Goldstein (2001) suggested that students must be able to move from the theoretical and conceptual nature of the classroom to real cases with real people. This may be best accomplished through experiential learning. Service-learning should not be limited, however, to applied professions; it can benefit all college students as they struggle to take their place in society. Parker (2007) believes that higher education has distanced itself from its students and from society. Service-learning can help bridge the gap between students and the society that they will help to mold.

Project Description

This entry describes the establishment of a community-based service center, which has provided experiential activities for future social workers, but also offers opportunities for university-wide projects.

The center incorporates service-learning opportunities for social work students beginning with the Introduction to Social Work course through the senior field practicum. BSW students answer phones, explore local resources, and provide case management to the homeless and other at-risk clients. Graduate students provide counseling to clients and some administrative oversight. All students are involved in grant-writing efforts, various psycho-educational groups, and program development as additional service needs are identified.

Project Timeline

A community needs assessment was conducted in a spring semester as the class project for a "stacked" (BSW and MSW) macro-level practice course. Students developed and conducted surveys of local stakeholders, and the responses were compiled during the spring semester. Student groups completed the semester by investigating resources to fund the identified needs of case management and counseling. Social work faculty then developed a proposal to a local foundation to develop the center, West Texas Family and Community Services (WTFCS). Faculty located space in a local outreach center, which houses a consortium of agencies providing services to the homeless and other vulnerable populations.

Senior students were placed in January to initiate services while stable funding was secured. Initially, social work faculty supervised the students by holding office hours on-site. Students in the Group Processes course developed and implemented psycho-educational groups at the center. Introduction to Social Work students provided child-care during the groups.

Funding was awarded through the local foundation in April, one year after the initial needs assessment. A Director was hired the following August, but only stayed three months. During the fall semester, two full-time and three part-time BSW interns were placed in the agency and several graduate students offered counseling. While unstable staffing and funding has been challenging, faculty and senior interns have provided a measure of continuity and stability. A main focus has been developing community relationships and collaborative efforts in order to use resources effectively and efficiently within the local community.

With a new Director in place, new services being offered, and outside funding secured, the center continues to grow and change. In the three years since the initial needs assessment, the center has provided services for clients and experiences for students far exceeding expectations. As current services and delivery systems are evaluated, additional changes will be made to meet newly identified needs of students or the community being served. The center is now poised to encourage the involvement of students across campus in various service-learning projects. Projects are planned to provide outreach to the elderly through a supplemental food program; to refugees through a local resettlement agency; and to a shelter for homeless women.

Steps for Implementation

1. Needs assessment developed and implemented.
2. Community needs determined.
3. Proposals submitted to appropriate funding sources.
4. Initial grant obtained from local foundation.
5. Policies and procedures, job descriptions and evaluation measures developed.
6. Director hired, service-learning students placed to provide services.
7. Community relationships developed, collaborative efforts initiated.
8. Continued funding sources explored, stable funding secured.
9. Ongoing assessment of services, needs, and programs.
10. Student evaluation of placement experience.
11. Expansion of project to include other university programs.

Outcomes/Assessment

Since first opening, the community-based center has served over 1000 clients, providing hygiene supplies, clothing and furniture vouchers, psycho-educational groups, Christmas gifts for families, counseling, case management, and a variety of other needed services. Although services have primarily been provided by social work students, other disciplines or classes have been involved in fund-raising, drives for donations of hygiene products and Christmas gifts, and some volunteer hours answering phones, etc.

In a recent focus group, students described their experience at WTFCS as confidence building. They believe they are better critical thinkers, and they enjoy having the flexibility to explore new interests. They are able to establish and grow programs or services as needed, and they enjoy stepping outside of their comfort zone. Also invaluable has been peer feedback on their various projects. In the reflection papers written every semester, students continually stress the "real world" learning they receive in this setting. They say it makes a huge difference in their sense of self-efficacy, and in how they view those in need.

Conclusion

Experiential social work education allows students to deal with what Goldstein (2001) called "the fluid, sometimes messy, and subjective nature of the client's story and circumstances" (p. 8), hearkening back to the Settlement House days when social workers went to where the clients were, learning about their needs, joys, struggles, and challenges first-hand. Goldstein perhaps summed it up best when he said, "It is in the field that learners can gain the confidence, the talent, the art, and the proficiencies necessary to become competent social workers not only in their encounters with clients, but also with agencies, communities, and other constituents of real-life practice" (p. 6). Although the project was built around the social work program, campus-wide involvement in the center is being implemented. The project offers a myriad of flexible opportunities for students, classes, or groups within the university community to design and implement service-learning projects to meet individualized learning needs.

References

Goldstein, H. (2004). *Experiential learning: A foundation for social work education and practice.* Alexandria, VA: Council on Social Work Education.

Parker, P. (2007). *The courage to teach: Exploring the inner landscape of a teacher's life.* San Francisco: Jossey-Bass.

...students described their experience as confidence building. They believe they are better critical thinkers, and they enjoy having the flexibility to explore new interests.

UGIVE: AN INTERGENERATIONAL SERVICE-LEARNING PROGRAM

SHARON M. BALLARD AND ANGELA LAMSON
EAST CAROLINA UNIVERSITY

Keywords: intergenerational, gerontology, social work, child development, aged population

Introduction

This entry outlines the essential components of the UGIVE (undergraduate interdisciplinary volunteerism experience) program, an intergenerational service-learning program implemented with undergraduate students, and provides implementation guidelines. Although the materials are specific to intergenerational service-learning, they can be adapted for other types of service-learning programs.

Project Description

The introductory gerontology course for which the UGIVE program was designed is a sophomore-level course cross-listed with the departments of Social Work, Gerontology, and Child Development and Family Relations. The service-learning component required all enrolled students to engage in 12 hours of service-learning with older adults in the community.

The learning objectives for the service-learning component of the course were that students will: (a) interact directly with older adults in meaningful activities, (b) integrate course material with service-learning experiences, (c) dispel personal myths and stereotypes about older populations, (d) increase knowledge about older adults and aging, (e) develop critical thinking and problem solving skills related to aging, and, (f) provide a needed community service.

Project Timeline

The service-learning component was implemented in the fall of 2002 and was initially funded by the Corporation for National and Community Service, Learn & Serve Higher Education through a grant to The Association for Gerontology in Higher Education in partnership with Generations Together (http://www.gt.pitt.edu/). Preparation for implementation occurred during the summer of 2002 including intergenerational service-learning training provided by the funder, assessment of community partner needs, and development of the service-learning manual.

Steps for Implementation

Based on existing research on service-learning, we identified essential components of service-learning: (a) Community Partnerships; (b) Training and Preparation; (c) Reflection; (d) Recognition; and, (e) Evaluation. Below, we outline the implementation steps for these components.

Step 1: Establishing Community Partnerships

To assess community partners' interest in a service-learning partnership, a needs assessment was administered. The assessment identified the number of students the site could accommodate, types of activities in which students would be engaged, and times that students must be available. This assessment allowed the community partners to better understand service-learning and to contemplate questions or concerns. Conversely, the assessment ensured a good fit between students and community partners. This step may be conducted in conjunction with a service-learning or volunteer center.

Step 2: Training and Preparation

We created a manual for students and community partners. The students received the manual with one hour of training during the second class of the semester. The community partners received the manual via a personal meeting at the service-learning site. This meeting facilitated communication between community partners and faculty. A brief description of each manual section is provided below.

Defining Service-learning. This section helped students understand the concept of service-learning, the distinction between service-learning and volunteerism, and the learning objectives for service-learning within the course.

Service-learning Requirements. Students provided service for 12 hours throughout the semester. Some faculty may choose to require more or less; however, with up to 65 students we didn't want to overwhelm the service-learning sites. We provided students with a timeline of hour completion to avoid having students wait until the last minute to complete their hours.

Classroom Assignment Requirements. This section provided guidelines and expectations for the reflection exercises, grading criteria, and instruction for electronic submission of reflection journals.

Disability Support Services. The inclusion of our university's statement regarding disabilities reaffirmed our commitment to having all students engage fully in the service-learning experience and provided students who needed accommodations assistance in obtaining them.

Dos & Don'ts of Service-learning and Tips on Aging. Both service-learning and interaction with older adults were new experiences for the majority of our students so we included a list of guidelines on professionalism and tips on aging.

Volunteer Act of 1997, Insurance Forms, and Confidentiality. The Volunteer Act of 1997 may offer some liability protection during service-learning. Additionally, our institution offers free liability insurance to students. This form, along with a confidentiality document to ensure that personal information is not shared during class or reflection exercises, was included.

Documentation of Hours and List of Placements. This section included the time sheet and a list of available service-learning placements.

Evaluation. The manual included the evaluation form that community partners completed on each student at the end of the semester.

Step 3: Reflection Activities

We included two forms of reflection: class discussion and journals. Class discussion occurred on scheduled days and provided an opportunity for students to share their experiences and to reflect on how these experiences coincided with class material. Reflection journal submissions were submitted every three weeks and followed an outline of (a) description: a description of their experiences with older adults, (b) analysis: an assessment of how course content related to their service experience, and (c) application; how service-learning experiences and relevant course content could be applied to their personal and/or professional life.

Step 4: Recognition

In an effort to recognize the accomplishments of participants, every student and community partner was invited to an end-of-the-semester service-learning appreciation day that included refreshments. Students were able to invite an older adult with whom they had been working that semester. All students who finished their service-learning hours received a certificate of completion. In addition, three awards were given: student learner of the semester determined by community partner nominations, older adult of the semester, and community partner of the semester. The students made the nominations for the latter two awards.

Step 5: Evaluation

We conducted both informal and formal evaluation of the service-learning experience through verbal and written reflection, student evaluations completed by community partners, objective exams, and a site visit and/or phone calls to community partners made throughout the semester. In addition to these more traditional pedagogical evaluation methods, we assessed the effectiveness of service-learning as a teaching strategy through a pre-test, post-test research study.

Conclusion

The components of the UGIVE program are essential to any service-learning program and can easily be applied to other types of courses. Implementing a successful service-learning experience can be time consuming and challenging. However, with careful planning, service-learning can provide tremendous benefits for students, faculty, and community partners.

References

Generations Together. Retrieved June 13, 2008 from http://www.gt.pitt.edu/.

THE PROFESSION OF SOCIAL WORK THROUGH SERVICE-LEARNING

CONNIE M. FOSSEN
VITERBO UNIVERSITY

Keywords: social work, reflection, profession, practice

Introduction

This article describes a course centered on service-learning activities, reflection and integration, which enabled students to discover the world of social work practice. The principles of service-learning and social work practice framed the design, assignments, class activities and content of the course.

Project Description

In 2004, the course *The Profession of Social Work through Service-learning* was added to the curriculum to offer an introduction to social work practice. The Wingspread Report of Practice Principles for combining service and learning —community identified need, active participation, reflection, learning goals and support—framed the course design (Honnet & Poulson, 1989).

Course Timeline

Students complete 30 hours of service over a 15-week semester with placement in the agency two to three hours per week. Class sessions are held twice a week for a total of three and one-half hours.

The beginning of the semester focuses on assisting the

HARPER COLLEGE LIBRARY
PALATINE, ILLINOIS 60067

student in service orientation; a series of case studies and discussion centers on appropriate volunteer behavior, service-learning concepts and professional expectations. The course content that supports beginning in the agency is self-awareness, social work careers, personal values, and professional ethics.

In the second half of the semester, the students' actual service experience is the basis of teaching social work practice. Class sessions support this integration of service into the academic content through a series of active learning strategies such as Four Corners group work, large group discussion, practice assessments, student diversity presentations and service 'sharing' sessions. In course activities students compare their service experience with the actions of professional social workers to understand together the ideal and the reality of social work practice. Both the midterm and final exam include a student assessment of the contributions of their service experience to the students' understanding of social work practice.

Steps for Implementation

Service-learning is successful if the service meets actual community needs (Honnet & Poulson, 1989). The service-learning agencies selected for the course offer the opportunity for students to work directly with clients and staff. The agencies identified through a community needs assessment offered a professional willing to provide student guidance including orientation, ongoing support, and evaluation.

The development and teaching of this service-learning course has been one of the most delightful experiences in my career. Students come to class prepared with in-depth questions, excited to talk about their service experiences and social work practice.

Important is the active participation of the agency and student in choosing and evaluating the service activities (Honnet & Poulson, 1989). Students are matched the first week with an agency based on their social work interest and past experiences. The student completes an interview at the agency and a written agreement is signed confirming the student-agency commitment to the placement. Both the student and agency supervisor complete service evaluations before a grade is awarded.

The International Partnership for Service-Learning recommends a journal as a structured method for students to think, talk, or write about what they experience in their agency (2008). Over the semester, the student writes eight journals reflecting on their service and integrating their experience to specific course concepts. Each journal entry describes a particular activity followed by the students' personal reflection of the experience. For example, in the unit on values and ethics, students are introduced to the National Association of Social Workers Code of Ethics. Students reflect how the Code guides service delivery in their agency and how the Code will guide their own practice. The final journal section, "further questions," provides the instructor an opportunity to monitor the student concerns and provide direction.

It is equally important for learning goals to be identified by the agency and the student (Honnet & Poulson, 1989). After students have completed self-awareness exercises and assessed their personal values, they develop a personal learning goal. The same framework that social workers use to devise a measurable plan for client goal achievement is used as students formulate their goal. Students share their learning goal with the agency supervisor to assure the availability of service opportunities for student goal accomplishment.

Service-learning happens with the collaboration and support of the course instructor, agency supervisor and the students as a group (Honnet & Poulson, 1989). Before the first course offering, 15 agencies participated in an orientation of the course and service-learning expectations to prepare supervisors for their supportive and educational role with students. Over the semester, agency support is provided in regular e-mail contacts by the instructor. At least once a week, class time is structured to allow students to consult with each other regarding their service experience. The role of "instructor" became less directive as the semester progresses with the students taking the lead in consultation and discussion, first in their service experience, and later in course content and assignments.

Outcome Assessment

As a newly designed course, multiple assessment strategies were used for course improvement. The most productive assessment tool was simply inviting students to provide course feedback as the experts of their learning. Students stated that the "course would be totally lacking if it did not require service" and "service really helped me understand class concepts." Further, students noted that they, "liked working with clients on a regular basis" and "I better understand what social work is—it's real with the service."

Student evaluations indicated that the integrative journal was the most helpful assignment to reflect on their service experience, analyze what was happening, and monitor their practice development. Over the four years of the course, university evaluations were positive in the area of course content, class discussion, assignments, service placement and the camaraderie-atmosphere of the class.

Conclusion

The design of this course was based on the service-learning principles of community identified need, active participation, reflection, learning goals and support—principals that could guide the development of service-learning courses in other disciplines (Honnet & Poulson, 1989). Over four years, the course design remained the same with changes focused on further integration of the students' service experience in assignments, content and exams. The

development and teaching of this service-learning course has been one of the most delightful experiences in my career. Students come to class prepared with in-depth questions, excited to talk about their service experiences and social work practice.

References

Honnet, E. P., & Poulson, S. J. (1989). *Principles of good practice for combining service and learning.* (Wingspread Special Report). Racine, WI: The Johnson Foundation.

International Partnership for Service-Learning and Leadership. *Principles of Good Practice.* Retrieved June 2008 from http://www.ipsl.org.

SERVICE-LEARNING: A SOCIOLOGICAL EXPERIENCE

JANICE G. RIENERTH
APPALACHIAN STATE UNIVERSITY

Keywords: sociology, experiential learning, Kolb's Learning Cycle, criminal justice, law, victims

Introduction

Service-learning can best be understood by reviewing the work of Kolb (1976). His learning cycle demonstrates the stages of complete learning: abstract conceptualization, active experimentation, concrete experience and reflective observation.

This type of experience is especially relevant to sociology students since they rarely have clear career goals. According to Ostrow, Hessner and Eons (1999),

> "...the instructor's task is to provide the sort of experience through which the sociological habit of mind can develop. Fieldwork projects that have community service as their frame are excellent vehicles for accomplishing this objective."

Students often work with populations they have not previously encountered and become aware of their community's social issues. They see class concepts "working" in real life; thus developing their sociological imagination.

Project Description

In my Women in the Justice System class, I implemented a project with the Community Law Center (low-cost law clinic). This class dealt with issues related to women as offenders, victims and practitioners. While mainly sociology majors, this upper-level class included students from a number of disciplines.

Project Timeline

I use service-learning projects in my semester-long classes. I feel this length of time is needed in order to adequately develop and implement a meaningful project.

Steps for Implementation

At Appalachian State University, we are fortunate to have a program entitled Appalachian Community Together (ACT). It helps faculty develop projects by contacting community agencies with needs. The following steps were used in project implementation:

1. I contacted an ACT staff member. We discussed the content of my class and the suitable projects.
2. I selected two projects; one was developing material for the Hispanic population served by the Community Law Center.
3. I included a statement about the service-learning requirement in the syllabus.
4. In class, I discussed the goal of service-learning, how it differed from volunteering, and what the class requirements were.
5. Group membership for the two projects, was based on self-selection.
6. I invited agency representatives to class to discuss their project. This allowed for questions and "brainstorming" about how to approach the project.
7. I allowed the groups to have limited class time for project work, because many students work outside of class or commute to school.
8. The groups gave oral reports and completed individual

reflective essays at the end of the semester. This is the syllabus statement.

Many students take classes without a clear understanding of the relationship between these classes and the 'outside world.' By being involved in a service-learning project you gain hands-on experience recognizing sociological concepts, thinking critically, overcoming stereotypical ideas and improving your interpersonal skills.

Your three page reflective essay must include a discussion of:
a. Your experience with the project.
b. How your experience relates to class material.
c. Three sociological concepts you experienced.
d. The value of this experience.

By looking back on their experiences, students were able to integrate new information into their knowledge base thus completing Kolb's learning cycle.

Outcomes/Assessment

Incorporating service-learning into a class is valuable in any discipline where students do not move directly from college to a career. For sociology majors, it forces them to "see" sociology in the outside world and think about career areas where sociological knowledge would be useful. Including a service experience into a class is not without its challenges, however. For example:
1. Students want direct contact with clients, which wasn't possible due to confidentiality issues.
2. In large classes, service-learning projects can be more difficult to implement unless students are divided into groups.
3. Group work is challenging when some students do not pull their share of the load.

The positive aspects, however, far outweighed the negative.
1. Students were able to provide services to an underserved community population.
2. Students were able to develop a brochure on the clinics' services for the Hispanic population.
3. Students became more culturally sensitive through assessing the needs of this population.

In addition to a reflective essay and an oral report, students also did a written evaluation for the ACT office. Their comments on the various forms of assessment showed that the students learned a great deal about the Hispanic population, their community and themselves from this project.

Conclusion

Service-learning follows a national trend in higher education; the movement toward a skill-based curriculum. This type of experience helps students improve the skills promoted by a liberal arts education. Specifically, my students cited enhancement in: interpersonal, communication, teamwork, listening and decision-making skills. As one student stated:
"WOW. I learned a lot about people and how they work. I saw so many different leadership styles..."

In conclusion, I plan to continue incorporating service-learning into my classes. The experience is educational to all parties involved. I would, however, make a few changes including:
1. dividing large classes into groups of no more than five, and
2. trying to develop opportunities for more "hands-on" experiences.

> Incorporating service-learning into a class is valuable in any discipline where students do not move directly from college to a career.

Specifically for sociology majors, students need to learn to apply what they have learned. According to Ostrow, Hesser and Enos:
"...the teachability of 'sociology' in its pure form, as a practice, rather than as a set of items that are detached and isolated from practice... we can and should teach sociology rather than a mock-up of it, and ... the service-learning course assignment is an extremely useful vehicle for doing so." (1)

References

Kolb, D.A. (1976) *Learning Style Inventory Technical Manual.* Massachusetts: McBer and Co.

Ostrow, J., Hessner, G., Enos, S. (Eds.). (1999). *Cultivating the social imagination: Concepts and models for service-learning in sociology.* Washington, D.C.: American Association for Higher Education.

A BETTER PLACE: COMMUNITY RESOURCE DEVELOPMENT THROUGH SERVICE-LEARNING

NANCY FRANCISCO STEWART
JACKSONVILLE STATE UNIVERSITY

Keywords: community, health, populations-at-risk, empowerment, rural, social work

Introduction

Personal, organizational and community change must connect to promote well-being (Prilleltensky & Prilleltensky, 2006). Making sense of "gemeinschaft and gesellschaft" presents theoretical and practical challenges when students see the serious personal problems people face and the overwhelming nature of those problems in the larger environment. Lohmann & Lohmann (2005) and Martinez-Brawley (2000) present community theory and practice as "ties that bond" noting the importance of context in understanding our own identities, power and leadership. Scales & Streeter (2004) emphasize "half-full" rather than "half-empty" in their asset-building framework. Relationship building is a necessary skill.

This service-learning project teaches community theory and assessment through a partnership with a national organization (American Cancer Society) to develop new local resources that can be accessed by area residents through the Cancer Resource Network. Undergraduate social work students unlocked the strengths of their communities, developing tangible resources for families with cancer in small communities with poverty, limited health care resources and educational opportunities, and a growing Hispanic population. The Community Resource Development project continues in the course on groups, organizations and communities and is appropriate for public health, nursing, psychology, planning, emergency management or economics as well as interdisciplinary perspectives.

Project Description

This assignment explored what individuals and agency personnel experience when accessing services designed to maintain health: identifying the barriers and learning community perceptions about resources and involvement. Students practice asset mapping, resource development and assess empowerment with a focus on one population group and specific geographic region: people with cancer within the local division of the American Cancer Society. Students analyzed census and public health data, met community leaders and identified formal (public, proprietary and nonprofit) and informal resources (churches, civic groups and individuals). The project stages include orientation to ACS, a literature review, defining the community and agencies currently providing services, development of at least one new resource per student and a report. ACS "Relay for Life" activities do not constitute resource development. Students submitted a printed document in addition to an electronic presentation. The compiled work was presented to the Health Initiatives Representative to be added to their national data bank.

Project Timeline

This five-week project began the second week of class:

Week 1: Introduce project. Students oriented to resource development network and responsibilities as volunteers. Attend library research orientation to obtain data from government documents, discipline specific peer-reviewed journals, local media and sponsored websites. Specific communities selected.

Week 2: Discuss homework assignment describing their community from various theoretical perspectives from obtained data and assigned readings. Submit literature review of journal article demonstrating relationship to the community project.

Week 3: Students, often as teams, visit community (outside of class) to gather information and develop a resource table. Resource table includes contact persons, address, phone numbers, information about waiting lists, fees, transportation, eligibility, and its status as an informal resource, nonprofit organization, church, local government, etc. During this data collection, students will also do "resource development" to identify potential resources and encourage individuals to become stakeholders in supporting community. Students complete forms developed by our partnering agency that will be entered into the data bank.

Week 4: Students develop a map of community resources and create a slide presentation of the research project, their experiences, analysis and results.

Week 5: Class presentations. Resource table submitted. Forms for ACS submitted.

After each semester: Instructor meets with ACS representatives to discuss outcomes.

Steps for Implementation

Articles on asset mapping provide framework for the assignment. Instructor must have familiarity with demography and literature or use reference librarian as resource. Before the course, the instructor should meet with the Health Initiatives Representative from the American Cancer Society to schedule class presentation. Familiarize students with ACS forms and networks so they can be Resource Development Volunteers. Make certain students have introductory letters on organization and university letterhead as well as nametags. Google Maps and GPS information are excellent tools for students. Provide opportunities for practice interviews. Have an "open door" for students to discuss fears and findings.

Outcomes/ Assessment

Academic work submitted in the departmental format (APA style) with correct grammar and citations. Students must be able to state the project problem and purpose, present the community from several perspectives: structural, human ecology, systems and strengths with supporting evidence from the census, presentation of available resources, a description of location and the opinions of its leaders and members, and develop at least one new community resource per student. Student analysis must include the limitations of the project and implications for social work practice.

Project outcomes: More new resources for ACS than any division in a six-state area, increasing national information for small communities. Students developed "tool box" for future practice and strengthened ties with underserved groups in their communities.

Conclusions

Students learned to assess their communities for their assets and strengths, relationships that exist and traditions that make them unique. The service project and rural perspective increased comprehension of elitism, dilemmas of few formal resources, political structure and sheer distance from healthcare, education or employment for many residents.

As they heard the priorities of those who face the difficulties of a potentially terminal disease, they began to uncover "hidden resources" to aid people in their local areas. Students developed new avenues to help with childcare, housekeeping, emotional, and social support, as well as tangible resources like gas and food far "outside the box" suggested by the national organization. This project promoted greater understanding of the significance of "place" and access to resources as fundamental to well-being. Students learned to analyze data from census and public health statistics, describe the structure of their communities from multiple theoretical perspectives and understand the pattern of relationships between families, government, churches, and employers. They learned to "see" their communities from new perspectives and practice their skills in developing relationships. The exceptional outcome of this project, more new resources than any division in a six-state area, is a tribute to the energies and investment these students made in their own communities.

This project promoted greater understanding of the significance of "place" and access to resources as fundamental to well-being.

References

Lohmann, N. & Lohmann, R. A. (2005). *Rural Social Work Practice.* New York: Columbia University Press.

Martinez-Brawley, E. E. (2000). *Close to home: Human services and the small community.* Washington, DC: NASW Press.

Prilleltensky, I. & Prilleltensky, O. (2006). *Promoting well-being: linking personal, organizational and community change.* Hoboken, NJ: John Wiley & Sons.

They learned to "see" their communities from new perspectives and practice their skills in developing relationships.

HOUSING AND QUALITY OF LIFE: STUDENT INTERVIEWS WITH FARM WORKER FAMILIES

ELIZABETH HARTUNG
CALIFORNIA STATE UNIVERSITY CHANNEL ISLANDS

Keywords: affordable housing, economic development corporation, farm labor, farm workers, social class, oral history

Introduction

Where people live, and the condition of their housing, is a fairly good proxy for social class. It affects the kind and quality of education one can receive, the ability to work and play, and physical and mental health. Sociologists have a long tradition of examining the impact of race and class in understanding the impact of residential segregation (Massey and Denton, 1995; Waldinger and Lichter, 2003).

This brief paper describes a serendipitous oral history project that examined how quality of housing impacts quality of life for farm worker families. Students in a Sociology/English class had the opportunity to interview farm worker families who in February and March of 2006 moved from overcrowded apartments, oddly subdivided homes, garages, or vehicles to a newly opened affordable housing development, Villa Cesar Chavez. Their stories make real the impact of a housing crisis that especially affects very low- and low-income families. The Villa Cesar Chavez research project is a snapshot of a moment in time. The conversations were completed only a month after the families moved into their new homes. The project was undertaken in the hope that such efforts will build a relationship between a new public university and a part of the community underserved by higher education, immigrant farm workers and their families.

Project description

According to the National Agricultural Workers Survey [NAWS], the average individual income of farm workers in 2001–2002 ranged from $10,000 to $12,499 per year; and total family income fell between $15,000 and $17,499 per year (NAWS, 2005). This income places home ownership out of reach for most farm worker families, and certainly in Southern California, where the median home price before the current market collapse was over $500,000.

The interviews with residents resulted from an interdisciplinary undergraduate class, Narratives of the Working Class, taught by Elizabeth Hartung (Sociology) and Renny Christopher (English) in spring 2006. We formed a research partnership with CEDC, the Cabrillo Economic Development Corporation, which builds affordable, high and medium density housing for low- and very low-income families to rent or to own. When we heard that a new community was opening in the spring of 2006, we proposed that our students interview the residents shortly after moving in and

ask them to talk about how their new home is making a difference in the quality of their lives. Initially we had planned to conduct interviews at several existing CEDC properties, but the opportunity to go to a newly opened development opened opportunities to look at how a community develops over time. The interviews were conducted in Spanish about a month after families had moved in. Their excitement, gratitude and desire to give back to others in the community are captured in the interviews. These eloquent conversations are now part of an oral and print record of the community's growth. They are available online as part of an electronic exhibit at http://www.csuci.edu/servicelearning/virtual-museum/. A year after the project was completed, the University brought the families of Villa Cesar Chavez to campus and honored them with a recognition ceremony. The goal was to emphasize to the farm worker families that the university is accessible to their children.

Project Timeline

Students had read David Shipler's book, *The Working Poor* (2004) and Tomás Rivera's *... And the Earth Did Not Devour Him* (1987). The class was designed so that each instructor would pose a major project/paper. The sociological interview project was slated for the second portion of the class. To prepare the students, in mid-March we discussed research ethics. Students generated a series of interview questions in class, which they tested on each other for organization and flow. Once the questionnaire was in rough form, the instructors edited, translated, and submitted it with the appropriate documentation to the university Institutional Review Board. We wanted students to understand the importance of human subjects review, and that they were representing the university to the community. Prior to going into the field, the Community Outreach Director came to class to discuss the history of Cabrillo Economic Development and the different communities it has built. She also dispelled a number of myths about affordable housing and spoke about being culturally sensitive.

The actual interviewing took about a month to complete, and posed a greater challenge to the students. Because few students were bilingual we had to be creative. We partnered with a Spanish translation class, explaining to those students what our project hoped to capture. The instructor of that class, Antonio Jiménez, allowed his students to work with us as part of their semester grade. He explained the role of the translator to our students: that is, our students were to be very clear that they would steer the course of the interviews. The Spanish-speaking student translator would contact households, and the monolingual English speakers were responsible for asking questions and probing beyond the open-ended interview schedule. While not ideal, English-speaking students soon realized just how much can be conveyed without words. In class, most of them indicated that communication was not the great problem they thought it might be. The interviews were transcribed in Spanish and later translated into English.

In February of 2006, 52 families moved into the Villa Cesar Chavez apartment home complex. The families were asked at one of their first community meetings if they would be willing to participate in a University class project and tell their stories to a student interviewer. They were assured that they could use a pseudonym if they wished, and that they could stop the interview at any time. All 52 families agreed to participate and to use their own names. Students contacted approximately 25 families and 15 interviews were successfully completed.

Individuals or couples were asked a series of questions about where they grew up and where they came from; how they came to Ventura County, how they found their new home, what hopes and dreams they had for the future, what they would say to the mayor about the needs of the poor, and how they feel about building their new community. The taped interviews lasted about an hour on average.

Outcomes/Assessment

The course syllabus listed several learning outcomes for students, including those directly tied to this project. We had hoped that upon completion of the course, students would (a) be able to explain class structures in the U.S.; (b) understand issues of classism; and (c) have completed their own working class narrative via the oral history method, among other things. Certainly the experience of conducting an open-ended interview in a language not one's own, in contact with a population that, by the students' own admission, had been largely invisible to them, was a useful learning outcome. Additionally, many of the students came away from their brief encounters with a respect for not only the work

of farm labor, but for the sacrifices the families had made so that their children would have a better life. As one student wrote, "I now understand the purpose of this project. It was to open our eyes to the injustices that occur … in our neighborhoods. People will continue to live in garages, in cars, crammed into small spaces or even on the streets. They will stay like this till people realize that more low-income housing needs to be built. Not in ten years, but now."

Conclusion

Certainly the stories that students collected were a first step in building a relationship between the campus and Villa Cesar Chavez. In the fall of 2007, a team of seniors in sociology began a homework club as a pilot project to help primary grade students with their school work in English. In the years since, other sociology students have participated in action-oriented research for their Senior Capstone experience.

As for the new community at Villa Cesar Chavez, it continues to thrive. All but three of the original families are still there, working hard to present the case of other families in need of housing to local city councils. In 2008, twenty-two families granted permission for a series of detailed interviews on community building and the outcomes of affordable housing in their lives so that the student project reported here did provide a baseline for more extensive research.

References

Massey, D. S. and Denton, N. A., (1993). *American Apartheid: Segregation and the Making of the Underclass.* Cambridge, MA: Harvard University Press.

Rivera, T. (1987). *… y no se lo tragó la tierra.* Houston, TX: University of Houston Press.

Shipler, D. K. (2005). *The Working Poor: Invisible in America.* New York, NY: Vintage Books.

U.S. Department of Labor, *Findings from the National Agricultural Workers Survey (NAWS) 2001-2002,* Research Report No. 9. March, 2005.

Waldinger, R. and Lichter, , M. I. (2003). *How the Other Half Works: Immigration and the Social Organization of Labor.* Berkeley, CA: University of California Press.

...many of the students came away from their brief encounters with a respect for not only the work of farm labor, but for the sacrifices the families had made so that their children would have a better life. As one student wrote, "I now understand the purpose of this project. It was to open our eyes to the injustices that occur…in our neighborhoods. People will continue to live in garages, in cars, crammed into small spaces or even on the streets. They will stay like this till people realize that more low-income housing needs to be built. Not in ten years, but now."

PHOTOVOICE PROJECT

BARBARA RICH
UNIVERSITY OF SOUTHERN MAINE

Keywords: refugees, photography, children, multicultural, race, ethnocentrism, affordable housing

Introduction

In the last 20 years, over 7000 immigrants and refugees have come to Maine to begin a new life. Many of these live in housing projects where they tend to be isolated physically, socially, and psychologically in small enclaves within the city. The children in these large families experience special burdens while striving to adjust to their new lives. For both old timers and newcomers, the cultural divide is difficult to bridge and the act of reaching out to understand, complicated by language barriers and cultural differences, can be confusing, time-consuming, and exhausting. For most, there is no common arena where they can come together, interact, learn about each other's culture, and explore their common human ties. Complicating these connections is the competition for scarce housing and jobs. The overarching issues of racism and ethnocentrism complicate all of these factors.

Project Description

The Photovoice Project was an ambitious service-learning program implemented in an undergraduate social work class at the University of Southern Maine. This project matched social work students with refugee children living in the housing projects to produce photographs taken by the children and to write narratives that answered the questions: Who am I? What do I value? The housing project's after-school centers were the community partners.

The aim of Photovoice Project was four-fold:
1. overcome the anxiety, fear, and hostility associated with the perceived differences of these newcomers by focusing on the resilient voices and viewpoints of their children;
2. encourage the children of these refugees and their parents to see themselves as valued members of the social fabric, each with unique gifts, special identities, and worthwhile dreams, and to increase their level of connectedness to the larger community;
3. educate university students and others about the strengths and the cultures of their near neighbors;
4. meet the specific goals for the social work students were tied to several of their course objectives which included their ability to:
   - apply communication skills of observing; active listening; interviewing; and collecting, analyzing, and synthesizing data at the service-learning site and in written assignments;
   - analyze the impact of differences such as ethnicity, culture, class, gender, age, color, family structure, national origin, race, religion, sexual orientation, marital status, and physical or mental challenges;
   - assess individual and environmental strengths, challenges, capacities, and resources for social systems of all sizes.

Project Timeline

Months	Activity
January	Planning Phase
February-April	Implementation Phase
April	Class Exhibition
May	Learning Evaluation
May-September	University Art Gallery and Housing Authority Exhibits

Steps for Implementation

These were the guidelines that the students followed to implement the project.

Week 1
Go to the housing project to become acquainted with the After-School Centers and the coordinators.

Connect with some kids for homework help and get to know them—perhaps ask coordinators for suggestions.

Week 2
Invite one of the kids (not under age 8) to become your Photovoice partner—explain program and timeline and give the handout—go over youth consent form and ask child to discuss project with parents—get permission slip signed by parents, with translator if necessary.

Week 3
Give camera and film to child—discuss how to take pictures and the guiding themes for the pictures—Who am I? What do I value?—tell child to take pictures of whatever they want and bring the film back next week.

Week 4
Meet with child and get the film back—talk about how the photography went—go over questions—get film developed

(always get 2 sets of prints—one for you to hold, one for child to take home).

Week 5 Discuss pictures with child—identify pictures that might answer questions—begin writing narrative about the pictures—give new film after discussing what other shots might answer the question—get film developed.

Week 6
Meet with child and get the film back—talk about the photos and work on narratives for each shot—get film developed.

Week 7–8
Prepare child for end of project—finish narratives for each picture and begin discussing which ones might be good for enlargements and framing—you and child can decide what ones will be exhibited (with parental and child permission) at the exhibitions.

Outcomes/Assessment

One of the tenets of service-learning is that there is reciprocity in the relationship between the educational institution and the community partner. The children received cameras and instruction books on photography, along with the special attention and homework help from their student mentors. Taking photographs encourages people to view their worlds through different perspectives, encourages self-expression, creativity, and self-esteem. In turn, the children helped the students to understand what it is like to be a stranger in a strange land, to understand their particular culture, and to help them become more culturally competent as professional social workers. The students had a chance to practice engaging with someone of a different culture and a different age and taking part in the Photovoice Project helped the students attain the course objectives.

One serendipitous outcome of this shared experience was that the students formed a strong group identity. They came to know each other well and learned how to function as team members. In addition, because we were all in this together, the students and the teacher formed a bond that does not usually happen in regular courses.

An evaluation of this project done by pre-and post-testing showed that students' knowledge about ethnic cultures different from their own and knowledge about the challenges facing refugees in Portland significantly increased by the end of the semester.

One of the tenets of service-learning is that there is reciprocity in the relationship between the educational institution and the community partner.

Conclusion

This project gave a voice to people who have been misunderstood, marginalized, stereotyped, scapegoated, and feared. The children and their families could see themselves in a new light, as unique and talented, and with valued viewpoints to share with their community. The Photovoice Project provided accurate information about people through their own voices and assisted us all to see their world through their eyes. We learned that they valued the same things that other children value: family, education, friends, sports, music, and dance.

The students were able to perform a service for the children, to be their assistants, to aid them in taking the photos and writing the narratives, and to help them with their homework. These students, many of whom had never even met a refugee, learned about working in a multicultural environment and about a particular ethnic culture.

In turn, the children helped the students to understand what it is like to be a stranger in a strange land, to understand their particular culture, and to help them become more culturally competent as professional social workers.

INCREASING CULTURAL COMPETENCY THROUGH REFUGEE FOCUSED SERVICE-LEARNING PROJECTS: BRINGING THE WORLD HOME

CAILE E. SPEAR AND AILEEN HALE
BOISE STATE UNIVERSITY

Keywords: cultural competency, globalization, personal health, refugees, diversity, tutoring, poverty

Introduction

Living and working in an increasingly globalized society, university students in the United States need to develop greater cultural awareness and competencies for interacting with people from other countries, including a growing population of refugees settling in their midst (U.S. Department of State, 2008). In an effort to help students develop global perspectives within the borders of the U.S., two education professors from Health Promotion and Bilingual Education have developed and taught Personal Health and Cultural Diversity courses, respectively, incorporating service-learning (SL) projects with local refugee agencies. This paper, designed for faculty interested in developing cultural competencies in students, discusses strategies and techniques for developing SL projects with highly diverse refugee populations.

Project Description

Most students have little to no knowledge of refugee populations living within their own communities; thus the learning curve is extremely pronounced in both its depth and breadth. The academic learning and experiential components of SL refugee projects help instill a greater understanding of other world perspectives. The breadth of diversity within refugee populations enables heightened learning opportunities. Each SL project is unique to its population and may incorporate issues such as literacy, poverty and/or health. The changing nature of refugee groups necessitates a high level of student critical thinking for designing creative and innovative projects to address the diverse and on-going needs of the refugees.

Common course goals for assessing and addressing community partner needs include: (a) increasing students' cross-cultural competencies, and (b) increasing awareness of social determinants and environmental factors that impact healthy living and learning for children and adults from multicultural backgrounds (National Center for Cultural Competence, 2008). Within the SL refugee program option, students are paired with refugee families serving as a mentor during the cultural adaptation process, tutoring in English as a Second Language (ESL), assessing and addressing health issues, assisting with case management, employment, and/or finding translated materials or interpretation services.

Project Timeline

One month prior to semester beginning, faculty:
- Complete a refugee orientation to gain cultural insights and learn about the complexities of refugee issues to help ensure successful projects;
- Discuss different perspectives of agency and student learning outcomes with agency supervisor; and
- Invite agency supervisor to class.

Week 1:
- Invited agency supervisor presents overview of refugee issues to class. Suggested topics include:
  - Personal testimonies of refugees, to captivate and motivate students;
  - Commonly encountered refugee challenges;
  - Importance of flexibility and adaptability when working with communication and cultural differences; and
  - Agencies' expectations of students for conduct and communication.

Students complete a pre-service reflection of their expectations and prior knowledge in preparation for their learning and service experience.

Week 2:
- Students complete a four-hour orientation prior to initiating service.

Weeks 3–14: (On-going service work and reflection activities)
- Students are assigned a refugee individual or family
- Students construct their own learning through extensive research on refugee cultures and histories. Compared to other service projects, working with refugees requires extra 'contact' time to learn about their cultures. This time also allows students to collaborate with refugees to tailor their SL projects. (Note: Some faculty structure class so students spend one third of their class time doing service).
- Students complete multiple reflections in class and online to facilitate personal and peer-to-peer education throughout the semester.
  Suggested topics include:
  - Researching the histories and cultures of the refugees;
  - Learning about current agency programs;

- Identifying environmental factors that effect successful refugee adaptation;
- Exploring the complexity of issues impacting adaptation; and
- Determining the extent to which students feel they are making a difference.

Throughout the semester, faculty maintain ongoing contact with the agency to assist in debriefing student/refugee concerns and questions. They also conduct a mid-semester site visit.

Weeks 15–16: (Completion of projects)

- Students present a final media-enhanced oral presentation and written referenced research paper. Oral presentations educate classmates and present tangible ideas for addressing refugee issues.
- Supervisor evaluates students' service and meets with faculty to discuss project and learning outcomes.

Steps for Implementation

In working with refugees, there are inherent challenges, which when facilitated, can generate optimal learning experiences. For example, service projects may frustrate students the first half of the semester as they wrestle with the overwhelming needs and how to best "help!" Ensuing connections that develop between students and refugees supercede the struggle to 'find an adequate project' as students discover that relationship building is the key to developing cultural competencies and serving others.

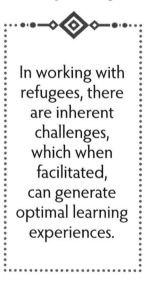

In working with refugees, there are inherent challenges, which when facilitated, can generate optimal learning experiences.

Faculty need to understand this dynamic and carefully facilitate the reflection and learning process for students as they struggle through these stages. The more faculty are engaged in understanding student-refugee relationships, the more effectively they can facilitate reflection that enhances student learning.

Outcomes/Assessment

- Close relationships develop between the students and refugees; thus, students often voluntarily extend their service both during the semester and beyond the class.
- Students construct their own knowledge through researching beyond course texts, learning how to learn about refugee situations, different cultures—religions, languages, customs and worldviews, the numerous barriers clients face trying to establish a new life in the United States, and the limited support provided to refugees by financially-strapped resettlement agencies.
- Students broaden life perspectives through awareness of refugee challenges.
- The peer-to-peer educational experience generates collaboration of ideas, critical analysis of community issues, and on-going initiatives for community involvement.

Students were assessed based on the projects required by their faculty member. The following are examples of different final products. In educational foundations class students created PowerPoint presentations and these were presented to their classmates. Each PowerPoint gave an overview of an agency working with refugees, an overview of one of the countries sending refugees to Idaho and finally each student included the story about a local refugee family they had worked with from that country.

In a health class the students created a community health resource guide for the local refugee agency. The students met with the director, she provided the format, students met with some of the refugee families to determine health needs and then the students created the guide including a map of the business locations overlaid on the local bus routes. The project was submitted in both paper and electronic format so it could be updated and translated into the various languages of the current refugee populations.

Students in a graduate Technical Communication class created Refugee Cultural Guides for Practitioners. The article was focused on how to set up SL projects with refugee agencies. Students were assessed based on the projects required by their faculty member.

Conclusions

In conclusion, the transformative impact of conducting service-learning projects with refugee populations has profound and long-lasting implications on students, refugees, and professors. Without having to travel across international borders, the experience propels students out of their "comfort zones" and greatly increases their cultural competencies. The nature of this service enables deep and formative relationships to develop, which inherently break down stereotypes. The extent to which students must research and construct their own knowledge develops heightened awareness of and advocacy for challenges refugees face integrating into their new community.

References

National Center for Cultural Competence. *Culturally Competent Guiding Values & Principles.* Retrieved June 2008 from http://www11.georgetown.edu/research/gucchd/nccc/foundations/frameworks.html

U.S. Department of State. *Refugee Assistance.* Retrieved June 2008 from http://www.state.gov/g/prm/asst/

CONFRONTING POVERTY'S IMPACT ON THE COMMUNITY

JUDITH I. GRAY
BALL STATE UNIVERSITY

Keywords: poverty, collaboration, civic awareness, Circle of Support program, social work, simulation

Introduction

What is needed to reduce or eliminate poverty in communities? A collaborative effort between various citizens and community leaders has been working to raise awareness and formulate initiatives to address poverty in Delaware County, Indiana, where Ball State University is located. These efforts have been led by organizations serving the poor and those living in poverty, in collaboration with the local Township Trustee and the Eliminating Poverty Initiative Committee (EPIC) from the agency TEAMwork for Quality Living. Recently, TEAMwork for Quality Living has been named a regional training site for the Circle of Support Program developed by Move the Mountain Center from Iowa. Using this model, the individual or family living in poverty becomes team leader of a circle of allies that provide consultation, guidance and support along their journey out of poverty.

Project Description

Social work students were trained to serve as volunteers with the aforementioned initiative and participated in planning, promoting and implementing a series of poverty simulations on the Ball State University campus and in the Delaware County community, where Ball State University is located.

The simulation entitled "Life in the State of Poverty" and was purchased by the local Township Trustee from the Missouri ACTION agency. The objective of the simulation is to sensitize participants to the realities of living in a low-income family facing month-to-month survival. Thirty to eighty-five participants assume the roles of up to twenty-six different families facing poverty. Families may be recipients of TANF (Temporary Assistance for Needy Families) or may be recently unemployed or deserted by the primary wage earner. There may or may not be additional sources of earned income. Others may be older adults living on Social Security or grandparents raising grandchildren. Given the limitations of their situation, each "family" must decide how to provide basic necessities and shelter. Family members must also interact with various "community representatives" at various resource and service tables. These services include a bank, super center, Community Action Agency, employer, utility company, pawn broker, grocery, DFS (welfare) office, payday and title loan facility, mortgage company, school, and child care facility. People who have lived in poverty or who are currently living in poverty staff the resource tables

and also assume the roles of police officer and a person engaging in "illegal activities." The experience includes an introduction, briefing, the actual simulation exercise, and a debriefing. During the debriefing period, participants, volunteers and those who have experienced living in poverty share their feelings and experiences. During this time, a transition occurs for many participants as the simulation becomes more than a "game," and they gain powerful insights about the lives of people in poverty.

Students were also involved in other EPIC initiatives such as community service in other settings addressing the problem of poverty such as the local mission, domestic violence shelter, food pantries or soup kitchens. Other goals were to increase campus student/faculty involvement, and expand social work students, and the faculty fellow's involvement in other EPIC initiatives. In addition to the benefits of community involvement for social work students, other students, faculty and staff participation helped to increase the community's awareness of the problem of poverty. Delaware County community members also benefited from their encounter with the simulation and contact with students. Implementing this project was funded through a grant from the Campus Compact's Faculty Fellows Program.

Steps to Implementation

1. Identified two senior level undergraduate, generalist practice social work practice classes to develop as service-learning courses. One focuses on working with small groups, and the other on individuals and social change
2. Identified course content and objectives to be emphasized through the service-learning experience: group work theory and practice skills, understanding the impact of diversity on groups, alleviating oppression and promoting social and economic justice through community task group efforts, understanding individuals and families living in poverty
3. Created contract with community partner, TEAMwork for Quality Living, EPIC Committee to assist with poverty simulations and other initiatives
4. Applied for and secured Indiana Campus Compact Grant to support the implementation of poverty simulations
5. Implemented poverty simulations on campus and in the community
6. Broadened involvement in other EPIC initiatives: Circles of Support providing support to people moving

out of poverty, eating for a week on food stamps public awareness campaign, and offering service to other poverty relief organizations

7. Completed reflection through class discussions and reflective papers

Course Integration. The faculty member integrated the aforementioned service-learning experience in two senior level undergraduate social work practice classes. The purpose of these courses is to prepare students for beginning level generalist practice with small groups, individuals and families focusing on individual, family and social change. Course content related to group work theory and practice skills, understanding the impact of diversity on groups, as well as alleviating oppression and promoting social and economic justice through community task group efforts, were tied to the service-learning experience. In addition, the emphasis on understanding individuals and families living in poverty was emphasized in a second social work senior level practice course. Students and faculty were involved in other EPIC initiatives such as: Circles of Support providing individuals

> Many students were transformed not only by the opportunity to interact with people who have experienced living in poverty but were inspired by the support circles approach to helping people move out of poverty.

and families with support to move out of poverty, eating for a week on food stamps public awareness campaign, and offering service to other poverty relief organizations.

Outcomes/Assessment

Measurement of outcomes was two-fold in focus. First, the evaluative data gathered from a questionnaire designed by the simulation committee has developed and gathered information from each group participating in the simulation. The evaluation was developed collaboratively with Purdue University Extension staff and approved by the Institutional Review Board for implementation. This measurement tool was completed by the social work students, and the Ball State University Campus and community site participants. Secondly, social work students completed a learning contract elaborating individualized learning goals, submitted a log of their hours through the campus Student Voluntary Services data base and verified by a TEAMwork for Quality Living staff member, and completed a series of reflective assignments. The reflective assignments will ask student to consider: (a) what they have learned about poverty and its impact on the local community, (b) what they learned about planning and implementing community task groups and, (c) the personal and professional insights they have gained.

Conclusion

Many students were transformed not only by the opportunity to interact with people who have experienced living in poverty but were inspired by the support circles approach to helping people move out of poverty. In addition to helping students to accomplish these objectives, the service-learning experience also assisted students in identifying professional learning needs and develop an ongoing plan for further development in relationship to their social work skills.

THE IMPORTANCE OF COMPETENCIES TO ALUMNI OF THE SOCIOLOGY/ ANTHROPOLOGY DEPARTMENT

LAURA KHOURY AND HELEN ROSENBERG
UNIVERSITY OF WISCONSIN-PARKSIDE

Keywords: competencies, ethnocentrism, teamwork, employment, alumni, social science, collaboration, civility

Introduction

This report traces a service-learning project that spanned two semesters and culminated in a report to the Sociology/ Anthropology department of the University of Wisconsin-Parkside as to the benefits alumni receive through the mastery of competencies developed for students in the

department. The faculty at UW-Parkside has focused their teaching on the basis of four stated competencies since 2000. These were revised and rewritten into three competencies in 2003. They were lastly modified in 2006 to encompass three dimensions: conceptual, methodological, and civic competencies. (See the competencies on the department website at: http://oldweb.uwp.edu/academic/sociology/

comp.htm.) We assess achievement of competencies when students develop their portfolios that complete their Senior Seminar class, but prior to this study, the department had no indication as to whether mastery of these competencies impacted students after graduation. The answer to this question seemed a good opportunity for a service-learning project in the Senior Seminar class. Our overall question was, "What impact do the competencies stated by Sociology/Anthropology have upon alumni?"

Project Description

In one semester, students developed, piloted, and finalized a survey to the population of alumni from Sociology/Anthropology since 2000 (N=267; a copy of the survey is at (http://www.uwp.edu/departments/teaching.center/laura_khoury/). Dr. James Robinson, Director of the Teaching and Learning Center published the survey on the web at the end of the semester. We allowed the summer for alumni to respond to the survey and sent a follow-up letter in the fall to increase participation. The following year in a second Senior Seminar class, students analyzed and summarized the data from respondents to the survey and reported outcomes to the Department, including challenging its faculty to consider curriculum changes based on outcomes from the survey.

Project Timeline

Semester 1:
- Presentation of project (one week)
- Discussion of competencies and their meaning (two weeks)
- Outline of sections to be covered in the survey, including background information on work history, questions about competencies, and questions about how the Department developed skills that helped students in their careers (three weeks)
- Writing the survey questions, discussion of format and self-piloting of survey (three weeks)
- Getting list of alumni from Alumni Relations Department (two weeks)
- Sorting list by year of graduation, cleaning of data, e.g., deleting duplicate names (one week)
- Contacting alumni to participate in focus group (one week)
- Meeting with alumni to take survey and ask questions about the survey (two weeks)
- Revising the survey (two weeks)
- Sending final survey to be published on web

Summer – alumni completed survey – Web entry of information on the survey was converted into an EXCEL file, which was read on SPSS 16.0. Thus, there was little data conversion required.

Fall – follow-up letter mailed to all alumni thanking those who completed the survey and asking those who did not complete the survey to do so.

Semester 2:
- Review of project (one week)
- Data cleaning and creation of meaningful categories in the data (four weeks)
- Practice in interpreting data (two weeks)
- Developing outline for final paper (one week)
- Report writing – two drafts were completed before the final including a literature review (four weeks)
- Power Point presentation (three weeks)
  - Organizing the presentation
  - Adding pictures and clip art, charts
- Presentation to Department (one week)

Steps for Implementation

Semester 1:
- Write letters to be mailed to all alumni notifying them of the survey
- Decide on incentives to be given to subset of those who respond to the survey
- Write an introduction to the survey
- Contact alumni to participate in focus group on survey
- Revise survey on the basis of alumni feedback
- Publish survey on the web
- Send out letters

Semester 2:
- Analyze data
- Decide on outline of paper and presentation on the basis of data analysis
- Literature Review
- Draft of paper
- Draft of presentation
- Practice presentation to Department
- Final presentation

Outcomes/Assessment

The following reports some of the important outcomes and findings from the alumni survey. The majority of alumni respondents were aware of the sociology competencies, especially after their junior year. Respondents felt that most of the competencies were easy to understand. About a quarter of the sample said that gaining competency in effective collaboration and teamwork and promoting the active exchange of ideas in a civil manner were also helpful in finding a job. Respondents also identified understanding cultures in their own terms and identifying and confronting ethnocentrism were both helpful in their current jobs.

The final product from this service-learning exercise was a report and PowerPoint presentation to the Sociology/Anthropology department regarding alumni perspectives on competencies they developed and the impact of these competencies on employment and their personal lives. (See the power points and the graph at either/or: http://oldweb .uwp.edu/academic/sociology/khoury/). In addition, the department received valuable information on the work history of alumni, including what jobs they currently held and for how long, how they got their current positions and the salary ranges they were in. Faculty learned which competencies alumni felt most helped them find a job, helped them in their current position, and helped them in their personal lives. In addition, faculty learned that most alumni understood the competencies, despite faculty concerns that competencies were difficult to understand.

Conclusion

Projects that involve service-learning should create purpose and meaning for all involved and be responsive to stakeholder needs. Projects should be challenging to students, yet connect classroom learning with real life experience. Sometimes, the connections between what students learn throughout their college years and service-learning experiences are not apparent. In such cases, we should make explicit the connections between service-learning projects and concepts learned from theory and methods.

This is an exemplar of a successfully implemented project. It was intended for higher education and thus appeals to almost all social science disciplines. It informed and motivated the sociology faculty at the University of Wisconsin-Parkside to think of ways to help students find jobs following the completion of their degree. It served as a self-reflection and self-discovery mechanism for both the community and alumni. Also, it was an experiential education for students who participated in service in both semesters. Students were able to reflect upon their own experiences. This project was a real testimony for the success of service-learning and its usefulness to both students and community simultaneously.

THE HEALING POWER OF MUSIC

CYNTHIA GREEN LIBBY
MISSOURI STATE UNIVERSITY

Keywords: music, healing, harp therapy, intergenerational

Introduction

Society's most vulnerable individuals, from children in life-threatening pain to our elderly confronting the end of life, need a special support network of care. Throughout human history, music has provided a unique form of therapy and healing, whether through relaxation, catharsis or to ease psychological pain. The folk harp, with its soothing properties and portability, has long provided that vehicle for relief and comfort. Introduction to Music and Healing was developed to give students the opportunity put their newly acquired knowledge of music's healing effects into the real-world settings of the hospital or hospice in order to better understand their role as a citizen, positively engaged in building a better community.

Project Description

Introduction to Music and Healing is a three-credit course devoted to the history and current practices in the field of therapeutic music, with an integrated service-learning component. Open to all majors, the only prerequisite is the ability to read music. In addition to completing classroom assignments, students learn to play the therapeutic harp and develop a portfolio including a reflection journal with time log, based upon the therapeutic harp music they provide in a local hospital and/or hospice.

People of all ages and circumstances benefit from the therapeutic harp. For example, children in hospital settings and with other special needs respond with a range of healthy outcomes, including appropriate excitement, joy, empowerment as well as relaxation. For people in intensive care units and in operating rooms, monitors show that the heart rate decreases and oxygenation levels increase when soothing harp music is played (International Harp Therapy Program, 2008). A recent study at Yale-New Haven Hospital proved that listening to music while undergoing outpatient surgery activates the flow of endorphins, which helps lessen pain. Harp

In all of these activities, both in and out of the classroom, students begin to understand their unique role as "musician-citizens," that they can communicate compassion through music to those most in need.

music provides sound focus other than the humming and beeping of hospital machines.

In hospices, transitional stages are often an area where the harp music can be very supportive. The sounds of the harp comfort and soothe the patient who may be in pain or experiencing fear or anxiety. Recent research by the International Harp Therapy Program revealed that 84% of 200 patients experienced relief of anxiety, 71% experienced easier breathing, 70% experienced decrease of fear and 63% found that their pain was lessened while harp therapy was being administered. The families of these loved ones also benefit from the reprieve and calming influence of the therapeutic harp.

Project Timeline

Introduction to Music and Healing is a full semester of sixteen weeks plus examination period. An in-class orientation to service-learning occurs in week one; by week six, students have made formal, contractual arrangements with their partner organization and have drafted a project schedule. The service project takes place after they have passed the playing test, usually by week twelve.

Throughout the semester in directed writings, students are asked to consider specific aspects of course content from the readings and class discussions. During the final four weeks they also document their thoughts and reflections following each service experience, analyzing how the course content related to each service experience and applying the overall service experience to their personal life, including their goals, values and attitudes.

Steps for Implementation

Procure funds to provide for the purchase of the 22-string therapy harps plus backpack cases and shipping/handling. Budget $800 to $1,000 per harp[1]. The more harps acquired, the more students will be able to enroll in the course, thereby increasing exponentially the impact of your community service for many years to come.

Design and disseminate a course recruitment brochure. In the semester preceding the start-up of the course, mailings to advisors in Music, Nursing, Counseling, Psychology, Gerontology and Religious Studies are encouraged. The brochure used by Missouri State University may be viewed at www.missouristate.edu/music/26607.htm. Click the sidebar "Introduction to Music and Healing."

Develop the course syllabus. Be sure to include a number of thought provoking questions to present throughout the

semester in the form of directed writings, to be added to the final journal project. Music and Soulmaking by Barbara Crowe (2008) provides a thorough context for the history and principles of music therapy. Class periods should also include musical development and group improvisation. Thus, two 75-minute sessions per week are more productive than three 50-minute classes.

Establish relationships with community partners by the sixth week of class. After students pass the playing test in the twelfth week, they may begin their 15 hours of service-learning in local hospitals and hospices. Your institution should assist in making and maintaining contacts with these organizations as a part of its outreach to the community.

Outcomes/Assessment

To assess the integration of the service-learning of this course during the last week of the semester, students complete an online survey conducted by the Office of Citizenship and Service-Learning. This information assists in the further development of this course as it relates to the service-learning project.

During the first and last weeks, the instructor distributes a pre- and post-project student self-evaluation to determine areas in which the students feel they have developed, such as bedside communication skills and confidence in their empathic abilities. This information is compiled as a research vehicle.

Students complete an anonymous, computerized evaluation form for the Department of Music to assess the course and instructor overall.

Community Partner Mentor's Report: students are responsible for collecting this report, which addresses their individual performance and documents their fifteen hours of therapeutic harp playing.

After the course is finished, the instructor sends out a one-page community partner questionnaire to assess whether the organizations are satisfied with the partnership, whether the service provided by the students helped fulfill their organizational mission, and if they would like the relationship to continue.

Conclusion

Transformational learning takes place not only as a result of the service activity, but also when discussing such topics as "Spirituality: Death and Dying in the Context of Diverse Religious Traditions"; "Socio-cultural Perspectives: Music for Diverse Populations"; "Identifying and Valuing Caring Behaviors"; "Developing Bedside Communicative and Intuitive Skills." The professor/facilitator schedules

---

1. Missouri State University received a quantity/educational discount from Triplett Harps for 15 Zephyr Travel Harps.

ample opportunity for in-class reflection and discussion throughout the semester.

Mutually beneficial relationships are developed between the students, the community partners and the patients in hospitals and hospices.

In all of these activities, both in and out of the classroom, students begin to understand their unique role as "musician citizens," that they can communicate compassion through music to those most in need.

References

Crowe, B. (2008). *Music and soul making: toward a new theory of music therapy.* Oxford: The Scarecrow Press.
International Harp Therapy Program. Retrieved June 10, 2010 from http://harprealm.com.

Perceptual changes through teaching others

Steve Willis
Missouri State University

Keywords: art therapy, correctional facility, art education, therapeutic, criminal justice

Introduction

This article discusses the experiences of Missouri State University art education students teaching at the Greene County Correctional Facilities (GCCF) in Springfield, Missouri through the Citizenship and Service-Learning (CASL) component of two art education methods courses.

Project Description

This project involves art educations students' visits to the GCCF to teach art to inmates while they are held in the county jail awaiting release or transfer to a federal facility. The CASL student group of three to five determines the curriculum, and the applications are multiple. Some lessons involve simple experiences in art while others focus on Art as Therapy with images that are narrative, symbolic, and therapeutic. As well, art for the larger community was produced and delivered to other CASL sites through a student-generated collaboration such as Culpepper Place and Cox Medical facilities.

The CASL experiences are directed through two art education methods courses, one focuses on elementary practices, the other on secondary methods. Because of the inmates' lack of artistic experiences, K-12 practices are applicable allowing student involvement for an academic year. Though the CASL office requires a minimum of 15 hours, the classes require a minimum of 20 hours. Frequently students extend their volunteer hours.

The CASL experiences must be a semester-long interaction, and through this, the students maximize benefits with time for reflection and implementation into course requirements of curriculum development, discussions concerning pedagogy, learning differences and management.

Project Timeline

Fortunately at Missouri State University, many of the initial connections are made through the tireless efforts of the Citizenship and Service-Learning (CASL) office. The Associate Director of CASL visits each class early in the semester to discuss guidelines, explain confidentiality, ensure proper placement, and clarify expectations.

To maintain continuity, students must allocate their 20 hours through multiple one to two-hour experiences distributed throughout the semester. This allows time for reflection of the learning experiences. The students begin the CASL experience the first week of the semester. Because CASL hours are required beyond class time, students need an opportunity to balance their schedule with other responsibilities. Starting early has multiple benefits.

Students must provide a minimum of four reflective documents in addition to multiple in-class conversations about their experiences and how these experiences translate into the course requirements.

The course calendar for ART 366: Elementary Art Education (Fall 07) was:

Aug 21 (First day)	Sept 4	Sept 25	Oct 2	Nov 6
Discuss CASL	First CASL entry	Second CASL entry	Third CASL entry	Fourth CASL entry

By expecting CASL entrees early and throughout the semester, students are not allowed to compress the required 20 hours into a less sustained interaction defeating the time needed to reflect and translate the experiences. Additionally, each student submits a summative report at the end of the semester.

The course calendar for ART 401: Teaching of Art (Spring 08) was:

Jan 15 (First day)	Feb 7	Mar 18	April 3	April 17
Discuss CASL	First CASL entry	Second CASL entry	Third CASL entry	Fourth CASL entry

In this class, all CASL entrees were posted in Blackboard including one reflective statement in the discussion board, and one critical-analytical paper in the digital dropbox. This allowed students to enter one, read all, reflect, and then respond at least three times to the peers' CASL narratives through critical peer-review. The internet component received positive student comments, and one of the benefits of flexible CASL reporting.

Steps for Implementation

The classroom requirements for successful CASL interactions in the methods classes are: motivated community partners, empowered student interactions, and faculty guidance.

For implementation, engage students early, monitor the interactions consistently with timely and meaningful feedback, use transparent applications to classroom expectations discussing openly the CASL experiences, and expect a clear integration between theory and practice.

Additionally, the CASL component must remain flexible and governance shared with students with the primary expectation that CASL is bidirectional and must be sensitive to student needs. This is easily noted through student entrees and classroom conversations.

It is important to note that CASL should not be an extra effort in the course structure but an integrated one. My role does not extend beyond developing and monitoring the interactions, providing critical feedback, and connecting cur-

rent practices and theories. CASL experiences are embedded and valuable to demonstrable student competencies.

Outcomes/Assessment

Assessment is qualified through two instruments. The reflective, critical journaling component is certainly the most valuable section. Dewey's (1934) action, reflection, and reaction guide the students' experiences. Each student must write reflective, critical evaluations of the CASL experiences and the applicability to art education. Journal entrees require: Expected (what is expected from the experience?); Actual (what happened in the experience?); and most importantly, Reflection (how is the experience transferable to contemporary practices in art education?). Through the semester, the typically larger first entry of Expected becomes smaller and the Reflection section becomes larger, more dense, and analytical. The narratives are the most significant component.

Secondly, the CASL office administers surveys and evaluates the responses. Community partners, students, and faculty each contributes to the data collected. Additionally, the CASL office publishes an annual report of the accomplishments of students, faculty, and community partners.

Conclusion

The CASL component is invaluable for the perceptual, socio-cultural exchanges that solidify the holistic education of the students' understanding of theory and practice. The CASL experiences move beyond the potentiality of what is teachable in the classroom. It places students in real-life situations and mandates they find the mechanism to transfer classroom conversations to their CASL experiences. Equally as important are the conversations between students as they share their experiences promoting good-practices, or seeking peer comments on well-devised plans that were poorly executed. Through this interaction, the students become the teachers galvanizing their beginning educational experiences prior to entering their own future classrooms.

Reference

Dewey, J. (1934). *Art as experience.* New York: Pedigree Publishing.

The CASL experiences move beyond the potentiality of what is teachable in the classroom. It places students in real-life situations and mandates they find the mechanism to transfer classroom conversations to their CASL experiences.

BUSINESS, INDUSTRY, AND THE HEALTH SCIENCES

INTRODUCTION

SHERRIL B. GELMON
CHAIR OF PUBLIC ADMINISTRATION DIVISION
PROFESSOR OF PUBLIC HEALTH
PORTLAND STATE UNIVERSITY

This chapter offers illustrations in service-learning in disciplines that can be referred to as business, industry and the health sciences. This introduction provides a brief overview of the articles, clustering them by profession/discipline and highlighting a key theme that may be unique to the profession, or in fact may be crosscutting for all professions or disciplines.

Business Education

Goetz and Palmer describe the Volunteer Income Tax Assistance (VITA) program, describing service-learning that addresses poverty in the context of taxation. College students provide tax-filing assistance to poor individuals in their local communities, learning through the experience about the economic circumstances of individuals and families, particularly low- and moderate-income households. Substantial benefits are realized by both the students and the community, but to be effective the experience requires planning and community partnerships.

Similarly, Alexander discusses the VITA program, articulating how hundreds of tax students nationwide each spring prepare thousands of tax returns for low income and elderly taxpayers through VITA. In addition, tax professors have created tax centers and outreach programs for low income and English-as-a-second-language taxpayers. After national disasters, tax professors and their students have disseminated important tax information to the victims through brochures and workshops. Tax faculty recognize the value that experiential learning activities provides the community and to students' educational experience.

Service-learning courses include student preparation, action/engagement, dissemination, and reflection – activities that are found across all disciplines.

Another example in business education is offered by Harris-Boundy, where students work on team projects that address social issues as consultants with real community-based organizations. Students gain valuable experiential learning while "client" organizations benefit from their fresh insights. What develops is a unique partnership between students, faculty and the community, where all become learning-focused problem solvers.

These three examples offer insight into a common element of the business curriculum where almost any faculty member could introduce service-learning, combining practical knowledge and skill development with important institutional commitment to address an urgent community need.

Nonprofit Management

In contrast to business education, Sarcone illustrates service-learning in nonprofit management studies in a course entitled "The Fundamentals of Nonprofit Management."

The instructor identifies nonprofit organizations with existing relationships (internship sites, community service sites) with the college. Students are attracted not only from the major but also through promotion to colleagues in political science, policy studies, environmental science, and international studies.

Health Professions

The health professions are another set of disciplines where there is a long record of service-learning as an effective pedagogical strategy. Young and Goodwin describe an integrated service-learning assignment for students to present a health fair in the local community, ideally with health/physical education students but also applicable to majors in elementary education, recreation, biology, business administration, or human resources.

Peters describes a dental education service-learning experience, where the focus is a community college dental assisting program and the focus of work is a free dental sealant clinic for children. In this case, the project is a collaborative effort involving a local community church and its members, a school corporation, and a students and faculty. Students gain hands-on experience participating in the clinic, and develop teamwork skills.

A third health professions experience is described by Cox, who illustrates a general studies experience that has helped undergraduate students change their thinking, feelings and attitudes toward people with HIV/AIDS in order to better understand societal decisions that are made in this arena. Course evaluations reveal the extent to which students grow in knowledge and understanding, by virtue of their engagement in service-learning. As Cox states, "Service-learning helps students, literally, "go outside of themselves" and relate to the suffering, joy, resilience, realities and complexities that people living with AIDS face almost daily."

Another relevant kind of experience in these disciplines is using service-learning to create opportunities for students to experience various careers that they might consider for the future. MacDowell et al. describe one example of a program to increase awareness of health career options among elementary-age students. Such programs are important to address concerns over the current and future shortages of workers in the health care sector, and are relevant in all of the professions covered here, not just the health professions. This is well-illustrated in the Wolvaardt et al. article that describes the experience of South African medical students in a service-learning course, where the intent is to "make things better" for the stakeholder groups of students, academic staff, service providers and the community. Evaluations confirmed that the service-learning enhanced students' sense of social responsibility and their integrative and reflective learning, and met the needs of the communities they were serving.

Design Professions

The final entries in this chapter address the design professions. Sturgeon describes an architecture experience that fulfills a programmatic need, makes better use of untended spaces in the city, and brings citizens with unique talents and backgrounds together through service-learning. In this case, he suggests that "a balance must be struck between producing a work of architecture and fostering a rich service-learning experience for the students"—wisdom that applies to all service-learning across the disciplines, and not just this one illustration. Dolan's article describes an "untapped community resource" that is a source of research, solutions, and strategies for affecting the community and society. The process of partnering between community and faculty allows a careful review whereby each project is carefully reviewed and mapped with the desired course objectives to match them with the needs of the community.

Conclusion

Students in a service-learning course move beyond traditional classroom activities by participating in community-based activities, and expand their learning accordingly, achieving the fundamental goals of service-learning related to attainment of content understanding as well as insights into personal and social issues and responsibilities. Sarcone describes how a "well-executed service-learning experience results from the collaborative efforts of an expertly lead and managed community network of students, community representatives and course instructor(s)." The attainment of the service-learning goals of the course will be feasible if the professor has the ability to align the resources, structures and processes necessary to deliver the course – and the evidence of goal attainment will occur when students demonstrate their understanding of the subject and an appreciation of the relevant social and community issues and values addressed through the experience. This is true for all of the disciplines represented in this chapter (and perhaps in the entire volume), and should be kept in the foreground by anyone designing and delivering a service-learning experience. As expressed by Young and Goodwin, "integrated service-learning enables [the students] to contribute to the quality of life in the community and to become ambassadors for the university." Not only are community needs being met through the education and application of how each of these disciplines affects society, but students are learning and practicing professional knowledge and skills while developing and understanding the importance of their potential future role as a professional in society.

INCREASING STUDENTS' AWARENESS OF VARYING SOCIOECONOMIC CLASSES AND THE INFLUENCE OF THE U.S. INCOME TAX SYSTEM

JOSEPH GOETZ AND LANCE PALMER
UNIVERSITY OF GEORGIA

Keywords: poverty, taxes, low-income households, IRS, VITA, taxation, accounting

Introduction

Millions of dollars of refundable tax credits go unclaimed each year because low-income households either fail to file their tax returns or fail to claim tax credits. Furthermore, low-income individuals often utilize tax preparation businesses that charge high fees and may encourage high-cost, refund-anticipation loans. To address these challenges, college students can provide tax-filing assistance to these individuals in their local communities. This service-learning (SL) activity may be particularly appropriate for courses that address the economic circumstances of individuals and families, particularly low- and moderate-income households. The Internal Revenue Service (IRS) provides the training and certification, and local community partners provide the infrastructure to enable students to provide free tax filing assistance. Substantial benefits are realized by both the students and the community.

Project Description

The IRS sponsors the Volunteer Income Tax Assistance (VITA) program (www.irs.gov; Search: VITA). The VITA initiative targets households that may be eligible for the refundable earned income tax credit (EITC) as well as other tax credits. The EITC phases out completely with earned income of $39,783 (2007) for married filing jointly taxpayers.

SL curricula incorporating VITA were adopted in the following courses at the University of Georgia (UGA): *Survey of Family Financial Planning, Financial Counseling, and Family Tax Planning.* Two of the three courses had minimal lecture time devoted to income tax concepts (< 3 hours) and the majority of these students had no previous experience with income taxation. Students acquired approximately 10 to 15 hours of further training through web-based self-tutorials along with four hours of live instruction, all offered through the IRS. Students did not sign returns and were not experts in all areas of taxation, but through certification became knowledgeable regarding tax issues specific to a lower-income population. Legal liability protection was provided under the Volunteer Protection Act of 1997.

Project Timeline

Incorporating VITA as an SL activity in undergraduate courses requires planning and community partnerships. Approximately one year prior to the semester of implementation, the course(s) and projected enrollments should be identified. Several communities throughout the United States have existing VITA programs. Establishing early contact with community partners—eight months prior to the course—is essential. The IRS maintains a listing of all VITA sites. Six months prior to the class starting, community partners, service locations, schedules, supervisory requirements, computer hardware (software is provided by the IRS), and advertising channels should be identified.

Just prior to the winter holiday break, students were given VITA certification and training materials. Within the first two weeks of the spring semester, students were required to pass the basic level certification test. Mandatory IRS training was provided on the Saturday following the start of classes, with one session in the morning and afternoon. Students provided tax assistance beginning the last week of January through the end of February, a peak filing period for low-income individuals. All reflective writing assignments and classroom discussions were completed during the first week of March.

Steps for Implementation

The course(s) selected should be upper division with enrollment of less than 30 students. Multiple courses from different disciplines can work together to enhance the experience and foster cross-discipline discussions. Smaller enrollments may be appropriate, depending on the number of qualified supervisors and scope of project.

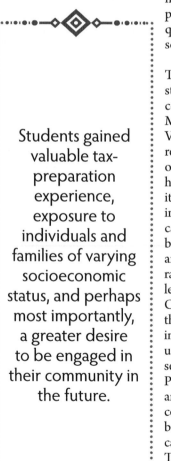

Students gained valuable tax-preparation experience, exposure to individuals and families of varying socioeconomic status, and perhaps most importantly, a greater desire to be engaged in their community in the future.

The next most important step is identifying strong community coalitions. Many already established VITA programs struggle to recruit sufficient numbers of volunteers. On the other hand, many faculty are hesitant to incorporate VITA into their coursework because of the administrative burden. Through faculty and community collaboration, both of these challenges can be overcome. Community partners for the UGA VITA SL activity included two local credit unions, two housing counseling agencies, and the Police Department's Weed and Seed initiative. Once community partners have been identified, logistical items discussed in the Timeline section above can be addressed.

Next, the students must be prepared. The process of

certification and providing the service requires approximately 30 to 40 hours outside of class. Care should be taken in developing the syllabus so that early in the semester students are not overburdened. Students in the UGA SL program signed up for six three-hour sessions. To schedule students for service sessions, we recommend a lottery process where students sign up for part of their sessions one round and part the next round with redrawing of lottery numbers between each round. Students had the option of participating in the SL activity or completing an alternative writing assignment; all students elected the SL activity.

At the time services were provided, students appreciated being paired to provide services, and clients appreciated attentive and involved supervisors. Students were assigned as greeters, interviewers, and preparers during each session. Multiple preparation stations operated simultaneously. The average return took approximately 45 minutes to complete. Complex, high-income, and uncooperative clients can all be referred to other tax preparation providers.

Outcomes/Assessment

Written student reflections on the SL activity were very positive. Using pre- and post-service surveys, statistically significant increases in students' intention to participate in future pro bono work were observed after participating in the SL activity. Furthermore, students indicated an increased desire to organize the establishment of VITA sites in the future. A total of 261 clients were assisted. Ninety-four clients were below the federal poverty level. A brief summary is provided:

Total EITC Claimed	$98,248
Total Federal Refunds Claimed	$278,417

In addition to the refunds claimed, providing the services at no cost resulted in significant savings to community members. Students gained valuable tax-preparation experience, exposure to individuals and families of varying socioeconomic status, and perhaps most importantly, a greater desire to be engaged in their community in the future.

Conclusion

The VITA program provides an effective and dynamic SL opportunity. Students come together with community volunteers and community members for a shared experience in furthering their understanding of the economic challenges low-income households face and how the United States income tax system currently assists those households. Increasing low-income community members' rate of claiming the EITC through VITA is an effective anti-poverty program and pedagogical tool for service-learning.

SERVICE-LEARNING IN THE TAX CURRICULUM

RAQUEL MEYER ALEXANDER AND ANDI WITCZAK
UNIVERSITY OF KANSAS

Keywords: accounting, taxation, research, VITA, IRS, taxes, low-income households, poverty, elderly

Introduction

The academic tax community has been engaged in experiential learning long before most universities formalized service-learning programs. Tax students have a tradition of service through participation in the Internal Revenue Services' Volunteer Income Tax Assistance (VITA) program. Each spring, hundreds of tax students nationwide prepare thousands of tax returns for low income and elderly taxpayers through VITA. In addition, tax professors have created tax centers and outreach programs for low-income and English-as-a-second-language taxpayers. After national disasters, tax professors and their students have disseminated important tax information to the victims through brochures and workshops. Tax faculty recognize the value that experiential learning activities provides the community and to students' educational experience. The following describes a service-learning project that can be implemented as a stand-alone course, or as part of an existing advanced tax course.

Project Description

Graduate tax research students conduct two workshops on tax and financial planning for graduate performing arts majors and faculty/staff in the School of Fine Arts. The presentations focus on minimizing self-employment tax, maximizing deductions, calculating estimated payments and establishing retirement savings.

Project Timeline

Two months prior to semester: Identify target organization. Make contact and schedule workshop date(s). Identify tax issues pertinent to this group.

Five weeks prior to workshop: Assign written research memorandum on tax issues related to workshop presentation.

Four weeks prior to workshop: Students turn-in research assignment and discuss findings in class. Groups are formed for additional research.

Two weeks prior to workshop: Students present initial in-class presentations and modify presentations based on feedback.

One week prior to workshop: Meet with student groups individually to critique final presentation.

Immediately after workshop: Assign reflection paper. The paper can easily be completed within one week. Faculty may also encourage journaling during the project.

Steps for Implementation

Instructor's Preparation. The instructor must first select a workshop topic and prepare the research questions. Faculty then contacts the targeted organization to arrange logistics and advertise the event. Faculty should consider multiple presentation times to accommodate conflicts and allow more students to present. Faculty with larger classes might consider topics that serve more constituents to allow for more workshops and presentation opportunities. See the table below for a list of alternative workshop ideas and potential target audiences. Faculty can require non-presenting students to conduct further research, prepare brochures for distribution, and attend the workshops.

Alternative workshops	Target audience
Business start-up issues	Small Business Development Office
Higher educational tax subsidies	Student groups on campus, local PTOs
Artist tax issues	University students, local art coalitions
Musician tax issues	University students, city philharmonics
Self-employment tax issues	Nursing students, hearing signers, architects
US tax fundamentals	Centro Latino
Kiddie tax, college savings, child care credit, and dependent spending	New moms and new parents clubs

Students' activities. Service-learning courses include student preparation, action/engagement, dissemination, and reflection. Each component is discussed separately.

Preparation Stage: The group presentations are compiled from each student's individual research paper on tax issues relevant to entertainers. This project requires students to identify tax issues, conduct research, provide a written analysis with appropriate citations, and then communicate the findings to a client.

> This project raises the stakes because outsiders will rely upon the advice presented. Faculty may notice that the students become more engaged, provide very constructive feedback, and ask each other tough questions to prepare for a real audience.

The individual writing assignment is designed to develop issue identification skills and is purposefully vague. Faculty can make this assignment less complex by providing specific tax issues to the students.

Action/Engagement: The students discuss their research findings in class. Teams are formed to complete additional research and prepare a brochure and PowerPoint presentation. To prepare for the workshop, the groups present to each other one week in advance. The students then complete an ungraded comment sheet to encourage constructive comments and feedback. The students are prompted to provide two positive comments, and identify two areas that needed additional work.

It is worth noting how these class presentations differed from other student presentations. Students are often quite collegial, and frequently do not challenge each other during class presentations. However, this project raises the stakes because outsiders will rely upon the advice presented. Faculty may notice that the students become more engaged, provide very constructive feedback, and ask each other tough questions to prepare for a real audience. This exercise is excellent for teamwork and communication skills development.

Dissemination: The students create separate PowerPoint presentations for two 60-minute workshops. Brochures distributed at the workshop summarize the law and provide references to websites.

Reflection: Students complete a two-page reflection paper. Students may either respond to directed questions or write on another aspect of their choosing. The directed reflection questions are:
1. How did this project connect to your learning in class?
2. How do you see your role in the business community upon graduation affected by this project?
3. How have you learned to communicate to a more general audience through this project?

Outcomes/Assessments

The students are graded on four components of the project:
1. Written individual research paper for accuracy, completeness, and format (individual grade);
2. Oral presentations for accuracy, completeness, and style (team grade);
3. Brochures for accuracy, references, and readability (team grade); and
4. Reflection papers for grammar, format, and content (individual grade).

Conclusion

Few universities offer an accounting course with a formalized service-learning component. The tax curriculum is an excellent place to apply tax accounting skills in a service-learning project. Graduate tax students at the University of Kansas find the ability to develop tax knowledge and apply it in a meaningful way very rewarding.

> This project defined the reason I chose this career to begin with…to help and serve others. It was rewarding to stand in front of strangers, explain tax advice, and observe their "ah ha" expressions or head nods.
>
> —KU graduate tax student

Service-learning courses include student preparation, action/engagement, dissemination, and reflection.

MANAGING TO ACHIEVE THE MOMENT

DAVID M. SARCONE
DICKINSON COLLEGE

Keywords: nonprofit, management, network, leadership, community development

Introduction

In a service-learning course students extend beyond traditional classroom responsibilities by participating in community-based activities. The goals of service-learning include attainment of a deeper understanding of course content and an increased sense of civic responsibility (Bringle and Hatcher, 1999). A well-executed service-learning experience results from the collaborative efforts of an expertly lead and managed community network of students, community representatives and course instructor/s. From a management perspective, the instructor's responsibilities include developing and maintaining network resources, structures and processes required to realize service-learning goals. The achievement of these goals is evidenced at that moment when students demonstrate a deeper understanding of the subject and a greater appreciation of civic engagement. This article provides strategies and techniques for the development and implementation of a nonprofit management course that achieves the goals summarized above. Experiences gained from offering a nonprofit management course at Dickinson College serve as the basis for these lessons. The article includes a project description, project time line, implementation steps, and outcomes.

Project Description

In support of Dickinson College's mission "to prepare young people, by means of a useful education in liberal arts and sciences, for engaged lives of citizenship and leadership in the service of society," the International Business and Management (INBM) Department offered a course entitled The Fundamentals of Nonprofit Management during the spring 2006 and spring 2008 terms. The course covers a broad scope of governance, strategic and operational aspects of nonprofits at an individual organizational level of analysis. The network supporting this service-learning project included nonprofits within walking distance of the Dickinson College campus, students from multiple disciplines, and an INBM instructor.

Project Timeline

Pre-course development required three months. Actions completed during this period included completion of the course approval process; service-learning training for the instructor; development of a detailed course syllabus;

development of an electronic course site; and, recruitment of nonprofit community partners and students. Students began field assignments during the third week of this fourteen-week course. Students were required to submit weekly reflective journal entries and produce and present the outcomes of their community project during weeks thirteen and fourteen of the course. Greater detail on pre-course and course activities are provided below.

Steps for Implementation

Effective management of the key stakeholder network is the basis for replicating course success. To achieve success, the instructor (course manager) must expertly complete four activities – activation, framing, mobilizing and synthesizing (McGuire, 2002).

Activation refers to "the set of activities employed for identifying and incorporating the persons and resources needed to achieve program goals" (McGuire, 2002, p. 602). The instructor identifies and recruits the correct sets of community partners and students. Seeking out nonprofits with existing relationships (internship sites, community service sites) with the college is an effective way to identify and solicit community participation. The instructor may also call on his/her professional network contacts to build the set of community partners. To attract students who might best benefit from the course, the instructor must promote the course to colleagues in other departments and secure agreements to crosslist the course. Suggested disciplines other than business for a nonprofit course include political science, policy studies, environmental science, and international studies.

Framing activities are "used to arrange and integrate a network structure by facilitating agreement on participants' roles, operating rules and network values" (McGuire, 2002, p. 603). A successful technique to reinforce values, roles and accountability among network members is the completion of a formal service agreement between the student/s and the nonprofit. The agreement should also be reviewed and formally signed by the course instructor. Ideally all three parties should execute the agreement at a joint meeting.

Mobilizing activities "develop commitment and support for network processes from network participants" (McGuire, 2002, p. 603). A key to effective collaborative process and outcomes is the creation of stakeholder specific rewards that are mutually supportive. Completing projects that directly improve the organization's management and/or program capacities can garner community participant commitment. Student buy-in to the process may be gained by assisting in the design of community projects that can be realistically completed within the term and serve as an integral aspect of a major course report and / or presentation. Examples of community projects undertaken by nonprofit course participants that served as the foundation for course assignments included the management of a fundraising event; the development of a volunteer management program; and, the development of both business and marketing plans.

> The instructor's (course manager) role is to direct and help students reach that moment when they attain two related goals - a deeper understanding of subject matter and greater commitment to civic engagement.

Synthesizing activities "build relationships and interactions that result in achieving network purpose" (McGuire, 2002, p. 603). Several techniques may be used to enhance these relationships. One management approach is meeting with relevant network members on site throughout the term to discuss progress on each community project. A second technique involves inviting nonprofit administrators to class sessions to serve as discussion facilitators and/or lecturers. The dialogue between practicing professionals and students in the nonprofit course on topics ranging from board /management relationships to volunteer management proved to be most valuable in achieving course goals and objectives.

Outcomes/Assessment

Community development outcomes from the most recently offered nonprofit course included the fulfillment of six separate service agreements. From a service-learning perspective, students reached that moment when experience and theory connect in a meaningful way. These student experiences were documented in post-service reflections; the content of term reports; and, results from the formal external course evaluation.

Conclusion

The instructor's (course manager) role is to direct and help students reach that moment when they attain two related goals - a deeper understanding of subject matter and greater commitment to civic engagement. One approach that worked in the case of a nonprofit management course involved the diligent management of the course's organizational network. The overarching service-learning lesson gained from this experience involves viewing the instructor's role as a network manager. As a manager, the instructor is responsible for selecting network participants; creating participant incentives; building trust and respect among participating members; and finally creating opportunities for the achievement of educational and community development outcomes.

References

Bringle, R. and Hatcher, J. (1999). Reflection in Service-Learning: Making Meaning of Experience. *Educational Horizons,* 77, 179-185.

McGuire, M. (2002). Managing Networks: Proposition on What Managers Do and Why They Do It. *Public Administration Review,* 5, 599-609.

Students reached that moment when experience and theory connect in a meaningful way.

‖‖‖

COMMUNITY SERVICE-LEARNING WITH STUDENT TEAM CONSULTING PROJECTS

JASON HARRIS-BOUNDY
SAN FRANCISCO STATE UNIVERSITY

Keywords: management consulting, student team projects, graduate students

Introduction

Student team projects are standard protocol in many business classes, often based on the claim that employers demand better team skills in graduates. They are used to reinforce the foundational knowledge of a particular discipline and to develop the professional skills of those headed into that field. Team projects requiring students to work as consultants with real organizations have become significantly more popular in recent years (Bowers, 2008). Students gain valuable experiential learning while "client" organizations benefit from their fresh insights. This article describes an innovation with this type of student project, the transformation into a community service-learning (CSL) experience without altering its primary objectives but resulting in increased student engagement and satisfaction.

In a persuasive critique of and recommendation for higher education, Altman (1996) identifies three domains of knowledge necessary for good citizens, the first two being well established in our system but the third far less so: (a) *foundational knowledge*, with its discipline-related history, content, theories and methodology combined with liberal or cross-disciplinary education; (b) *professional knowledge*, with its technical information and practical skills training; and (c) *socially responsive knowledge*, with students learning and directly acting on society's problems in their communities. This third domain is aided by the first two, but according to Altman must become "an integral part of our educational offerings" (375).

"Even in business courses?" some might ask. "Especially in business courses," I say. In fact, it might be with business school students and faculty where the greatest paradigm shifts can occur. Previously focusing only on technical business information and skills, they might suddenly see that this third type of knowledge can be pursued without harm to the other two. In my experience, business students appreciate this conceptual model because it powerfully frames the assignment described below, and possible paths to greater satisfaction in their classes, programs and careers. Other influences on CSL receptivity might include economic effects (recession-related enrollment by those re-evaluating their career direction and values) and the "millennial" generation's values, described as more concerned with work-life balance and social issues (Needleman, 2008).

Project Description

This project has been successfully implemented in a first-year "management principles" MBA course. It could easily be implemented in a host of other business courses. The basic idea is for student teams to engage in consulting-like projects with real organizations. Rather than working with just any organization, however, student teams must work with community-based organizations or on projects that address social issues (not necessarily limited to not-for-profit organizations). If similar team assignments already exist, their discipline-related learning objectives and content need not be diminished; the added value is for students to also apply themselves to real problems in the community.

It can help if instructors have consulting experience—and many faculty do, but it's not required. What develops is a unique partnership between students, faculty and the community, where all become learning-focused problem solvers. It might help to prepare a set of potential projects in advance (identified from the instructor's or colleagues' networks, CSL databases, or cold-calling), yet the most successful projects seem to happen when students identify their own. An early task can be for teams to brainstorm and discuss at least 10 potential projects, which increases their commitment and enthusiasm for their eventual choice. Some teams might need extra coaching in clarifying the focus and scope of the project with their community partners. Deliberate configuration of diverse teams usually ensures a favorable mix of more and less experienced students. Interim reports or milestones will help teams advance their projects and keep the instructor informed. Final reports and presentations can involve the organization's representatives.

Examples of successful projects include a strategic planning project for an environmental organization, a technology assessment for a community services organization, a mentoring program analysis of a disadvantaged youth organization, organizational design work for an HIV-AIDS prevention non-profit, recommendations about underserved communities for a guide dog provider, a needs assessment and soft skills training program for local crime prevention, etc.

Project Timeline

This CSL student team consulting project is designed as a primary course assignment for a 16-week semester, but could be shortened. **Weeks 1–2:** intro of assignment objectives and guidelines, configuration of teams, brainstorming of potential projects; **Weeks 3, 6, 9, 12:** interim reports that show status of project management tasks and analysis/management of team dynamics; **Week 15:** written/oral presentations; **Week 16:** project and team evaluations.

Steps for Implementation

The course syllabus should include project information and performance guidelines. A set of potential projects can be secured in advance for teams unable to identify their own projects. Altman's (1996) model described above can help frame the project's importance. In-class discussions about the projects allow the teams to learn from each others' experiences and the instructor to guide the process as a whole. Utmost professionalism should be required and taught. At minimum, community partners should receive an executive summary of the team's work. These "clients" might also attend the teams' oral presentations. Adequate time should be set aside for student team feedback and evaluation, as well as for instructor follow-up with the community partners.

Outcomes/Assessment

Long-term relationships with community partners should be developed when possible. Team projects can result in subsequent and improved ones, evolve into cross-departmental projects, or trigger multi-semester course innovations or student thesis projects. These projects and relationships also can generate research opportunities and good press coverage. In the short term, various deliverables such as written and oral reports should be clearly specified. If team-building skills or satisfaction is deemed important, then corresponding evaluation methods should be used to assess them. For students, projects should achieve all the associated course learning objectives while providing value to the partnering organizations.

Conclusion

This article identified a call for more social responsibility in higher education and described designing student team consulting projects for CSL opportunities. The assignment has increased team satisfaction, commitment and engagement. Many teams have even continued working on their projects after the semester and grading, I believe primarily because of the extra enthusiasm and satisfaction caused by socially responsive knowledge.

References

Altman, I. (1996). Higher education and psychology in the millennium. *American Psychologist,* 51(4): 371-378.

Bowers, B. (2008, May 8). Student consultants supply fresh insights to businesses. *The New York Times.*

Needleman, S.E. (2008, April 29). The latest office perk: Getting paid to volunteer, bait for millennial generation. *Wall Street Journal, pp.* Eastern edition, D1.

SERVICE-LEARNING IN PROJECT MANAGEMENT

SHARYN HARDY GALLAGHER
UNIVERSITY OF MASSACHUSETTS LOWELL

Keywords: business management, project management, nonprofit management

Introduction

Project management (PM) is the application of tools and techniques to most effectively complete projects usually constrained by time, money or resource allocations. As such, it is a field that is useful in many disciplines. The combination of PM service-learning is a good solution for providing projects which have real value, and thus, have more impact on student learning.

Project Description

Most projects in business are performed by teams of people, so a team-based approach must be used in a PM course. The kind of project that could be used is influenced by the relatively short time frame of a semester compared to that of most corporate projects. Teams should be less than six people so that each person can have the chance to make a significant contribution to the end result. Students should be expected to spend at least five hours per week on the projects themselves (classroom time can be allocated for some team meetings).

Two recent projects present good examples. The first was a project for a home health care agency that served many towns. The agency needed to update their media database so that they could keep their service providers and the public aware of their activities and encourage volunteers to help.

This project included gathering updated contact data on the local media, creating a new database (the agency had no central database for this data), training the database users and documenting actions so the agency could maintain the database and obtain reports after the semester was over.

The second project was for an agency whose mission is to provide short-term support to non-profits by connecting them to professionals who could provide free targeted assistance. This project included developing a list of all non-profit organizations in its service area and surveying them to see what kinds of staff training was necessary. The students had to research contact information, develop the survey, choose the best way to administer it, and collect and analyze survey data.

Project Timeline

Two of the key tenets for project management are planning and monitoring; these are also necessary when using service-learning as a pedagogy. The instructor will spend more time personally on the projects in the planning phase.

1. **Introduction to Project:** These projects are the major portion of the student's grade, so they must be described in the first class, along with the concept of service-learning. Students should be asked to indicate first and second choice projects in the second class; you match students with interests.
   The project-specific documents that should be handed out in the first class are:
   a. Project Descriptions including contact and web site information for the agencies.
   b. General Description of Service-Learning Project: This spells out the course-related assignments, such as Work Breakdown Schedule, and the weight of each assignment in the final grade calculation. Each person's obligation to the project team to perform timely, high quality work must be clearly articulated since the entire team will receive the same grade.
2. **Project Commencement:** Week two of semester.
3. **Project Monitoring:** Monitoring projects throughout the semester is a difficult balance of ensuring students make progress without telling them what to do. Once per week, ask each group to report in class about their progress and pitfalls; this provides "teachable moments" where you can reinforce points from the curriculum or ask the entire class to brainstorm solutions. You may want to meet with each group one to two times per semester to probe any major issues; for example, approving any surveys before they are sent. You should also check in with the sponsoring agency once or twice in the semester to make sure they are satisfied with the project progress and amount of communication.
4. **Team Monitoring:** It is common for interpersonal conflict among teammates to derail things. One tool is having students fill out midterm and final evaluations of each teammate, asking them to grade the others using a scale of 1-10 on cooperation, timeliness, quality of work, preparedness and communication skills. You may need to intercede where major problems with communicating and expectations arise.
5. **Reflections:** Assigning three one-page reflections ensure students are connecting their service to the curriculum. Suggested prompts include:
   a. Describe the mission of the organization, the goal of the project, and your impressions of the project sponsor.
   b. How is communication working within your team; should anything be done differently?
   c. How has your project made a difference to the organization, how did you add value yourself and what surprised you most about this project?
6. **Project Conclusion:** Week 14 of semester. Each team should write a paper and make a presentation on their project and agency. Project sponsors may be interested in attending, which will give you a chance to thank them for participating.

Steps for Implementation

Project planning begins two to three months before the semester begins; meet with the Service-learning Center Director (SLCD) to talk about the course and the learning outcomes desired. Depending on your institution, the SLCD may offer suggestions for agencies you can contact or may pre-qualify the contacts for you. (If you don't have a SLCD, you may want to send out a letter to area nonprofits to ask if they have any projects that they want some help with.) You should talk with the agencies yourself in more detail about the course and set mutual expectations for the project and the interaction required.

Two of the key tenets for project management are planning and monitoring; these are also necessary when using service-learning as a pedagogy.

Like any other course assignment, you need to decide how to measure progress in mastering the course content against the project deliverables. Some project submissions will be graded and others not; choose what makes the most sense for your class.

Outcomes/Assessment

In a PM course, there are several documents that must be created to adhere to professional standards. These become natural opportunities for formal assessment on the more critical documents, such as a work breakdown structure and schedule. Formative assessments help to provide quality control throughout the project.

A mid-term exam and personal reflections will measure mastery of content and relevance of the project experience. The completion of the project itself should be a component of the final grade to ensure that all students actually do the project and not just the paperwork assignments.

In our experiences, all of the students who have taken this course are business majors. Working in a nonprofit setting and seeing the management issues they face is very enlightening for them. The students express satisfaction knowing that they made a difference for their agency, and they devel-oped more empathy for the missions of nonprofits and their importance in our society. The agencies have reported they are happy to have the help because otherwise these projects would still be on their "to do" list.

I also felt satisfaction that the students have "done good" and that this may be sowing the seeds for future engagement with volunteerism.

Conclusion

A project management course needs real projects to effectively reinforce the course content. Service-learning projects provide added richness by exposing students to issues facing the non-profit sector. Good planning and monitoring will ensure that students connect their service to their learning and complete projects successfully.

REACHING AND TEACHING: BRINGING HEALTH CONCEPTS TO LIFE

JANICE CLARK YOUNG
TRUMAN STATE UNIVERSITY

BRENDA GOODWIN
MISSOURI STATE UNIVERSITY

Keywords: reflection, assessment, health education curriculum, contemporary health issues

Introduction

Service-learning in the classroom intentionally links the academic component of a course with relevant service in the community. To be successful, academic study and community service must be equal in importance. Studies show without reflection, students view community service simply as added work. All this can be accomplished with an integrated service-learning assignment for students to present a health fair in the local community. Health fairs provide opportunities for students to work in the public schools, community, or the university setting, and offer practical experience while applying health teaching methods, making professional business contacts, and using organizational skills.

Health education and physical education students best implement this project. However, with minor changes and a little creativity, this project could be adjusted and presented by student majors in elementary education, recreation, and biology. In addition, students majoring in business administration or human resources could benefit from developing a health fair for the university or community.

Project Description

The initial step for implementing this activity into a college course is securing a host site for the fair. An especially good health fair site is a local elementary school receiving Title I funding. Generally, students in these schools lack some of the basic necessities and welcome the presentations and the information. A health fair can also be planned for an entire community or a university. Consider using a senior center, community center, or a civic auditorium when planning for a community health fair, or using a gymnasium when conducting a health fair on a university campus.

Topics for booths can be selected by or assigned to student groups. Popular topics for health fair booths include bicycle safety, nutrition, dental health, physical activity, sun safety, stress management, and/or recycling. The topics are limitless, constrained only by the age of the participants and relevance to health education.

Project Timeline

Weeks 1–2: students form working groups.
Week 3: groups submits health fair booth proposal.

Weeks 4–5: groups plan booth/activities.
Week 6: students submit the first project evaluation.
Week 7: continue booth planning/preparation.
Week 8: students submit second project evaluation and continue booth preparation.
After health fair: students submit final project evaluation.

Steps for Implementation

Once the health fair site and date are secured, the booth preparation, presentation, and contact of health sources is the students' responsibility. Early in the semester have students form groups of two or three, or assign groups. By the end of the third week, each student group must submit a proposal including the following information: topic/title of booth, health subject, educational objectives, description, activities, type of "freebies," and special needs (electrical outlet, near door, etc.) of the booth. The instructor must review the proposals and accept or modify them based on variety, available resources, and alignment with the health curriculum.

Students should compile a list of available resources (community organizations and businesses), and then contact them to request donations of health items, pamphlets, and "freebies." Professors should discuss the significance of using proper contact protocol when asking involvement from businesses, the importance of good organization, the value of hands-on activities, and colorful eye catching booth backdrops.

By the end of the sixth week of the semester, students submit their first pre-health fair evaluation. This evaluation should address the following items: personal preparation/involvement, an assessment of each group member's involvement with a suggested grade, acquisition of freebies, how freebies are being obtained and who is responsible for this, description of the hands-on learning that will occur at the booth, type of age-appropriate informational handouts, plans for an eye-catching backdrop, and what needs to be completed to create a successful health education booth. Without reflection, students view community service simply as added work.

By midterm, the students will submit a second pre-health fair evaluation. Again, students will describe their own preparation and involvement, and that of other group members. They will assess what still needs to be finalized for all aspects of the booth. The students must explain what they will wear to support their booth's theme, and describe the backdrop. Lastly, students will assess the learning activities, worksheets, and freebies that will be used and distributed at the booth.

Throughout the semester, professors must continue to emphasize the importance of responsibility, teamwork, sharing of duties, and organization. Periodically, devoting some class time for group work/discussion of their booth's needs and activities is also helpful.

On the day of the health fair, students must arrive at the school early to set up their booths. The elementary students will visit as a class with children divided into groups of three to four. Each elementary group begins at a different booth and groups rotate every three to four minutes. This rotation schedule allows an entire class to visit each booth in 30–45 minutes. For a morning health fair (8:30–11:30 a.m.), approximately five classrooms can visit the booths.

Outcomes/Assessment

During the health fair, the professor evaluates each booth. A previously-circulated rubric containing the following information should be utilized: set-up and take-down of booth, use of creative ideas, appropriate and creative dress, accuracy of information, hands-on learning, organization of learning activities, educational value of the booth, positive reinforcement given to children, enthusiasm of team members, appropriateness of booth to grade levels, handouts/freebies bagged for easy distribution, and equal participation of all members. Points for the health fair are equal to those of a course test.

After completing the health fair, the college students submit one final evaluation. For this assessment, they discuss their personal involvement and preparation during this project. They also describe each group member's involvement and suggest a grade for each of their team members. In this final reflection paper, students assess the educational value of the health fair and how it will help them as future educators. It is also helpful for them to describe the response of the participants. Finally, students should offer constructive suggestions to improve the health fair as a service-learning experience for future students.

Conclusion

Allowing students to organize and present a health fair booth is an opportunity to create relevance in a health course. Continually evaluating the process and reflecting on the outcome helps students to understand the importance and value of their efforts. Integrated service-learning enables them to contribute to the quality of life in the community and to become ambassadors for the university.

THE HAPPY TEETH SEALANT CLINIC: ENGAGING STUDENTS, SCHOOLS AND COMMUNITY

LAURIE PETERS
IVY TECH COMMUNITY COLLEGE OF INDIANA, KOKOMO REGION

Keywords: dental sealant, partnership, dental health, pediatric dentistry

Introduction

Community involvement and service-learning projects are integral to education and training in a variety of healthcare fields including dental assisting programs. Ivy Tech Community College health programs strive to provide students with the skills needed for marketable employment while at the same time focusing on improving the health and welfare of the communities served. The *Happy Teeth Sealant Clinic* presents an ideal opportunity to provide service-learning activities for the dental students, while helping young children overcome fears about going to the dentist, providing free dental services to at-risk student populations, enhancing knowledge of dental care and disease prevention through provision of educational materials for children and their parents, and collaboration with individuals and groups throughout the community to provide a unique and beneficial service.

Project Description

The *Happy Teeth Sealant Clinic* is a collaborative effort involving local church members, a school corporation, and Ivy Tech Community College, Kokomo Region, dental assisting program students and faculty with a goal of providing improved dental services to at-risk children. Due to the age when first molars appear, second-grade students were targeted for this project. If the child's biting surfaces have no dental caries present, sealants are applied free of charge. If decay is found, a written follow-up report is generated by the school nurse and sent to the child's parents so they might seek further assistance for their child. The school nurses also work with area dentists to find those who provide low-cost or Medicaid eligible dental services for needy children. A steering committee of church members, college faculty, dentists, and a school system nurse and administrator identified and outlined the following project objectives:

1. To enable regional second grade students to receive a dental exam to identify any serious dental problems.
2. To provide free sealant protection to molar surfaces to prevent decay as indicated.
3. To engage Ivy Tech dental students in service-learning activities that provide hands-on learning with area dentists to meet an identified need.
4. To provide a method for a variety of stakeholders including an area church, a local school system, volunteer dentists, and college dental students to participate in a collaborative effort to improve the dental health of school children in the community.

Project Timeline

The *Happy Teeth Sealant Clinic* project planning begins each spring semester, with implementation the following spring. Steering committee meetings are held following each annual event and beginning six months before the next year's event to determine supply needs, identify which schools will be participating each year, and identifying the anticipated number of second grade students to be involved. The initial event began with two schools of second grade students from more impoverished areas of town during year one of the clinic. The first sealant clinic was held over two half-days, included two dentist volunteers, and was conducted in the dental lab at the college. Since that time, the *Happy Teeth* project has grown to include all second-grade children from a large school system (over 540 participants), four dentist volunteers, and is held over five full days at the college dental lab.

Ivy Tech dental assisting students and faculty prepare the learning experiences for the participants and set up the clinic beginning the fall semester before the spring clinic commences. Presentations, games, and dental health videos are developed and used by the dental assisting students to educate the children on proper oral hygiene and encourage them to take care of their teeth. College dental assisting faculty work with the school system staff and nurse director to coordinate bussing and lunches for the children. The dental assisting students develop methods to manage traffic flow in sealant clinic, schedule rotations for working with and assisting the dentists, and create a variety of fun and educational activities for students waiting to be seen by the dentist.

Steps for Implementation

The steps for implementation of the *Happy Teeth* project include the following:

1. One year in advance: Meet with the dentists, church representatives, nurse director at the school system, and the college dental faculty to identify dates, times, and schools to be selected for the project. Identify any supply or equipment needs.
2. Six months in advance: Order any necessary supplies and deliver to college dental lab. The school corporation

nurse director begins coordinating bus delivery of the children to the clinic and student lunches.

3. Two months in advance: Lab supplies are received. School nurses send notices home to parents seeking permission for their child to participate in the event.

4. Two weeks in advance: The school nurse director contacts the college dental program chair and confirms the final number of participants for the event. College dental students and faculty complete final preparations and complete assembly of the "goody" bags.

5. One week following the event: Project coordinators meet to discuss outcomes, dates, funding issues for future clinics and to identify areas for improvement. Identified dental problems are reported to the parents following the sealant clinic and the school nurses work with families to find affordable follow-up dental care.

Outcomes/Assessment

The *Happy Teeth Sealant Clinic* project provides service-learning opportunities for students, the opportunity to develop and enhance workforce skills, and the establishment of strong collaborations with a variety of stakeholders who come together to make a difference in the health of children while providing a greatly needed service. Dental students gain valuable experience in developing educational strategies to promote good dental health for the children and hands-on experience participating in the clinic, developing teamwork skills in managing preparing for the event. The school nurses and parents are very appreciative of this free service, which many families may not be able to afford. The children learn that it's not "scary" to go to the dentist, and it can even be a fun and educational experience. The project has been a huge success and is expected to continue for many years to come.

The *Happy Teeth* project has been remarkably successful. Depending on the condition of a child's teeth, nearly 98% of those examined receive sealants. Many children reported it "wasn't as scary" as they thought it would be going to the dentist. Parents and teachers reported how much they loved the project and their excitement about participating in future events. Church members built a wooden tooth and pass it around each week to gain funds for upcoming clinics, which continue to increase in size. Follow-up meetings are held following each annual event to discuss evaluations by parents, school nurses, principals and administrators, college faculty and students, dentists, and church members. Plans for the following year are discussed as well as current community needs regarding dental care for children.

Conclusion

The award-winning *Happy Teeth Sealant Clinic* project (Kroeger, 2009) has continued to grow substantially since its inception and provided preventative dental sealants to hundreds of children. This unique partnership involves a diverse group of stakeholders coming together, developing a single vision to provide a much needed community service, and making it a reality. The Happy Teeth project is an example of how collaborative efforts between the college and community can lead to the development of a successful service-learning project that benefits many individuals.

Reference

Kroeger, V. (2009). *State recognizes outstanding career technical education students, programs, personnel.* Retrieved from http://www.in.gov.

SERVICE-LEARNING CREATES EPIPHANIES IN A GENERAL STUDIES HIV/AIDS COURSE

LISA E. COX
THE RICHARD STOCKTON COLLEGE OF NEW JERSEY

Keywords: undergraduates, general studies course, HIV/AIDS content

Introduction

For eight years now, I have required service-learning and used novels to teach an upper-level general studies course about HIV disease. As HIV disease has become part of the fabric of our national history, service-learning experiences have helped my undergraduate students change their thinking, feelings and attitudes toward people who have the disease and understand societal decisions that are made in the HIV/AIDS arena. During the 15-week semester course, students complete 20-30 hours of service-learning at organizations involved

in service delivery, health care provision, and policy/research dimensions related to HIV/AIDS. Consistently positive course evaluations reveal the extent to which students grow in knowledge and understanding, by virtue of their engagement in service-learning.

Project Description

Our college catalog lists my values/ethics subscripted course as *GIS 3628 HIV/AIDS: The Epidemic*. In addition to two objective tests, and one AIDS Biography assignment, students must complete a service-learning experience that includes volunteering, recording learning log entries and writing a final reflection paper.

As the course evolves, the attention-getting novels help students gain empathy about the predicament and societal prejudices that people who have lived and died with HIV/ AIDS encounter, and the readings convey scientific explanation about immunology and disease progression. However, it is service-learning where students have epiphanies and observe the art of helping people cope and survive. When students come back from working at South Jersey AIDS Alliance, the local methadone maintenance clinic, or Heartland Hospice their book learning comes alive as they share great insights and observations related to their service-learning. In class, such spontaneous thinking and sharing creates spirited debates about service-learning observations and textbook content.

Project Timeline

Across the 15-week semester, a community organization placement, that is close to the college or the student's residence is found by our college's Service-learning Coordinator and approved by me, the course instructor. By design, the intent is for students to spread out their hours across the entire semester so they can integrate their service-learning experiences with their book knowledge. Around mid-semester, in class I have students sit in a circle and process how their service-learning experiences have evolved since the first time they showed up at their organization. Learning log entries are kept weekly, and the formal reflection paper—that draws upon these entries—is assembled and handed in the last day of class.

Steps for Implementation

On the first day of class, a syllabus that earmarks my course as mandatory service-learning and values/ethics focused is distributed to students. Because the format is seminar-style, attempts are made to cap the course at 25 students. Students are next introduced to the main text (Stine, 2008), AIDS Biography assignment, and told that next class session they will need to commit to being interviewed and placed at a college approved service-learning site.

During the second class session, the Service-learning (SL) coordinator talks with my class, distributes requisite forms, and reviews rules and regulations for communication and completion of hours. Afterward, students call and visit service-learning sites and decide where they will spend time learning. Successful implementation for students, faculty member, SL coordinator, and agencies alike is contingent upon a good orientation, ongoing processing and feedback, and a final qualitative reflection paper.

When the SL coordinator comes into class, students are given a Service-Learning Student Handbook and told where to download a PDF version on the college service-learning website. These handbooks define service-learning and its history and requirements at our college. The handbooks also give communication tips, outline student responsibilities, and inform about ethical codes, clothing policies, grievance/incident procedures, and requisite forms (e.g., registration form, agreement, liability release & timesheet).

Faculty are also given a Faculty Service-Learning Handbook when they embark upon teaching a course that either requires or includes service-learning. In addition to the student information noted above, faculty get content about the role of service-learning in classes, Principles of Good Practice, course development basics, and the service-learning placement process for students.

Liaisons at community organizations and agencies also receive a copy of the college's Community Partner Service-Learning Handbook. This resource describes the service-learning process and requirements, gives samples of our required student paperwork and forms, and gives tips for beginning and working effectively with students.

Outcomes/Assessment

By the semester's end, students will have completed requisite forms and community partners are responsible for completing the student evaluation form. From even a cursory perusal of data collected on these forms, one can usually see that service-learning is beneficial for students, faculty, and community organizations. Service-learning gives students practical, hands-on experience, provides welcomed help to local agencies, gives students glimpses of job possibilities, and allows students to have service-learning credit appear on their transcripts.

As the professor who teaches the HIV/AIDS class, I have observed how students go beyond surface learning when they do service-learning. In class, they'll communicate more about readings and they will reflect more deeply and intimately about taboo topics that HIV/ AIDS tends to engender, related to addiction/injection drug use, sex, faith, and death.

Service-learning gives students practical, hands-on experience, provides welcomed help to local agencies, gives students glimpses of job possibilities, and allows students to have service-learning credit appear on their transcripts.

Service-learning helps students, literally, "go outside of themselves" and relate to the suffering, joy, resilience, realities and complexities that people living with AIDS face almost daily. When student evaluations of teaching are administered, at the end of the HIV/AIDS course, the service-learning component gets rave reviews.

Conclusion

The purpose of this service-learning course is to present an understandable scientific explanation of what has been learned about HIV/AIDS over the last three decades. The textbook presents science, epidemiological and historical/political trends about HIV/AIDS; however, it has been the AIDS Biography assignment and the service-learning component that have touched student's hearts and minds. Service-learning experiences that transform student prejudices, because they can now put a face on an illness and touchy societal issue, are a delight to behold!

References

Stine, G. (2008). *AIDS Update 2008*. New York: McGraw-Hill.

EVALUATION OF A CAMPUS: COMMUNITY PARTNERSHIP TO PROMOTE WELLNESS AND INTEREST IN HEALTH CAREERS AMONG OLDER RURAL ELEMENTARY SCHOOL CHILDREN

MARTIN MACDOWELL AND MICHAEL GLASSER
UNIV. OF ILLINOIS COLLEGE OF MEDICINE

MADONNA WEESE
STATE 4-H OFFICE, UNIVERSITY OF ILLINOIS URBANA-CHAMPAIGN

MARY DEATHERAGE
KATHERINE SHAW BETHEA HOSPITAL

Keywords: rural, youth, health, education, careers, health professions, community education

Introduction

Concern over the current and future shortages of workers in the health care sector, especially in rural areas, has led to the need for programs to increase awareness of health career options among elementary-age students. Rural communities continue to experience disparities in access to and quality of health care; thus it is important to offer programs that can inform and educate young people on healthy lifestyles, as well as health career options in rural settings. The interactions described during this event between health professions students with younger students from similar rural/small town backgrounds is a service-learning project that is mutually beneficial and part of the fall course activities for each participating health profession.

Project Description - 4-H Jam Component

In 2006 and 2007, five rural elementary schools in Northwest Illinois participated in a two-day event with follow-up called '4-H Health Jam' that involved 166 fifth- and sixth-grade students. This event increased the participating elementary students' knowledge about health topics (focusing on fitness and wellness) and health career options.

One elementary school was selected by 4-H Youth Educators in each five rural Illinois counties based on the demographics of the school, and the school's proximity to the camp and hospital where the Health Jam was conducted. The students are the type of students from rural backgrounds that the National Center for Rural Health Professions (NCRHP) seeks to encourage to consider working in a health career. A partnership involving academic training programs (university and community college), county and state 4-H educators, local classroom teachers, and a rural hospital planned and conducted the event with support from a large agribusiness company grant.

Project Timeline and Steps for Implementation

Day 1 - Camp White Eagle, near Adeline, IL: Elementary students rotated through five 50-minute classes focusing on personal health and physical fitness. The five classes were: (a) basic strength training for youth; (b) introduction to the Walk Across Illinois Program; (c) preventing diabetes through a healthy lifestyle; (d) kickboxing for beginners; and (e) 4-H cooperative games.

Health Professions students working in teams (some interdisciplinary) developed a lesson plan for each of the five rotations the elementary students attended. The focus is on using "hands-on" engaging activities to achieve the learning objective they established for the elementary students. Specific goals for the health professions students were to:

(a) formalize and implement a lesson plan that contained a goal, learning objectives, and specific educational activities for the rotation; (b) initiate or increase their experience working with other health professions students to develop and complete an educational program for younger students; and (c) develop perspectives about the multiyear aspect of health workforce development that could be applied in communities where they practice in the future. Elementary students did five 25-minute rotations with a dental, nursing, and pharmacy students group, and three groups of rural medical students to learn about body systems, the roles and responsibilities of the specific health professions, and the profession's educational requirements. Each of the five small group activities lasted 25 minutes. Fun camp activities occurred after supper.

Day 2 - KSB Hospital in Dixon: Students rotated through five stations while at the hospital to observe and learn about various roles responsibilities: Dietary, Imaging, Physical therapy/Audiology services, Emergency Medical Services (EMS) and the Lee County Health Department discussed protection of health (focusing on hand washing to avoid risk of illness).

Each of these five rotations in the hospital was taught by a trained, certified hospital or health department staff member. Each rotation lasted 25 minutes with five additional minutes allowed for travel time between departments. In all the learning activities the students were engaged in experiencing a topic directly.

Follow up activities at each school: Once a week for eight weeks following the 4-H Health Jam, the students met with the 4-H educator at their individual schools. At meetings, students chart their daily physical activity. Each team of four students plots their progress on the 448 mile "Walk across Illinois." This group served as the student's support group in reaching their goals of 30 minutes of daily physical activity that was converted to step equivalents. At the end of the eight weeks, each student who completed the Walk across Illinois receives a t-shirt saying, "I walked across Illinois," which shows the path they took on their "walk."

Outcomes/Assessment

Using a survey process approved by the Urbana and Rock-ford Univ. of Illinois IRB committees an identical survey occurred before and after the education event in fall 2006 and 2007. Paired t-tests were used to assess the statistical significance of changes in 25 questions, n = 166 children.

A unique anonymous participant identification number was used to match pre- and post-surveys. At the end of the eight weeks, students completed the School Health Education Evaluation (SHEE) test in their school classroom.

Analysis of responses to the 25 questions using paired t-tests indicate that 13/18= 72% of the common survey questions used in both 2006–07 to assess pre-post event changes showed statistically significant change (p <0.05) in knowledge of health concepts and health career options. Of the questions unique to a given year, 7/15 = 47% showed statistically significant change (p <0.05) pre-post.

The health professions students benefited as well from Health Jam participation. Faculty advisors evaluated and provided informal feedback to the health professions students regarding their educational rotations for the elementary students based on qualitative observation of lesson plan implementation and the reactions/engagement of the young students. These are comments from two of the health professions students:

> Student 1: I found this event very beneficial. It made us think how we could work with children if we were trying to explain something medically-related to them at their level. It was fun devising hands-on activities that could help the kids actually see how things work in their body. The kids seemed to really have a good time and participated very well in the activities and with answering questions.

> Student 2: The kids surprised me about how much they already knew about our topic, even at their age. They asked some very intelligent questions and seemed to be interested in what we had to say, and in actually learning from us. Among their main concerns, I believe, was the effect smoking has on their family members who smoke.

Conclusions

The findings indicate that a special two-day experiential education event can substantially improve the knowledge of wellness behaviors and health careers among older rural elementary children. In addition, teachers, students, hospital staff, and health professions students report subjective benefits from interacting in this application oriented educational partnership. The Health Jam was continued in subsequent years with similar positive results, and in 2009 was offered in other locations under the guidance of the State 4-H office.

INCORPORATING SERVICE-LEARNING IN AN INTERDISCIPLINARY MEDICAL ETHICS COURSE

NANCY B. MARTHAKIS
PURDUE UNIVERSITY NORTH CENTRAL

Keywords: medical ethics, ethics consultation, interdisciplinary, ethics committee, health care

Introduction

Healthcare professionals often lack formal training on how to approach solving medical ethical dilemmas (Gordon, et al., 2004). For this reason, a three-credit hour undergraduate college course entitled "The Biology and Controversy of Medical Ethics" was developed and implemented. The creation of the course has offered students a unique perspective in the application of ethical theories and principles. Traditionally, ethics courses are taught in the classroom, with class lectures supplemented by discussion of assigned readings as being the mainstay of course instruction. By adding a service-learning component to the traditional form of ethics pedagogy, this unique course has inspired students with questions of justice, equity, power and access, and introduces students directly to the civic process. The course is designed to provide a service-learning component in such a way that promotes valuable critical thinking skills in the moral-ethical-biological aspects facing modern medicine.

Project Description

In addition to the conventional ethics lecture and study of textbook precedent cases, students were involved in service-learning activities designed to provide them with real patient case studies and development of ethics consultation skills. Emphasis of the course is placed on an introduction to medical ethics based problems commonly encountered in the modern medical setting. All students that enrolled in the one semester 16-week course were fulfilling an undergraduate elective requirement for their specific discipline of study. Introducing clinical ethics experiences on the undergraduate level is unique because students usually do not gain this type of insight into a case based approach in medical ethics until they are near completion in health professional programs. There were no prerequisites for the course, and students that participated declared their area of study to include nursing, business, social work, pre-medicine, pre-pharmacy and liberal studies. For the service-learning component, a variety of healthcare institutions partnered to provide students access to a select group of diverse patient cases. For example, ethical dilemmas included topics ranging from patient competency and informed consent to decisions concerning withdrawal of care and palliative medicine.

Project Timeline

Prior to arrival at their assigned service-learning site, students were placed in small groups or teams, and each team contained students from different disciplines of study, thus creating interdisciplinary teams. The purpose of the student interdisciplinary teams, in addition to fostering student collaboration and reflective discussion, was to mimic actual hospital ethics committees, since ethics committees are often composed of individuals from a variety of professional backgrounds. Near the end of the course, the students had an opportunity to act as a mock ethics committee in presenting their cases.

Steps for Implementation

Early in the course development and construction, collaborations with a variety of healthcare providers were established. The course was designed to provide students with experience at several locations to include a care spectrum ranging from local acute care hospital environments, to more long term care settings, such as nursing homes, reduced fee health clinics, and hospice settings. In this way, the students collectively have been introduced to the full range of continuity of care that a patient may encounter. Interdisciplinary teams consisting of two to five students were assigned to one provider location for the entire semester. Each team received a mandatory orientation at their assigned health facility, prior to beginning their case studies. To

By adding a service-learning component to the traditional form of ethics pedagogy, this unique course has inspired students with questions of justice, equity, power and access, and introduces students directly to the civic process.

further prepare students for their clinical experience, the students completed sections in their ethics student study manual detailing the four box approach to ethics consultations (Kenny, et al., 2001). Patient cases assigned to the teams of students at the provider locations were pre-selected by the healthcare staff to include those with an identified medical ethical dilemma. Once a case had been selected by a pre-appointed facility coordinator, the team of students began by identifying the moral nature of the selected case, discussed the medical issues impacting the patient, and formulated questions pertaining to the ethical issue. Throughout the course of the semester, students visited their assigned facilities up to five times in two to three-hour time blocks. The first visit consisted of the student orientation, visits two to four were actual patient case assignment and analysis, and the last visit consisted of a wrap-up session. During the final session, the team formally presented their case to the facility. Prior to beginning the presentation, the students creatively decided on assuming various roles and role playing, such as the role of the physician, the ethicist, the patient, and the floor nurse. By doing this, the student driven team acted as an actual ethics committee would during an ethics consultation.

Outcomes/Assessment

The definition of service-learning also highlights the importance of reflection. Reflection is "intentional consideration of an experience in light of particular objectives." (Student manual Biology and Controversy of Medical Ethics). Therefore, structured reflection time was also a crucial dimension of the course. The students, in addition to writing

a paper on their service-learning patient case, presented the case to their assigned facilities and to their fellow students in the classroom setting. The collaborator facility sites had the opportunity to critique the student panel presentations, thus providing direct professional feedback to the student. The students, by offering several solutions to the patient's ethical dilemma, had a positive impact on the facility sites and allowed the healthcare staff a chance to retrospectively analyze and reflect upon the various resolutions to the patient's medical ethical dilemma.

Conclusion

Across the undergraduate and graduate medical education, there is a call for better preparing students for common ethical dilemmas they will likely encounter. One way to bridge the knowledge gap is to offer courses in medical ethics that have a service-learning component, and that engage learners in doing, discussing and reflecting.

References

Gordon D., Clarridge, B., Gensler, G. & Danis, M. (2004). A National Survey of U.S. Internists' Experiences with Ethical Dilemmas and Ethics Consultation. *Journal of General Internal Medicine,* 19(3), 251-258.

Kenny, N., Sargeant, J., & Allen, M. (2001). Lifelong learning in ethical practice: a challenge for continuing medical education. *Journal of Continuing Education in the Health Professions,* 21(1), 24-32.

Student manual biology and controversy of medical ethics. Retrieved June 10, 2010 from www.rlsimonson.com.

Across the undergraduate and graduate medical education,
there is a call for better preparing students for common ethical dilemmas
they will likely encounter. One way to bridge the knowledge gap
is to offer courses in medical ethics that have a service-learning component,
and that engage learners in doing, discussing and reflecting.

DESIGNBUILD STUDIO: A CASE STUDY IN FORMING COLLABORATIVE SERVICE-LEARNING INITIATIVES

KYLE ANDREW STURGEON
BOSTON ARCHITECTURAL COLLEGE

Keywords: design/build, architecture, risk-based learning, collaborative learning, community partnership

Introduction

Urban designBUILD (UdB) is an advanced workshop founded at the Boston Architectural College (BAC) that seeks to develop young architects' design and construction skills while cultivating strong community partnerships to improve Boston's built environment. Each spring, students collaborate with a pre-selected community-based client to create a work of architecture that fulfills a programmatic need, makes better use of untended spaces in the city, and brings citizens with unique talents and backgrounds together through service-learning (SL).

Project Description

During the spring of 2008, students in the first UdB studio paired with two organizations based in the Boston neighborhood of Roxbury to design and fabricate an amphitheater and shade canopies for a reclaimed park. Members of the neighborhood played a significant role in both the planning and construction of the work. In the final design, three concrete benches stow red boxes that can be used as portable seating or can be assembled into a platform for performances. Overhead canopies are designed to provide shade to performers, and they double as a projection surface for film screenings at night.

UdB Project Goals:
- To lead students in hands-on construction combined with a design studio education to teach the intersection between design and fabrication in architecture.
- To foster a collaborative studio environment such that students engage more fully with peers, practitioners and communities.
- To implement architectural research and design as stewardship of our built environment and social contexts.

Project Timeline

Background: Several years prior to the initial UdB Studio, the *"United Neighbors of Lower Roxbury"* secured the rights to utilize and maintain a series of spaces in their community through another non-profit, the "South End – Lower Roxbury Open Space Land Trust." These two organizations worked together to clean up these abandoned lots to establish shared gardens and usable open-space. Community

members agreed that these spaces would be best utilized with proper design and planning, and they sought assistance from the BAC. Mixed faculty began to reorganize several ongoing design/build efforts to found Urban designBUILD to focus on the community in Roxbury.

Typical Project Structure: The program runs over a 16-week spring semester and extends as required into the summer on a volunteer basis. As each class must form a cohesive team and each annual project requires a different set of solutions, much responsibility is given to the studio instructor and the students to define their working models and assessment. Several community meetings, such as a design workshop, design selection meeting, and an on-site 'build' day are scheduled in the neighborhood to ensure a partnership throughout the process.

"...Above all, working with a real client/ community to define the specifics of the program, discuss design, and implement our ideas in a built form that could be appreciated by a grateful neighborhood was an unparalleled learning experience."

Rebecca Grace,
BAC thesis student

Steps for Implementation

Establishing Program Goals: As the founding project for an SL program, it is crucial to schedule ample time to define critical goals of the course. Mixed faculty began meeting two months prior to the class to establish the program's responsibilities to the student, the school, and the community.

Acquiring Funding: Funding needs to be secured relative to the scale of each annual project. Over the course of the '08 spring semester, an educational grant was written and awarded to cover the majority of the program's cost (typically between \$6,000–\$12,000) and to ensure funding for next year's project. Additional fundraising was undertaken by the BAC to ensure adequate contingency, and the program has now been given an annual allowance in the BAC's faculty budget.

Establishing a Collaborative Classroom: SL initiatives are most successful when there is a comfortable environment for team members to produce both individual and group work, and to participate in constructive feedback sessions. At the first meeting, students review the grading rubric (focusing on collaborative initiative, conceptual production, and communication skills) to ensure that expectations are clear and to emphasize the role of collaboration throughout the course. During the design phase, each student rotates between several focus groups, establishing all work as intellectual property of the group. As the studio shifts from the classroom to the field, students undertake project management roles. At the mid- and end-points of the semester, self- and peer-to-peer assessments are conducted.

Fostering Community Engagement: A balance must be struck between producing a work of architecture and fostering a rich SL experience for the students. Scheduling moments of community/student partnership during both design and fabrication were critical in reaching this goal. Construction lessons are open to community members and often occur at the neighborhood site. All student work must be legible, presentation-quality work that can easily be understood by those outside of the design profession.

Outcomes/Assessment

Success of the first UdB Project has catalyzed a far-reaching increase in activism within the Boston community. The United Neighbors of Lower Roxbury has seen a significant increase in membership, and has begun the planning stages to build a community center with help from the BAC and other organizations. A Village At Work has used the '08

project to host fundraising event and farmers' markets. The BAC continues its relationship with the community through the National Organization of Minority Architect student chapter, and is currently hosting an urban design competition to rethink the master plan of the neighborhood. Several BAC students have focused their thesis projects on the area, and the UdB studio is working in Roxbury again during the '09 project.

Students report a variety of learning and developmental outcomes from the service-learning experience, including:
- Development of leadership and collaboration skills working with other peers, the client and the community.
- Development of presentation skills from submitting their designs to the community.
- Exploration of methods in pre-fabrication techniques.
- Critical thinking regarding construction strategies.
- Ability to manage time, project and budget constraints.

"… Above all, working with a real client/community to define the specifics of the program, discuss design, and implement our ideas in a built form that could be appreciated by a grateful neighborhood was an unparalleled learning experience."
—Rebecca Grace, BAC thesis student

Conclusion

Urban Design-Build Architecture is a powerful and fulfilling SL activity. In this model, students and instructors constantly reinvent methods of collaboration with peers, co-workers and whole communities. Students develop their professional skills by confronting multiple facets of architecture—implementing design concepts in the construction process and fostering client relationships, and acting as stewards of their environment. By focusing this research in an urban context, this form of service-learning promotes dialogue across socioeconomic borders while having a positive physical impact on our cities.

Designing change

Timothy D. Dolan
Appalachian State University

Keywords: architecture, design, interior design, homelessness

Introduction

Though service-learning is not new, its popularity continues to increase as colleges and universities incorporate, and even require, participation in service-learning courses. However, utilizing the curriculum of design programs is considerably

newer to this best practice application. Precedents do exist combining design and service-learning; Auburn University's School of Architecture has been integrating service-learning through the Rural Studio to international acclaim for over fifteen years. Its greatest success, though, is the life-changing impact it has had on the residents of Hale

County, Alabama, and the students that participate in the Rural Studio programs (http://www.cadc.auburn.edu/soa/rural-studio/mission.htm).

> Not only are community needs being met through the education and application of how design affects society, but students are learning and practicing professional knowledge and skills while developing and understanding the importance of one's role in society.

The design disciplines, Architecture, Graphic Design, Industrial Design and Interior Design, have long been viewed as luxuries few could afford. Utilizing service-learning in the classroom has not only enhanced achieving course goals and outcomes, but has allowed an untapped community resource to be a source of research, solutions, and strategies for impacting the community and society.

Following integration of service-learning into the Interior Design Program at Appalachian State University approximately four years ago, the request for services has been unprecedented. The community's interest in partnering with the design students has allowed faculty to critically review each project to appropriately align with the desired course objectives and match those with the needs of the community. The success of service-learning in the interior design program cannot be overstated. Not only are community needs being met through the education and application of how design affects society, but students are learning and practicing professional knowledge and skills while developing and understanding the importance of one's role in society.

While this article specifically explores one service-learning project in a given semester, the processes, organization and execution of each project is very similar and would be applicable for most design-intensive service-learning projects. The design program has completed over fifteen such projects, each unique in scope, but similar in application and approach.

Project Description

In addition to panoramic views of surrounding mountains, clean air, and an abundant supply of outdoor activities, Boone, North Carolina is home to approximately 14,000 full time residents, Appalachian State University, second-home retirees, and the Hospitality House that serves the needs of homeless individuals and families. In 2007 alone, the Hospitality House provided 15,783 shelter nights.

With a twenty-year history and now operating four separate facilities, the decision was made to combine these locations into one new freestanding facility. Having utilized the service-learning program for a number of years, the executive director of the facility inquired as to other avenues with service-learning participants while contemplating this new facility. Following discussions between the executive director and instructor, the project was selected and paired with the appropriate course. The project was an assessment and research of the proposed facility, its functions, operations, residents, unique needs and recommendations for enhancement and development of spaces and aesthetics appropriate for intended use, desired behaviors, and outcomes.

Project Timeline

A sixteen-week semester housed this project that also included two additional in-class projects. The timeline was as follows:

- End of fall semester 2006, instructors review possible projects for inclusion in spring courses. Following additional research, final project is selected and organization is contacted for initial meeting.
- **Weeks 1–4:** Instructor meets with Executive Director to determine specific needs and goals of project. Class participants are assessed as to ability in conjunction with course goals. Communication between instructor and executive director fine-tune project program and project schedule. This project was scheduled as the last project of the semester incorporating approximately four weeks.
- **Week 10:** Instructor contacts executive director to discuss any program changes. Meeting is scheduled between students, executive director and residents to introduce project.
- **Week 13:** Project Introduced, Student teams formed.
- **End of Week 14:** Class review of progress, Executive Director is contacted with student questions
- **End of Week 16:** Final project is presented to Executive Director

Steps for Implementation

Clients:
- must understand the unique nature of service-learning
- must be willing to work with students
- must be willing to be educated
- must recognize a give and take relationship
- outcomes must be win/win
- needs must be met

Students:
- must understand and believe design can be an impetus for change

- must accept responsibility for their actions as a designer and a member of society
- must be taught and led; this isn't a "trial by fire" exercise
- begin to understand design as a profession

Professors:
- must maintain objectivity between the classroom and the boardroom
- must understand out time is limited
- Does the project meet course outcomes?
- Does the product meet client needs?
- Are students learning? What specifically?

Outcomes/Assessment

This project resulted in a class compilation effort composed of specific design guidelines for the proposed facility bound in an 8.5" X 11" document as well as an 11" X 17" bound document including design solutions based upon the guidelines.

For service-learning to be truly effective, students must be engaged in some form of journaling and response based upon their experiences. A series of open-ended questions were proposed to the students based upon their perceptions of homelessness prior to their involvement as well as after the completion of the project. Additionally, a comprehensive survey is conducted by the service-learning office regarding the students' experiences with the project. Unequivocally, initial student perceptions were considerably altered. The experience of having real clients was unique, providing education a classroom alone cannot offer. Students overwhelmingly expressed satisfaction in the project, an increased understanding of societal issues, and a deeper desire to further explore areas in which they can use their skills and knowledge to benefit their communities.

Formal project assessment was achieved through a standardized grading sheet designed based upon specific project objectives.

Conclusion

Design students provide a resource that most non-profits and service organizations cannot afford but desperately need. Utilizing service-learning with design creates a win-win situation. Service-learning is an invaluable resource for studio instruction and a connection to community important for all designers.

HOW WE MADE THINGS BETTER IN MEDICAL EDUCATION: FROM SERVICE DELIVERY TO SERVICE- LEARNING

LIZ WOLVAARDT, JULIA BLITZ, AND GERDA BENDER
UNIVERSITY OF PRETORIA

Keywords: medical students, public health, primary care, healthcare, medical educators

Introduction

The purpose of higher education in South Africa should be not only "education for the market place" but also "education for good citizenship." This is vital for medical education in a resource-limited country under pressure to produce and retain skilled professionals for the public good.

The key challenge facing medical educators who wish to adopt a service-learning strategy is that the recent history of medical teaching is dominated by large group didactic sessions. Any interaction with patients and the community is sporadic and focuses on developing the students' medical skills while service providers and the community are passive enablers of this learning experience. In our health sciences setting, the long history of students providing service as part of their practical requirements distorts discussions about service-learning as a teaching and learning strategy. To change from service delivery to service-learning we have implemented an integrated curriculum model for service-learning. The focus is to demonstrate the "Plan, Act and Evaluate" of using the specific curriculum model to integrate service-learning in a fifth-year medical module.[1]

Project Description

At the University of Pretoria, Faculty of Health Sciences, one of the fifth-year medical modules1 is a collaborative effort between two academic schools in the same faculty. The module deals primarily with clinical skills in ambulatory family medicine and an understanding of the South African healthcare system. The moderate dissatisfaction among the academic staff, particularly with the teaching strategy, was the impetus for the changes described in this article.

---

1. The term 'module' can be replaced with the term 'course' in the USA context. Academic, undergraduate and postgraduate program can be replaced with a study course in the USA context.

This paradigm shift from service delivery to service-learning is reflected in the subtitle of the module, "Making things better," as the intention was that a service-learning module could make things better for the stakeholder groups of students, academic staff, service providers and the community.

Project Timeline

This project was implemented over a standard semester from January to May 2008.

Preparation (Plan). The 200 medical students were divided into four subgroups of 50 for the four-week module. These four subgroups worked in sequence so that there was never more than one group at a service-learning site (clinic) at any given time. As long-standing partnerships already exist between the university and the public sector, the placements were easily facilitated.

As the placement is relatively short, a single clinical topic (type 2 diabetes) was chosen as the illustrative disease for the care of patients with chronic diseases.

Students had seven preparatory sessions in their subgroups before going out to the service-learning placements. This orientated them to the sites as well as ensuring that they had revised the skills necessary for their clinical and non-clinical work. The sessions covered the following topics:

Personal skills: preferred learning styles and communication; introduction to teamwork skills, and reflection.

Technical briefings: the academic, service-learning and personal growth objectives of the module; an introduction to the South African healthcare system and quality improvement.

Clinical skills: revision, peer teaching and self-assessment of clinical skills essential for the management of patients with diabetes.

Steps for implementation

Implementation   (Act). The service-learning sites were primary healthcare clinics serving the local community. The 11 sites varied slightly in their capacity regarding infrastructure and learning opportunities, so smaller sites had two students and larger sites 12 students. Primary healthcare clinics were chosen as the ambulatory care sites. Before this block, the students' clinical exposure had been predominantly in academic hospitals.

The three-week period spent by each student at one site enabled the possibility of team relationships to develop. Students completed 64 hours of service-learning which was

structured to include clinical and non-clinical components. Clinical components included substantive patient consultations under the direct or indirect supervision of the clinic doctor or primary healthcare nurse.

Non-clinical components required students to investigate the clinic's operational management; health program; or a community/NGO service doing prevention and/or care. Each of the groups also conducted a quality improvement project that they and the clinic staff had jointly identified. Each successive group implemented a subsequent step of the project cycle. Students were encouraged to focus on projects that would address a real need and could feasibly be completed by the fourth group.   Examples of the projects include the creation of health promotion material, health promotion sessions at the local schools and repair of equipment.

Academic facilitators visited the students to facilitate the learning experience. They also assessed each student's competence at conducting a consultation with a patient, and gave immediate feedback and suggestions for improvement if necessary. Administrative staff dealt with operational issues and communication, and clinic managers were the local resource for students. A key success factor was a single liaison person that represented the interests of the service-providers and who facilitated the placements.

Besides the individual reflections, students participated in facilitated exercises for group reflection (before, during and after the placement), where issues of learning and service were discussed.

Outcomes/Assessment

Assessment and evaluation (Evaluate). Various assessment methods were used. Student's self-assessed their competence with the relevant clinical skills, a mentor from the Department of Family Medicine assessed the students' consultation competence; members of the clinic team completed the mini-Peer Assessment Tool; students' clinical knowledge was assessed using a computer-based multimedia test; their experiences of service-learning was captured in their reflection portfolios; the students submitted handover quality improvement reports and

Academics with an interest in educational strategies are the most likely change agents who could make the small shifts that would make a difference.

they did a group presentation of their findings on the non-clinical components.

All the stakeholders gave evaluations of the module to ensure that there was sufficient breadth of information to make appropriate adjustments for when the module is run again next year. The students evaluated the outcome of the module through semi-structured questionnaires as well as individual and group reflections. Service providers gave feedback via questionnaires. Academic staff participated in a focus group discussion to make suggestions for future improvements to the module, such as greater integration of theory and practice, mentorship for students, better alignment of the clinics' needs to the university's academic needs, and enhancing reflective engagement.

Conclusion

Health sciences faculties have a rich potential for contributing to good citizenship by transforming service delivery into service-learning, but the initial changes have to come from within. Academics with an interest in educational strategies are the most likely change agents who could make the small shifts that would make a difference. It is essential to share the lessons learnt and the outcomes of the project with colleagues to encourage others to reassess their teaching methodologies. Evaluations obtained from all the stakeholders confirmed that the service-learning used in this module did enhance students' sense of social responsibility and their integrative and reflective learning, and met the needs of the clinics.

Academics with an interest in educational strategies are the most likely change agents who could make the small shifts that would make a difference.
It is essential to share the lessons learnt and the outcomes of the project with colleagues to encourage others to reassess their teaching methodologies.

The Teaching of Research and
Other "Tools of the Trade"

Introduction

Robert G. Bringle
Indiana University-Purdue University Indianapolis

When I discuss civic engagement to higher education audiences, I always display and discuss the Venn diagram in Figure 7.1 (Bringle, Games, & Malloy, 1999). This figure is useful because it bases the analysis of civic engagement on the three areas of faculty work: teaching, research, and service. Much of faculty work takes place on campus, but it illustrates how civic engagement is teaching, research, or service in and with the community, not just service (Bringle, Hatcher, & Holland, 2007). The figure is also useful because it situates service-learning as the intersection of teaching and service, demonstrating how service-learning has the dual purposes of meeting the learning objectives of the course and also being beneficial to the community. Similarly, the intersection of service and research, participatory action research, has the dual purposes of meeting the scholarly interests of the faculty and also being beneficial to the community. Every time I present this figure, I am quick to point out that, when Rich Games and I drew the diagram, we both knew that it did not represent the triple intersection of teaching, research, and service, even though we knew that it could exist. We did not draw the figure to include that element because it would not clearly represent other aspects of civic engagement in the figure. Nevertheless, as I point out to all my audiences, the triple intersection of teaching, research, and service in and with the community is the most integrated type of civic engagement and it can exist. That is, a service-learning class on participatory action research can be conducted in which students engage in participatory action research with the community partners in order to learn research skills and other course content, the research is beneficial to the community, and the research also makes a scholarly contribute to the discipline or the profession.

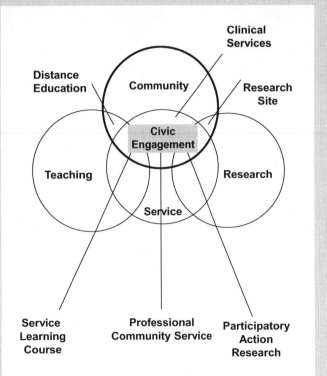

Engagement of Faculty Work in and with the Community

Figure 7.1. Civic Engagement as Faculty Work in the Community (adapted from Bringle et al., 1999b, p. 5).

All practitioners of service-learning understand the integral role that reflection plays in providing the indispensible mechanism for learning to occur. Eyler, Giles, and Schmiede (1996) note its essential role, "It is critical reflection...that provides the transformative link between the action of serving and the ideas and understanding of learning" (p. 14). The entries in this book and service-learning practice across the nation illustrate that reflection has many different forms that help students learn from their experiences. However, all reflection may not be equally effective in fostering student learning. Eyler et al., (1996) note that reflection "need not be a difficult process, but it does need to be a purposeful and strategic process" (p. 16). Bringle and Hatcher (1999) posit that reflection activities should (a) clearly link the service experience to the course content and learning objectives; (b) be structured in terms of description, expectations, and the criteria for assessing the activity; (c) occur regularly during the semester so that students can develop the capacity to engage in deeper and broader examination of issues; (d) provide feedback from the instructor so that students learn how to improve their critical analysis and reflective practice; and (e) include the opportunity for students to explore, clarify, and alter their personal values (Hatcher & Bringle, 1997). Bringle, Hatcher, and Muthiah (2004) also found that three characteristics of reflection independently predicted course quality: (a) reflection activities that clarified personal values, (b) reflection activities that were a regular part of the course, and (c) reflection activities that were structured with clear guidelines and directions.

To bring all of these points together, the entries in Chapter 7 of this volume illustrate how reflection is important to the design of optimal service-learning courses. Furthermore, many of the entries go beyond this and show how service-learning provides an excellent vehicle for teaching about research. To add a research component to a service-learning course creates a component that aligns very well with the qualities of good reflection: it links theory and practice, it is a highly structured activity that provides regular opportunities for feedback as the research is developed, and it allows the students to explore not only the technical aspects of the work but also the civic aspects. Furthermore, it provides a meaningful and authentic way to teach research skills and to do so in ways that benefit the community. This creates a very powerful pedagogy that more instructors need to explore.

Conclusion

I admire the creativity of the educators who have contributions in this chapter; they demonstrate the myriad of ways in which community service can enhance different kinds of courses. They also demonstrate imaginative approaches to building community partnerships, teaching research, designing effective courses, detailing learning objectives, and being beneficial to communities.

References

Bringle, R. G., Games, R., & Malloy, E.A. (Eds.) (1999). *Colleges and universities as citizens.* Needham Heights, MA: Allyn & Bacon.

Bringle, R. G., Hatcher, J. A., & Holland, B. (2007). Conceptualizing civic engagement: Orchestrating change at a metropolitan university. *Metropolitan Universities,* 18(3), 57-74.

Bringle, R. G., & Hatcher, J. A. (1999). Reflection in service-learning: Making meaning of experience. *Educational Horizons,* 77(4), 179-185.

Hatcher, J. A., Bringle, R. G., & Muthiah, R. (2004). Designing effective reflection: What matters to service-learning? *Michigan Journal of Community Service-learning,* 11(1), 38-46.

Eyler, J. S., Giles, D. E., & Schmiede, A. (1996). *A practitioner's guide to reflection in service-learning.* Vanderbilt University: Corporation for National Service.

Hatcher, J. A., & Bringle, R. G. (1997). Reflections: Bridging the gap between service and learning. *Journal of College Teaching,* 45, 153-158.

PROVIDING REFWORKS TRAINING FOR THE UNIVERSITY LIBRARY

TEENA A. M. CARNEGIE
EASTERN WASHINGTON UNIVERSITY

Keywords: technical communication, library, technology training, peer-to-peer instruction, writing procedures

Introduction

For this service-learning project, teams of students from an introductory technical communication course partner with the university library to provide training to other students. The project meets the needs of the library building connections with the university community. As a Benton foundation report on libraries notes, libraries can "provide a forum through which community members interact with each other, both through the use of meeting space and through the collection, dissemination, and implementation of information" (1996).

Current research, however, suggests that for many students, the library is losing its relevance. In the Benton Foundation study, focus groups "placed libraries at the fringes of modern life" (1996). A survey conducted at a regional, university library showed that this perception of decreasing relevance was prevalent among undergraduates. When asked how often they used library resources, only 20% said they used the library on a daily basis.

Concerned, the library consulted with faculty. The faculty concluded that to remain relevant, the library needed to foster interactive relationships, serve as a focal point for university intellectual life, stimulate vital campus culture and life, and support faculty research. Amongst the objectives for achieving these goals, the faculty recommended the following:

- collaborate with faculty to build information literacy skills
- increase and update faculty and student knowledge of library services
- engage faculty and students in actively using the library
- help faculty incorporate library use into the curriculum

This service-learning project was designed to address these four objectives and to meet the library's need to provide training for an online service called RefWorks. RefWorks is a citation management program that allows students to record reference information from various indexes and databases, incorporate those references into essays, and create bibliographies.

While addressing community-defined needs, service-learning must also meet course objectives. In this project, students create a series of technical communication documents, conduct a 50-minute training workshop (both a trial session and a final session), and write and present a reflective report. The project is effective for enabling students to learn the following objectives:

- collaborating with others to manage, complete, and deliver instructions and training
- analyzing audiences' needs
- demonstrating effective design and communication of technical information
- delivering informative and professional oral presentations

Project Description

This project is designed for one ten-week quarter. In the first three weeks, the teams develop a project proposal. The proposal analyzes the library's needs, outlines how the workshop will meet these needs, details the tasks required to complete the project, assigns team members to tasks, and indicates when tasks will be completed. The proposal is approved by the faculty and the librarians, constituting the service-learning contract for the project.

In the third week, the teams write a letter or formal e-mail to invite an instructor to bring a class to the training session. Inviting other classes guarantees an audience for each workshop. In the past, open workshops, even if well-advertised, have had poor attendance. To facilitate the invitation process, the course instructor identifies classes and asks the designated instructor to participate prior to the start of the project.

In the fourth and fifth week, students learn the RefWorks program, so they can teach others. Each student writes instructions for one RefWorks' task. Teams combine the instructions to create a

> The RefWorks project teaches students how to work together to effectively communicate technical information to a specific audience, and it demonstrates to students the central role of the library in the culture and life of the university community.

unified reference guide that participants can use during and after the workshop.

In the sixth week, each team creates an evaluation form to assess the effectiveness of their workshop. Teams also create a script to coordinate the workshop activities and create PowerPoint presentations to introduce and conclude their workshop. In the seventh week, teams present trial workshops, receiving feedback from their peers, the librarians, and the faculty. In the eighth week, teams present the final workshop to the invited instructor's class. The workshops are interactive with participants following a live demonstration given by team members.

Finally, in weeks nine and ten, students write a reflection/recommendation report. In the report, students assess if they were successful in meeting the community's needs. They report on how the project did or did not enhance their learning; what they learned about writing and presenting technical information and working in teams. Students combine material from their reports to create a final team presentation, which they deliver to their peers.

Steps for Implementation

To implement this project, instructors will need to (a) verify that the university library subscribes to RefWorks, (b) determine if the library needs training workshops, (c) identify a librarian who is both familiar with the program and willing to participate in service-learning, and (d) identify and schedule training facilities (a computer lab with reliable online access, LCD projector, and computers for participants). If these four criteria are met, instructors will need to familiarize themselves with the RefWorks program

and contact other instructors to request the participation of their class in the workshop (classes should be scheduled concurrently).

Outcomes/Assessment

Students are assessed based on criteria established for each of the documents they produce and for the presentations they deliver. In addition, students complete an assessment of their collaboration and of the service-learning project. The librarians also complete an assessment of the project. Overall, students view the project as an effective and engaging approach for learning technical communication. The librarians also view the project as beneficial.

Conclusion

The RefWorks project supports both the learning objectives for the technical communication course and the objectives from the library's action plan: it teaches students how to work together to effectively communicate technical information to a specific audience, and it demonstrates to students the central role of the library in the culture and life of the university community. In addition, the project is sustainable: the influx of new students each year means an ongoing need for training. This project could also be adapted for other online services offered by the library.

Reference

Benton Foundation (1996). *Buildings, books, and bytes: Libraries and communities.* Washington, D.C.: Benton Foundation.

Teaching research skills through service-learning

Brenda Moore
Texas A&M University-Commerce

Keywords: social work research, community assessments, research skills, research methods, needs assessment

Introduction

Service-learning has become institutionalized in many programs of higher education, but at our university, we only offer a few courses that include a service-learning component. However, in the field of social work, service-learning is a natural fit with our profession's commitment to service. So, in the spring of 2006, a partnership was formed with our community's United Way to implement a service-learning project to enhance undergraduate social work students' learning of research skills and provide United Way with their

requested community assessment to help them establish funding priorities and guide their allocations process.

Project Description

The course instructor for the Research Methods for Social Work class was contacted by the United Way Board President and the agency's Executive Director about the possibility of using students to conduct a community needs assessment. This initial contact provided the impetus for subsequent meetings to plan and develop the project. It was decided that input would be sought from community agencies, elected officials, school administrators, and the general community on their perceptions of community needs.

Project Timeline

There were almost 50 students in two sections of this 15-week class, which met on Mondays, Wednesdays, and Fridays for 50 minutes. The United Way Board President, Executive Director, and another member of the board presented the project to the students during the first week of class. This provided an opportunity to impress upon the students the importance and value of this project to United Way. The organization funded about 20 agencies that provided a wide array of services, but did not have any clear guidelines or criteria for their funding decisions. The community assessment would provide the board with some direction of perceived importance of community needs. The meeting between the students and the United Way representatives allowed the students to ask questions, brainstorm, and begin to take ownership of the project.

During the second week of class, the students began to research what other United Ways were doing for community assessments and various surveys that were used for collecting data. Some class time was devoted to sharing information, continued brainstorming about how to carry out the project, and identifying what information would be important to collect. During the third week, the class had narrowed down the specific tasks and student assignments were made.

As a group, students developed a survey instrument that would be used for interviews with key informants and the public. Each student was assigned two to three key informants (health and social service agency personnel, elected officials, school administrators, etc.) to complete survey interviews with. Students were also required to obtain secondary data from various communities reflected in United Way's catchment area on demographics and key social problems. The third component of data collection involved scheduling times to go to Walmart in two different communities to conduct public surveys. Students decided that in our rural area, there was a fairly representative sample of the population who shopped at Walmart. Permission was obtained from the Walmart managers and the students willingly solicited Walmart shoppers for their input in completing surveys. There were two bilingual students who translated the public surveys into Spanish for non-English speaking shoppers. A total of 102 key informant surveys and 80 public citizen surveys were completed.

Throughout the course, specific research content was continually linked to various aspects of the community assessment project. After the data was collected, the students then coded the data, entered it into SPSS (software for data analysis), and did some initial analyses by the end of the semester.

Steps for Implementation

There were several critical steps to implementing this project. The first step involved contact with United Way prior to beginning the semester. This provided the instructor and the organization an opportunity to clarify expectations and responsibilities. The second step required having an organized plan for relating class content with the project. As students were carrying out various activities, these were purposely linked to relevant course content (and vice versa). A third step focused on spending time every week assessing progress and learning objectives. Related to this was the importance of monitoring interactions of students with outside professionals (key informants) via phone calls and e-mails. This monitoring function provided some quality assurance and validity to the information brought back by the students.

Outcomes/Assessment

Student learning and growth was assessed through students' qualitative and quantitative responses on class evaluations. Students reported enjoying the project and benefiting from using their social work communication skills while learning research skills. They liked networking with professionals in the social service community through their key informant surveys.

In addition to student learning, United Way provided feedback on the project. They scheduled a special board meeting for the presentation and discussion of findings. Each of the board members expressed appreciation for the work of the students and the benefit of the data. Their plan was to use the findings from the community assessment in their subsequent funding discussions the following year.

Conclusion

This was an extremely valuable learning experience, for both the students and the instructor. It was time consuming in terms of project design and implementation; however, it was worth the effort because of the reported learning outcomes for the students and the benefit to United Way.

The instructor also learned that good planning, organization, and time management are essential, especially when working within the constraints of an academic semester.

After completing this project, the instructor realized how important it was to make the various components a requirement for all students. For example, not all students were required to conduct the public surveys. Some of the students were allowed to research secondary data instead. However, after completing the project, all of the students would have benefited from the survey experience. The instructor also learned that good planning, organization, and time management are essential, especially when working within the constraints of an academic semester. Judgments were required weekly regarding how much class time to spend on course content versus processing the field-based learning experiences of conducting the research. And ultimately, the class ran out of time before concluding the project, which resulted in the instructor having to put together and present the final report. Overall, it was a wonderful experience and there are plans to conduct a follow-up needs assessment for the United Way every three years.

QUALITATIVE METHODS IN THE SERVICE OF LEARNING

NICOLE L. JOHNSON
MOUNT UNION COLLEGE

Keywords: qualitative methods, nonviolence, religious studies

Introduction

In a service-learning workshop I attended years ago, and during a rather contentious group discussion of what constitutes "true" service-learning and what does not, one participant stated: "Well if everything is service-learning, then nothing is!" While I have come to agree with this statement, I also believe that "true" service-learning in higher education, in simple terms, can be any activity which at least (a) provides service of some kind to some intended person or group of people and (b) provides a unique and concrete type of learning that a student will not likely find in the classroom.

While initially I was a bit skeptical of my own idea for the service-learning project described below, conversations with students along with their written reflections prove the project's nature as an authentic service-learning project based on the simple guidelines above. This project is unique in its use of qualitative methods and in its service not directly to a particular demographic of needful people, as service-learning is normally conceived, but to those individuals who regularly work for and on behalf of that broader demographic.

Project Description

In my upper-level Religious Studies seminar, *RE400: Theologies of Nonviolence,* students were challenged by course materials to consider nonviolence as a comprehensive and intentional lifestyle choice, which moves beyond the conception of nonviolence merely as a political position on issues of war and peace. To that end, I designed an assignment that asked students to do the following:

1. Choose a local organization from a list of "Community Partners" previously established by Mount Union College's Office of Service-Learning;

2. Contact and personally interview a volunteer or paid employee at that organization;
3. Submit a 500-word reflective report of the conversation, describing whether and how the individual interprets her or his work as contributing to broader understandings and efforts toward nonviolence.

The overall goal of the project was to broaden and, to some degree, concretize students' perceptions of nonviolence through the interpretations of people who actually work against violence in its various manifestations. For example, in what ways does the mission of a faith-based no-kill animal shelter potentially reflect a broadly-conceived nonviolent worldview? How might an after-school tutoring program for inner-city kids confront the violence of an urban context and, through education, encourage children to seek a better path for their lives? These and similar types of questions formed the rationale for the project.

Project Timeline

The project was easily completed within one semester. To assist students in avoiding procrastination, firm deadlines were provided for each step of the process. Confirmation of an interviewee, location, and time was due from each student by March 1, with reflective reports of the interview due in mid-April. This timeframe gave students all of March and the first two weeks of April to conduct their interviews, and left time at the end of the semester for class discussion and reflection on the experience.

Steps for Implementation

A. Approval from Human Subjects Committee
Most institutions require approval from a Human Subjects Committee for any project which asks students to gather data in the public realm. Because the interview questions

did not cover sensitive or highly personal topics, the project was easily approved by the HSC.

B. Generating Interviewee Options

The next step involved providing a list of local organizations from which students could choose an interviewee. Thankfully, my institution maintains an Office of Service Learning, where the current Director keeps an updated list of local "community partner" organizations that are open to involvement with our students.

C. Designing the Interview Grid

In recognition of the fact that most undergraduate students are terrified of conducting a personal interview, parts of several class sessions in February were devoted to brainstorming and developing an interview "grid" of guided questions that each student would utilize in the interview. During this time we also practiced interviewing techniques such as transitioning, moving a side-tracked interviewee back to the original question, and following-up on potentially important insights. By the time they set out to conduct their interviews, students were sufficiently confident in their interviewing abilities.

D. Conducting the Interviews

Students were on their own to conduct the actual interview. I was careful to impress upon students prior to the interview that their goal was not to persuade the individual that her or his work qualifies as the work of nonviolence, but to investigate how people in this line of work actually think about their own jobs.

E. Student Reflection

Finally, students were required to submit a 500-word reflective report of their conversations. Students were asked to summarize their conversations and to describe whether and how the individual interpreted her or his work as a contribution to the work of nonviolence. These reports were brought to class and formed the basis for our reflection session toward the end of the semester.

Outcomes/Assessment

Based on this conversation and the reports themselves, it is clear that this project impacted both students and community partners in significant ways. In their written and oral reflections, students noted feeling genuinely moved by their interviewees' passion for their line of work and for the people they serve. The assignment also made tangible the classroom concepts that were more abstract and theoretical. One student suggested that in the future, the project should be implemented earlier in the semester in order to help students grapple with the more abstract materials in the classroom. Of particular interest to me was that a few of the stu-

dents, supporting their arguments with course materials, felt confident in interpreting the work of their interviewees as reflective of a nonviolent worldview and lifestyle even if the interviewee did not like the term "nonviolence" and did not describe her or his work that way. The assignment allowed students to delve further into classroom materials, and to make comparisons and connections that they would otherwise not have had the opportunity to make.

> ...it is clear that this project impacted both students and community partners in significant ways. Students noted feeling genuinely moved by their interviewees' passion for their line of work and for the people they serve. The assignment also made tangible the classroom concepts that were more abstract and theoretical.

Second, the assignment provided an opportunity for the interviewees themselves to reflect on their current jobs, which proved reaffirming for these individuals. A majority of students reported that through the course of the conversation, their interviewees mentioned appreciating the opportunity to reflect with some intentionality on the nature of their work, which in turn led them to feel proud about or otherwise renewed in their current positions. This comes as no surprise to practitioners in the field of qualitative research, which recognizes the transformative potential of intentional reflection involved in in-depth qualitative interviewing. And yet it was meaningful for students to see that they were in fact providing an important service in the midst of seeking to increase their own learning.

Conclusion

The uniqueness of this service-learning project lies in its focus on service to and learning from a somewhat neglected population—the individuals who regularly volunteer or work for social service organizations. As an experiment in service-learning which utilizes qualitative methods, this project was successful both in providing a service to these individuals and in providing a concrete learning opportunity for students as they grappled with theoretical ideas in the classroom.

▕▏▎▍▌▋▊▉█▏▎▍▌▋▊▉█▏▎▍▌▋▊▉█▏▎▍▌▋▊▉█▏▎▍▌▋▊▉█▏▎▍▌▋▊▉█▏▎▍▌▋▊▉█▏▎▍▌▋▊▉█

COLLABORATING WITH COMMUNITY PARTNERS ON COURSE DESIGN: FROM INCEPTION TO DELIVERY TO FOLLOW-UP

NANCY ZACHAR FETT, LISA R. GRINDE AND MAGGIE W. BAKER
LORAS COLLEGE

Keywords: community partnerships, course design, advisory board, reciprocity, experiential, poverty, simulation exercise

Introduction

How does one attempt to impact a complex societal issue while simultaneously trying to educate and inspire undergraduate students to be catalysts for future social change? At Loras College in Dubuque, Iowa, an interdisciplinary undergraduate course has been developed that focuses on researching the plight of the working poor, while utilizing a community partner advisory board in a transformative manner.

Utilizing community partner advisory boards to assist program development in higher education has become more common in recent years. These collaborative partnerships allow professors and programs to enlist the assistance of experts in the field to assure that they are teaching and researching the most current data and programming in the field, are on track with realistic practices, and are addressing all of the facets of the most pertinent issues. While beneficial in many respects, too many of these relationships are linear and transactional with a focus on utilitarian purposes rather than being built with a spirit of reciprocity.

In response to a call for experiential courses for the inaugural three-week January term at Loras College, the authors developed a plan to design a course focused on plight of the working poor in the U.S., utilizing community partnerships in a more intentional and transformative manner. The vision was to design a course informed by the lived experiential text of the working poor population and the agencies working with them.

The course was completely designed in partnership with representatives from Dubuque community-based organizations (CBOs). The result was a community-based undergraduate endeavor that (a) respected and relied upon CBO voices in course design from inception to post-assessment and on-going course revision (b) provided an opportunity for faculty, students and community partners to be active learners and thoughtful contributors, and to work collaboratively to create a path to social change in their community.

Project Description

Ten community professionals in related fields were invited to serve as the advisory board for the new course entitled, *The Working Poor.* The board members, along with the two

faculty teaching the course, met on a monthly basis over the course of the ten months prior to the first offering of the course. In the initial meetings board members and the two professors shared, brainstormed, and discussed ideas on how to present each of the courses' main topics in an engaging and understandable approach for the students. Later meetings focused on structuring the content and experiential pieces by converging the ideas brought forth throughout earlier meetings. Board input was instrumental in the formation of the key components of the course, including the community-based and service-learning components. The board thoroughly critiqued each course assignment in terms of its usefulness and poignancy due to their intense desire for the course to be reality-based, current, and experiential.

In between meetings, advisory board members read the text from the course, David Shipler's *The Working Poor* and sent afterthoughts, new materials, ideas they had discussed in agency staff meetings, and other information that might be useful as a technique or aid in steering a discussion or creating an experience. Most importantly, ownership of the course lay in everyone's hands as a collaborative team.

The team produced a syllabus, which included readings and related journal questions, guest speakers, documentaries, community-based learning activities, simulations, and group projects. In the second offering of the course, based upon results from course evaluations and assessment, a number of changes were made including, most noteworthy, the replacement of the main simulation project with a community-based learning project and the addition of a poverty simulation.

While the course was being taught, board members continued to impart their knowledge and experiences by being involved in various capacities: sharing knowledge as CBO representatives about their experiences serving with the working poor population and the mission and philosophy of their respective organizations, co-sponsoring a community-wide workshop board members and students attended together, referring consumers from agencies to serve as experts from the working poor population, assisting with publicity coverage, leading the final discussion, and assisting with overall course evaluation.

During the course, the students engaged in dialogue with members of the working poor over a meal the students had prepared. They engaged in conscious-raising activities such as serving a meal at a local shelter, taking public transportation, creating a monthly budget for a working poor family, and purchasing an interview outfit for $10. Students benefited from a number of high-quality guest speakers and powerful documentaries, and from participation in a three-hour poverty simulation. While students in the course taught the first time did visit a number of the CBOs that had representation on the advisory board (as part of a larger group simulation project), students in the class taught the second time around were engaged in a community-based learning experience by working with and completing a needed project for a CBO. Examples of student work included the creation of a logo and informational flyer for a new community health center and revamping, administering, and assessing the results of a consumer satisfaction survey for a mental health agency.

Project Timeline

November 2006–January 2007
Outlined idea for course; Proposed course for new January term

February 2007–March 2007
Recruited ten professionals in community to serve as advisory board

April 2007–December 2007
Monthly meetings of board and faculty; creation and constant collaborative revision of the syllabus

January 2008
The three week course is offered; Board members involved throughout

February 2008
Reconvene board members to analyze successes and challengesNoted possible revisions to future course offering

Summer 2008
Faculty worked on syllabus revision

November 2008–December 2008
Reconvened board for two meetings to critique revised syllabus

January 2009
Course taught for 2nd time; Board members involved throughout

Steps for Implementation

The first crucial step in facilitating this successful collaboration was to select ten professionals representing key CBOs serving this population in various capacities and covering a mix of experience. A letter of invitation was sent out ten months before our class was scheduled to be taught. All ten professionals readily accepted the invitation and were excited about the opportunity to be at the forefront of the course, not only as professional experts but as active participants in a collaborative endeavor they felt, would simultaneously benefit their organizations, educate students, future professionals and community members.

The second step was finding a convenient monthly meeting time and location. Prior to our first advisory board meeting, members were provided with the selected text from the course, a skeletal outline of the course, and the college's requirements for January-term courses. An agenda was sent a week in advance of each meeting and minutes of the meeting were shared after. The agenda included the topics to be discussed, relevant texts to be read, and two to three discussion questions. Having monthly meetings kept everyone engaged in the process, yet also respected busy schedules by allowing time to complete tasks and prepare for each meeting. E-mail allowed for continued dialogue and feedback to occur between professors and board members in between meetings.

One month after the course was completed, the board met to discuss and evaluate the successes and challenges of the current course and to consider changes and additions which would better serve all constituencies involved in this collaborative effort. The two faculty members worked with this information to revise the course over the summer and then convened the advisory board again in the fall to critique the re-designed course to be offered the following January.

Outcomes/Assessment

Assessment of this approach includes quantitative and qualitative data from the students, the professors, advisory board members, and additional community members, both professionals and members of the working poor population. Student learning was assessed via a pre-/post-formal essay exam, informal discussions, a pre-/post-Poverty Simulation evaluation, a final group presentation, and a final qualitative and quantitative course evaluation. These measures indicate student learning was greatly enhanced and deepened by the advisory board's expertise and knowledge of community resources and tools. Students especially valued the realistic picture they gained of the challenges, limitations and strengths of the working poor population through in-depth dialogues with members of this population. This learning was evident in their exams, presentations, and evaluations. The diversity of materials, assignments, and experiences from varying perspectives was key to the course's success as students reported multiple different "a-ha" moments. This course would not have been as rich and diverse if only designed by the two faculty members.

The collaboration between the two faculty (from psychology and social work) strengthened the learning outcomes for themselves and the students because it allowed each to reach beyond their own disciplinary paradigms when researching and examining this complex and multi-faceted issue in the community. Both faculty recognize that their professional knowledge and skills were improved through this process.

All of the advisory board members and the majority of additional professionals involved reported that this was a worthwhile, insightful and beneficial process. They reported that they felt included and that their lived experience was valued and utilized. Members of the advisory board identified and labeled changes in the relationship (between academia and CBOs). Several board members wrote in follow up evaluations that they felt a relationship that was previously exchange-based, (supervising students on-site), had evolved into to one that focused beyond utilitarian ends and was transformative in nature. An unplanned outcome for the advisory board members was the sharing of knowledge, ideas, including differences of opinion and agency perspectives, and resources amongst the board members. In addition, board members shared information from these discussions with other colleagues in their agencies and across an array of forums, including conferences and other board meetings.

Conclusion

The work of this advisory board before, during, and after was essential to the success of this course and depth of student learning. It is a useful model that can be applied to a variety of courses, an entire discipline or even a division of disciplines. By acknowledging the experiential texts available throughout our community and by fully integrating community members into the educational process and experience, we were able to enrich the learning and understanding of all involved- students, faculty, and community members.

EFFECTIVE SERVICE-LEARNING REFLECTION: HARNESSING THE POWER OF BLOOM'S TAXONOMY

ANNEMARIE VACCARO
UNIVERSITY OF RHODE ISLAND

Keywords: reflection, Bloom's taxonomy, reflection prompts, journaling, reflective writing, critical thinking

Introduction

Effective reflection is paramount to successful service-learning (Pascarella & Terrenzini, 2005). Yet, there is little available information to guide faculty in creating meaningful reflection assignments. The dearth resources may be due to the fact that course content and service projects vary by university, course, and professor. This chapter provides a framework which can be utilized by faculty from any discipline to enhance the depth and complexity of student reflection.

Project Description

The taxonomy described in this chapter has been used to teach a variety of service-learning courses including: sociology, women's studies, multicultural studies, and general education classes. While this chapter could describe any one of those classes in detail, it is intentionally written with a broader audience in mind. Thus, instead of a specific project, this chapter offers suggestions on how to implement effective reflection in any service-learning class.

Service-learning reflection is most insightful and moving when it combines personal experiences with educational depth and cognitive complexity. What is often referred to as "Bloom's Taxonomy" provides a useful framework for rich service reflection (Bloom, et al., 1956). The taxonomy suggests there are increasingly complex cognitive domains through which learning (and in this case, service reflections) can be structured and assessed. The taxonomy includes knowledge, comprehension, application, analysis, synthesis, and evaluation.

Project Timeline

College and high school instructors can implement the framework in any service course. However, it is most effective when used with long-term (as opposed to single day or short term) service projects. A lengthier timeframe allows for cognitive growth to occur over. Whether used in a semester- or year-long class, the following timeline issues should be considered:

- Prior to the start of the course: Collaborate with local agencies to create service opportunities. Construct a syllabus that embeds Bloom's taxonomy in course objectives and learning outcomes.
- First week of class: Review taxonomy with students.
- Ongoing: Shape assignments and class discussion to reflect the taxonomy; Revisit the taxonomy with students prior to each assignment.

Steps for Implementation

The initial step for implementation is to embed the taxonomy into course objectives and assignments. It is important for students to know that their service project is not merely about "doing good" in the community. It is also about comprehending, applying, analyzing, synthesizing, and evaluating course materials. The syllabus, course requirements, and class activities should reflect this emphasis. To implement this taxonomy, instructors should craft assignments (reflection papers, journals, and test questions) to reflect increasingly higher levels of the taxonomy over the course of the class. For instance, early reflection assignments should require students to apply course material to their service site while later assignments should require students to synthesize and evaluate.

Since this framework can be used for any course, other steps for implementation will vary by course and instructor. Of course, collaboration with community sites about initial placements, student performance reviews, and appropriate assessment should be considered when implementing any service course.

Outcomes/ Assessment

Service-learning experiences can be quite difficult to grade. This is especially true when student reflections rely solely on personal experience and opinion. By using the following framework, faculty can more objectively grade reflection papers. With Bloom's taxonomy, writing prompts can be constructed to encourage personal reflection and higher order thinking.

> It is important for students to know that their service project is not merely about "doing good" in the community. It is also about comprehending, applying, analyzing, synthesizing, and evaluating course materials.

In the following paragraphs, Bloom's Taxonomy is summarized and sample service-learning writing prompts are suggested. The four highest domains of Bloom's taxonomy are used to exemplify potential ways service-learning reflections can be structured. The lowest domains (knowledge and comprehension) are a prerequisite for adequate reflection, and thus are not included.

Application reflects a student's ability to comprehend a concept or abstraction and put it to use in a variety of given situations. In the case of service-learning, students are typically expected to apply course content to a particular service-learning site. Unfortunately, many service-learning reflections go no deeper than mere application of course concepts.

Sample Reflection Prompts
- What class concepts can be observed at the service-learning site?
- Select two to tree concepts from the textbook and describe the ways they can be applied to the service project.

Analysis happens when students break down a concept into its many parts. Good analysis also requires a student to compare arguments, conclusions, and factual data to a particular thesis. Students at service-learning sites have a unique opportunity to analyze course materials through action.

Sample Reflection Prompts
- What are the main components of the Theory X? How are they inter-related? What activities, events, or issues at the community site relate to Theory X?
- Reflect on the main topic of the chapter. How are the hypotheses and arguments from the textbook visible in the daily workings of the site? Describe anything in the community that is unexplained by, or counter to, course materials.

Synthesis requires students to take different concepts or ideas and arrange them into an understandable whole. It requires more than regurgitating parts of an already constructed whole- such as an already proposed theory or model. Instead, students must take seemingly incongruent concepts to form a new and unique whole.

Sample Reflection Prompts
- Reflect on the topics covered in Chapters X-Y. Compare and contrast the similarities and differences between these concepts to observations from the service project.
- Keep a reflection journal. Are there themes or trends in the reflections? Is there a level of congruence or incongruence between journal reflections and the essential aspects (mission, values, services) of the service site? In a visual representation, synthesize major course materials, service experiences, and the functioning of the service site?

Evaluation of particular theories, course materials, and service-learning sites is a standard part of many service classes. However, evaluation should be considered only after students have mastered course concepts, spent adequate time in the community, and synthesized the two.

Sample Reflection Prompts
- Given theories A, B, and C, which most effectively describes the workings of the service site? Explain why a particular theory is most effective and provide specific examples of policies, practices, or observations to support the argument.
- Discuss the shortcomings of theory. For instance, are there experiences or events that happened at the site that cannot be adequately explained by course theories? Why might this be?

Conclusion

Thoughtful and structured reflections are paramount to meaningful service-learning. Faculty can utilize the taxonomy suggested in this chapter to inspire cognitive growth and deep reflection in their students.

References

Bloom, B. S., Englehart, M. D., Furst, E. J., Hill, W. H., & Krathwohl, D. R. (1956). *Taxonomy of educational objectives. Handbook 1: Cognitive domain.* New York, NY: Longmans, Green.

Pascarella, E. T., & Terrenzini, P. T. (2005). *How college affects students: A third decade of research.* San Francisco, CA: Jossey-Bass.

STRATEGIES AND TECHNIQUES FOR IMPLEMENTING COMMUNITY-BASED RESEARCH SERVICE-LEARNING PROJECTS IN ADVANCED COURSES IN AREAS OF STUDY THAT ARE NOT TRADITIONALLY RELATED TO PUBLIC SERVICE

DR. BILLIE J. A. FOLLENSBEE
MISSOURI STATE UNIVERSITY

Keywords: community-based research (CBR), advanced courses, art history, community partners, civic responsibility

Introduction

While the implementation of service-learning projects has proven useful for enhancing teaching and learning in a wide range of lower-level college courses, service-learning programs are sorely under-utilized in the advanced courses of most academic areas. An important reason for this is that higher-level courses typically require research projects, but research opportunities available through service-learning are viewed as primarily appropriate to fields such as the social sciences, education, and political science, which conduct research on the performance, evaluation, and educational benefits of service work. Creative application of community-based research (CBR) service-learning, however, opens up invaluable opportunities for higher-level research projects in virtually any field.

In its most simple definition, CBR service-learning involves a course-appropriate service-learning research project that serves to promote social justice, done in collaboration with a community partner (CP) who expresses a need or desire for the project (Strand, Marullo, Cutforth, Stoecker, and Donohue 2003). Institutions with needs for advanced research exist in virtually all fields, and helping non-profit or public institutions of this type promotes social justice; alternatively, public dissemination of project results can promote social justice through education. By designing targeted, social-justice-oriented course projects that apply student re-

search to CP needs, instructors may create highly enhanced advanced curricula.

Project Description

Identifying and developing CBR course projects for advanced classes begins with locating potential CPs. In my case, as a professor of art history, I desired to offer an engaging course project for an advanced art of Africa course that would emphasize the importance of proper research and public dissemination of knowledge about African art and cultures. Because museums, galleries, and historical societies with financial means employ art historians to research their art and artifacts, I began by researching public and non-profit art institutions in the region. I located several with collections of African art, and upon contacting them, I found that these institutions are typically understaffed and would welcome gratis, professor-guided undergraduate research projects and public exhibits of their collections.

I arranged to borrow a collection of African art for one year and to store the collection at a secure facility on my university campus, where the students would have access to the objects upon request. I also arranged for an exhibit of the collection during the semester following the course.

I prepared my students for their service-learning projects by developing a course unit on museum practices and on researching and writing about art for museum exhibits and catalogs. After this training, the class was given a private viewing of the CP's collection and provided with the existing curatorial information.

Each student was then allowed to choose one of two final projects: S/he could either study and research an object, write exhibit text and a label, study the materials and methods for making the object, and create an accurate reproduction; or s/he could study and research five objects, write exhibit text and labels, and create a themed exhibit for the objects. To ensure that the students developed their projects appropriately and punctually, detailed guidelines were provided and the project was divided into three stages: (a) A project proposal and starting bibliography; (b) a mid-term research report; and (c) the complete final project. The students received detailed feedback after each stage, enabling them to correct initial problems and to produce high-quality final projects.

The following semester, I placed the student projects on display in my department. The CP's collection was placed on exhibit in a public gallery space on campus, along with the edited labels and exhibit texts researched and written by the students; this created an informative, educational exhibit of the collections for the university and the community. The collection was then returned to the CP, along with the exhibit labels, texts, and copies of the students' course projects.

Project Timeline

Developing and implementing this CBR course project requires approximately eight months to one year. As listed below, step 1 should take place three to six months before the course; steps 2-3, one to three months before the course. Steps 5-6 take place after the course.

Steps for Implementation

1. Begin identifying and approaching potential CPs. Explore CP needs/desires; develop appropriate research projects.
2. Arrange for student access to the research materials through either visiting the CP institution or borrowing the materials and arranging for student access at a secure facility.
3. Develop in-class training, detailed project guidelines, and feedback/guidance methods.
4. Implement the course.

5. Disseminate the project results to the CP and, if appropriate, the public.
6. Compile and review student reflections, course evaluations, and comments from the CP, the public, and colleagues. Revise and refine the course and project design.

Outcomes/Assessment

Several methods were used to assess the success of this CBR project. In addition to formal course evaluations, in their project proposals, students developed learning goals and proposed benefits for the CP and the public, and in their final projects, they reflected upon their successes, problems, and how the experience could be improved. A comment book was also placed in the exhibit, and I discussed the project results with the CP and with my colleagues. Reviews of the project from all parties involved were enthusiastically positive.

Conclusion

As advanced undergraduate art history course projects typically require students to conduct in-depth research of specific works of art, these CBR course projects closely correlated with traditional art history research projects. Further, the projects greatly enhanced learning by providing actual art for students to research hands-on and by requiring thoughtful, focused application of research to the practical, real-life situations of developing exhibit labels and texts. The students also developed personal civic awareness, as their research provided a concrete service to the CP, as well as a public, educational exhibit for the community that promoted understanding and appreciation of foreign cultures.

In sum, CBR is an invaluable resource for developing highly enhanced, applied advanced research projects in virtually any field, with the added benefits of promoting social justice, civic awareness, and improved academic-community relations. Similar applications of CBR service-learning in other advanced undergraduate courses can be modeled readily upon this example.

Reference

Strand, K., Marullo, S., Cutforth, N., Stoecker, R. & Donohue, P. (2003). Principles of Best Practice for Community-Based Research. *Michigan Journal of Community Service Learning*, 9(3), 5-15.

Creative application of community-based research (CBR) service-learning, however, opens up invaluable opportunities for higher-level research projects in virtually any field.

||||||||||||||||||||||||||||||||||||||||||||||||||||||||||||||||||||||||||||||||||||||||||||||||||||||||||||||||||||||||||||||||||||||||||||||||||||||||||||||||||||||||||||||||||||||||

CHECKLISTS FOR AN "ALL-OR-NOTHING" SERVICE-LEARNING PROJECT

KEN VOLLMAR
MISSOURI STATE UNIVERSITY

PETE SANDERSON
OTTERBEIN COLLEGE

Keywords: deliverables, productivity, goals, outcomes, planning checklist, production-enhancing software

Introduction

Service-Learning projects may be divided into two broad categories. The first type is an *"incremental-value"* project, in which students and community partners each directly benefit from the amount of time and effort expended. In the event of termination or redirection of the project, each party would have already benefitted from the time or material expended thus far. Project success is more or less a result of time-on-task.

Other projects are *"all-or-nothing"* projects, in which the project's success is dependent upon satisfactory completion of some defined, tangible product. In the event that the project is not completed as planned and scheduled, the S-L students as individuals will have learned from the positive and negative aspects of the project, but the community partner's mission or clients will not benefit from the expended effort. All aspects of an all-or-nothing project (such as goals, personnel, technology, duration, and support) must be determined at the start, and also must be correct and proportional to the other aspects of the project.

Computer Science projects are usually all-or-nothing projects because of notorious difficulty in completion of partially finished software by formerly uninvolved personnel. Recent Computer Science S-L projects have been "nearly successful" and "wildly successful." We believe the two projects are interesting in their illustration of the need to pay close attention to detail in all-or-nothing projects.

Project Description

The "nearly successful" project, a game for preschoolers to learn their phone numbers, was designed with particular attention to implementation difficulty and schedule. The preschooler users would move a photo of their own face through a maze toward the goal, which was the next successive digit of their phone number. As each digit was reached, the next digit popped up elsewhere. The game was age-appropriate, non-competitive, etc. University guidelines were followed for protection of the human subjects (the preschoolers), in that no S-L students or faculty had access to the preschooler's data, physical access to the preschool, etc.

The implementation was technically correct and met all known goals – but clearly there should have been at least one more consideration. When our team visited the preschool to present the software, the preschool students sat down together at the computer. They loved the game, but they were learning their friend's phone number! In the preschool setting, the project failed in the need to associate each student with only his/her own phone number.

In the "wildly successful" project, five S-L students partnered with the US Department of Agriculture's Natural Resources Conservation Service to write software for digital media storage. Their need was that thousands of digital photos were stored on many CDs, with no indexing or cataloging for later retrieval and use. Prior to use, the software would be subject to an inspection and certification process at the USDA's Washington, DC office. Students designed a solution largely using standard Java features but with additional database operations.

Project Timeline

The project was one component of a typical one-semester course. Software engineering practices include requirements, design, coding, and testing, which may be repeated. Several software development practices are possible while incorporating these steps.

Steps for Implementation

The factors that contributed to the success of the project:
- Community partner had a clear goal and supported S-L students well.
- Project was well-suited to the Computer Science course area.
- Project was the correct degree of difficulty and lent itself to Java code libraries.
- Community partner was flexible and willing to adapt project goals, and championed the software through the certification process.
- Students took "ownership" and were motivated to complete the project (including donation of time after the end of the S-L course).
- The requirement for software certification was an obstacle right up until the point it turned into an accomplishment.

Outcomes/Assessment

The following checklists can assist in the careful planning required by the nature of an all-or-nothing S-L project.

Checklist for Community Partners regarding a proposed S-L project

- ☐ Have the correct university departments been approached for this project?
- ☐ Are the capabilities of S-L students a good match for my organization's needs?
- ☐ Are my expectations of S-L students and faculty realistic?
- ☐ If completed on time, would this project fill my organization's need?
- ☐ Is the scope of the project flexible? Can the project be scaled back in the event of schedule problems?
- ☐ Have I disclosed any unusual needs or expectations of my organization?
- ☐ Is my organization committed to providing adequate support to the S-L project team?
- ☐ Is failure an option?

Checklist for students regarding a proposed S-L project

- ☐ Am I willing to commit to extra time required by this project?
- ☐ Have I accurately communicated to my instructor my level of knowledge, skills, and commitment regarding this project?
- ☐ Am I aware of the benefits to my own learning and portfolio of completion of this S-L project?
- ☐ Am I aware that the community partner has some need that will be met by this project and which will be unmet in the event of its failure?

Checklist for faculty regarding a proposed S-L project

- ☐ Is the project task appropriate to the course material?
- ☐ Will the project contribute to student learning for the course? How will the student learning experiences be assessed?

- ☐ What are the obstacles to successful completion? (For instance, lack of clear goals, partner site visitation restrictions, human subject research guidelines, health/safety/security, critical timeline or schedule, etc.)
- ☐ Is completion of proposed project by a team of S-L students realistic in the given schedule?
- ☐ Is it likely that the project can be completed despite typical difficulties?
- ☐ How will this project's implementation minimize the need for post-completion maintenance? Who is responsible for maintenance?

Conclusion

We believe that S-L projects that deliver products rather than services require particular attention to planning. The additional care in planning the S-L project will benefit both the students and the community partner by increasing the likelihood of project success.

References

Honnet, E. P. & Poulson, S. J. (1989). Principles of Good Practice for Combining Service and Learning. Reprinted by the National Service-Learning Cooperative Clearinghouse with permission from the Johnson Foundation, Inc. at http://www.servicelearning.org/instant_info/online_documents/service-learning_standards/principles_of_good_practice_for_combining_service_and_learning_a_wingspread_special_report/index.php.

Sanderson, P. & Vollmar, K. (2000). A primer for applying service learning to computer science. *ACM SIGCSE Bulletin*, 32 (1), 222 – 226.

A Tool-Kit for Service- Learning Partners. Missouri Service-Learning State Advisory Council. http://dese.mo.gov/divcareered/Service-Learning/Community-based_Organization_Toolkit.pdf. Also see a list of toolkits at http://www.servicelearning.org/instant_info/tool_kits/index.php.

We believe that S-L projects that deliver products rather than services require particular attention to planning. The additional care in planning the S-L project will benefit both the students and the community partner by increasing the likelihood of project success.

||||||||||||||||||||||||||||||||||||||||||||||||||||||||||||||||||||||||||||||||||||||||||||||||||||||||||||||||||||||||||||||||||||||||||||||||||

Successful integration of a university service-learning class into a community coalition

Sandra D. Byrd and David B. Byrd
Missouri State University

Keywords: community coalition, financial literacy, IRS, taxes, undergraduate and graduate education

Introduction

In this article, the successful integration of a university service-learning class into a community coalition will be discussed. The students in this class work with older adult volunteers and administrators of various community organizations to provide financial literacy and tax assistance to the most vulnerable members of the community.

Project Description

Undergraduate and graduate accounting students participate in a community coalition as part of integrated service-learning classes. The participation has been very successful with an estimated $38 million local economic impact since 2001. More than 200 service-learning students have provided over 20,600 hours of service to the community coalition. The number of individuals directly assisted by the coalition each year has increased from 500 in 2001 to over 48,000 in 2008.

In class, members of the community coalition work with faculty and discuss tax law related to low income and older adults, tax anticipation loans, interview techniques, privacy issues, communicating with clients who do not understand tax laws, and different cultural perceptions of U.S. tax law. Students have a project during the first weeks of class in which they do mock interviews, research tax law, and prepare tax returns. Each tax return is prepared by hand, and then on two different tax software packages. The students have to research and prepare the returns until the returns are accurate. As the semester progresses, the students work weekly with coalition members interviewing clients, researching tax law, preparing tax returns, providing financial literacy information and recording their impressions in their service-learning journal. Each tax return is reviewed for accuracy by a different student. This enables students to better understand tax and financial policy and their impact on individual taxpayers. Weekly, students participate in class by reflecting on problems they have encountered working with clients and their solution so that other students may learn from their experience. At the end of the semester all students do another project consisting of a mock interview, tax research and tax return preparation. They record in their journal the time it takes and insecurities they have with these projects both at the beginning and at the end of the semester.

At the end of the semester, each student turns in their journal and a reflection paper. All students have reported in their journals that it took them less than half the time to complete their projects at the end of the semester and they were much less insecure about actually researching and preparing a return and the accuracy of the return. End-of-semester reflection papers also discuss how much students have learned working with the coalition. Excerpts from student's reflection papers include the following:

- "This class gave me real work experience…and assured me that it is the field that I want to go into."
- "I learned how to communicate with a range of different people."
- "Changed my outlook on low income, English as second language and older adults …and the laws pertaining to them."
- "I learned how to ask questions."
- "I was able to interact with students and people in the community both old and young."
- "I closely touched American society. I know a lot more about culture, thought, etc."

Project Timeline

April: Meet to discuss community problems
June: Determine goals and objectives for current year project
July: Raise funds for current year project
September: Discuss participation opportunities with students
November: Distribute training material to student participants
January: Training and testing of student participants
February: Implement current year project

Steps for Implementation

1. Identify community problem that the use of service-learning students could help alleviate while contributing to the student's academic success. The community problem we identified was the very large population who could not understand tax laws and who needed assistance with financial literacy issues. The student academic problem identified was their need to learn to understand tax law, its effect on society and how to communicate with non-accountants. Service-learning

classes on Public Service Tax Accounting appeared to be the answer to both problems.

2. Determine if the problem could be solved by the university working alone, or if there is a need for a community coalition. We decided that while the university could provide services in this area working alone, the students would benefit more by working within a community coalition, interacting with older adult volunteers and community organization administrators. Our coalition presently has 15 member organizations.

3. Determine the role each member of the coalition will have in providing learning opportunities to the students.

4. Develop short-term and long-term goals and objectives. In our coalition, we started with the long-term goal to provide services and education to decrease financial illiteracy in our community and increase savings. The initial short-term goals were to provide free electronic tax preparation and free tax controversy assistance. Each year we are progressing toward the long-term goal.

5. Communications between coalition members is vital to the success of the coalition and to provide maximum learning opportunities for the students. Weekly e-mails are used in our coalition to coalition member organizations and students.

6. Assess the results of the services provided. We do not just assess the learning of the students; we also look at the numbers of individuals assisted and the quality of services provided. We want our students to learn the importance of providing not only service but quality service to low-income and older adult clients.

Outcomes/Assessment

An anonymous survey is administered each semester by the university service-learning office. Of the 50 students in these classes answering this survey in spring 2008, 100% stated their experience in this class "Would motivate them to participate in another service-learning experience"; 95% said that "Compared to regular classes, in this course I learned much more"; and 85% stated that "The service-learning project made the class discussion much more stimulating." Student evaluations of the course were also given anonymously by the School of Accountancy. The results for these classes in spring 2008 were above 4.7 on a 1 to 5 scale, with 5 being the top rating.

Conclusion

The successful integration of service-learning classes in a community coalition provides an excellent learning experience for students and a valuable service to the community.

||||||||||||||||||||||||||||||||||||||||||||||||||||||||||||||||||||||||||||||||||||||||||||||||||||||||||||||||||||||||||||||||||||||||||||||||||

CREATING AN ENGAGED PROGRAM: THE BENEFITS OF SERVICE INTEGRATION ACROSS THE CURRICULUM

DONALD A. RODRIGUEZ AND PILAR PACHECO
California State University Channel Islands

Keywords: service infusion, curriculum development, graduation requirement

Introduction

The Environmental Science and Resource Management (ESRM) discipline at California State University Channel Islands (CSUCI) is designed to be a true interdisciplinary major spanning the life sciences, physical sciences, and social sciences. Seventy-three percent of the courses taken toward degree are outside the major. This results in a variety of unique interdisciplinary course offerings involving water, international field studies, history, geography, chemistry, communication, biology, and political science.

Since the major is rather diffuse, integrating student effort into a cohesive program of study has been challenging and requires careful structuring to insure students "get what they came for." A strategy that we have used effectively has been the integration of service, in its various forms, throughout the curriculum.

Project Description and Timeline

Freshman Year: Volunteerism is used as a strategy to introduce students to service and the community based on their environmental interests. Students choose from a list of community partners with the expectation they complete 15 hours of service in the environmental community. Each of the community partner's mission ties to one or more of the chapters in the text. Students are given the latitude and the responsibility to select the organization, topic, and type of service that is of interest to them.

Sophomore Year: Students are directed to a range of community service activities that builds on the freshmen volunteer experience and interest. Students are organized into community service activities with the National Park Service (NPS) that directly articulates with the course components. The instructor works with the NPS to design a variety of community experiences that resolve management issues within the park units. Students may work on a variety of park projects under the supervision of the NPS.

Junior Year: Students are engaged with a range of field work projects that reflect individual and group for an array of community partners including the Coastal Conservancy, National Park Service, the Minerals Management Service, the U.S. Forest Service, and local water districts. Also the environmental field studies concept is integrated during their junior year (University 392 and ESRM 492) that allows students a level of immersion in national and international settings where community engagement is an integral part of the course.

Senior Year: The culminating senior capstone brings students' educational experience into sharp focus. Students shape their capstone project in combination with faculty and community partner mentors. This capstone experience reflects a complete immersion and often results in a community-based service-learning/research project that responds to a need of the community partner and the community. Essentially, the student moves from a model where the program directs the student experiences, to the student taking initiative for the learning experience that provides a high level of student and community engagement

This stepwise progression model allows us to move the service paradigm from "me and I," to "we and they." Our students' increased involvement of engagement provides built-in exposure to the community and to their interests; our community partners now view the University as a resource and our students as potential employees.

One of the benefits from this type of program has been a much clearer career development type of focus within the discipline. Since the discipline offers students a multitude of career options, immersion in the field and development of one's expertise is critical to a successful school to work transition.

Steps for Implementation

Utilizing Furco's (1996) experiential education continuum that "operationalizes" service as spanning volunteerism to internships, as a model, the ESRM discipline has created a stepwise progression of service that begins freshman year and continues throughout the students' tenure in the program. The utility of this strategy is two-fold: create an engaged program and provide increasing levels of community/civic engagement that enhances students' educational development.

One of the key elements for implementing this program is the establishment of a community advisory board. This advisory has served our students curricularly and professionally. More importantly, the board has reaffirmed that service-learning is an important core value of the ESRM program and has provided important external support for the program's outreach strategies.

Outcomes/Assessment

Table 7.1 illustrates the outcome and methods of assessment utilized within the program. This assessment structure is embedded in the program design and the data serves to evaluate the programmatic impact on student's academic performance and civic behaviors.

Table 7.1. The outcome and methods of assessment.

Student Outcomes	Assessment Method
1. Students will become increasingly knowledgeable about environmental issues and engaged in local, national, and international communities	Ongoing classroom reflection and critical thinking exercises.
2. Students will engage in a high level of community involvement where the goals include leadership roles in designing, initiating, implementing, and assessing environmental community based projects.	Professional peer mentors work with students and program faculty to design meaningful learning experiences and provide faculty with assessment and unique perspective on student performance.
3. Students will move from a program directed model to student initiated learning experiences.	Professional mentors attend student poster sessions and act as outside reviewers for student assessment. Rubrics are used to evaluate level of student performance
4. Students will have a clearer career focus within the discipline.	Student Service Learning Survey is administered at the end of each semester. Specific to this outcome students are asked, "As a result of my service-learning experience, I have a clearer idea of my educational/career goals." http://www.csuci.edu/servicelearning/studentresources.htm
5. Students will find a professional network through the ESRM program, allowing them to secure work in the field once they have graduated.	Outcomes assessment survey administered to program graduates at 3 year intervals to identify valuable program elements, and curricula strengths and weaknesses.

Conclusion

Utilizing Furco's model of service, as a continuum for experiential education, has allowed the ESRM program to build an engaged program. This cohesive infrastructure allows the major to develop a learning environment that builds upon itself, becomes incrementally more student focused, creates an environment conducive to learning and growth, and gives students the skills to be leaders in promoting and managing their own educational and civic growth within the program and the environmental community.

References

Furco, Andrew, (1996). *Service-Learning: A Balanced Approach to Experiential Education. Expanding Boundaries: service and Learning.* Washington DC: Corporation for National Service, pp. 2-6.

INVOLVING UNDERGRADUATE STUDENTS IN COMMUNITY-BASED RESEARCH

MARCIE COULTER-KERN
MANCHESTER COLLEGE

Keywords: education for conflict resolution, community-based research, research design, psychology, student research, correctional facilities

Introduction

Seven psychology students and their professor are collaborating with a community partner to study the impact of training inmates on how to resolve conflicts constructively. The training program is entitled "Productive Communication and Conflict," and the psychology students are analyzing its impact on more than 100 inmates in two county jails.

Project Description

Education for Conflict Resolution (ECR), a non-profit organization in Wabash County, provides mediation and conflict resolution services to a wide variety of individuals, schools, non-profit organizations and correctional facilities. One program conducted by ECR that has received considerable attention is a training program entitled "Productive Communication and Conflict." In this training program, correctional officers, inmates, and their families, participate in practical workshops that train them how to use non-violent methods of reducing conflict. Thus far this program has received considerable accolades. Correctional officers report fewer incidents of violence among program participants, and inmates report improvement with anger management and satisfaction with the training. Unfortunately, most of this data has been anecdotal, and ECR has lacked more systemic research to support the effectiveness of their program

Project Timeline

Community-based research takes place in community settings and involves community members in the design and implementation of research projects. Engaging students in this type of research promotes active learning and deeper engagement in course material through involvement in community issues. To get started, faculty need to explore potential agencies in the community that might benefit from their disciplinary expertise. The next step is to identify a class or group of students that could benefit from this type of research experience. For this particular project, a class in research design was chosen. Research Design I is a course that all psychology majors take, usually in their sophomore or junior year. In the current example, students in this course had the choice of two research projects, both of which promote active scholarship and meaningful connection with the course material. One of the choices was the community-based project with Education for Conflict Resolution in a prison population.

Community-based research takes place in community settings and involves community members in the design and implementation of research projects.

Students who participated in the ECR research found themselves changed by the experience. The relationships they developed with the community leaders were powerful in helping students sustain their involvement in research and awareness of community needs. Through the ECR project students had the opportunity to work closely with the Executive Director of ECR and the county sheriff. The advantage of offering students a choice in service-learning with research projects is that students are better able to embrace the project as their own and consequently find it more meaningful.

The project also had a profound effect on students' civic awareness and responsibility toward the judicial system. The students were aware that they were taking leadership in a research project that had a direct effect on rehabilitation programs, inmate recidivism, and even prisoners' relationships with their families.

During the course students learned to design and implement a research project, analyze data, and write a research report. In the case of the ECR project, class time involved learning research methods, becoming familiar with the "Productive Communication and Conflict" program, designing ways to measure the impact of the program, learning to quantify behavior, analyzing data, and presenting research findings.

Steps for Implementation

The following steps are important for creating a successful community partnership that furthers student learning and meets the needs in the community:

1. Identify community agencies that have research needs (such as programs evaluation and program impact studies).
2. Find community directors that are excited about working with students and are willing to spend time collaborating.
3. Develop close working relationships with community partners prior to the beginning of the semester.
4. Begin working on the project and consider potential obstacles in advance of student participation.
5. Involve students as early as possible in the planning of the research so they have a sense of ownership in the project.
6. Set aside time in class and labs to work on the project.
   a. Invite community partners to class.
   b. Encourage communication between students and community partners via email, meetings, and phone calls.
   c. Provide time for students to interact with participants.
   d. Walk students through the Institutional Review Board application process.
7. Encourage students to form small research groups (3–4 students) around a common research question.
8. Make daily connections between the research methods curriculum and the community-based project.
9. Help student develop abstracts and proposals to be submitted to appropriate research conferences.
10. Be sure to collaborate with partners to create research projects that clearly benefit the community partners.

Outcomes/Assessment

The major goals of this project are to engage students in learning while connecting them in the community through community-based research. The case discussed in this article focused on research in the social sciences but the same model can easily be implemented in other disciplines. The initial experience has been very successful. Students are better able to grasp abstract principles of research by applying them to real community problems. Students have learned more about community-based partners through the research than through participation in other service-learning experiences.

In order to evaluate ECR's program a mixed method program evaluation model was used that incorporated both qualitative and quantitative measures. After conducting the program evaluation we wrote a professional research report documenting the program's effectiveness. This report is currently being used by the ECR staff to apply for funding to expand the program to other correctional facilities.

Conclusion

Engaging college students in applied research provided benefits for both students and the community agency that we served. When students were able to see the immediate impact of their research in tangible and predictable ways they became committed to the intellectual and scientific process in a way that rarely happens when completing textbook research projects. In addition, students learned important skills that are transferable to many professional challenges that they will face in the future.

The community agency we served benefited from this type of project because they received the scientific resources that they needed to evaluate their programs. The additional time needed to construct a practical and applied research experience for students is worth the effort because the benefits are so substantial.

Engaging college students in applied research provided benefits for both students and the community agency that we served.

The research partnership model

Jeanette Harder
University of Nebraska at Omaha

Keywords: research, graduate-level, social work, incremental learning, research methods, human subjects

Introduction

Research Partnership is a service-learning model utilized to teach research and data analysis knowledge and skills to graduate students. It provides hands-on activities within an authentic context, group support and individual accountability, and structured and incremental learning opportunities. To date, this instructor has used this model six times, with 64 students and 14 community agencies and/or projects with very positive results.

Project Description

The *Research Partnership* model is used in teaching a graduate-level social work course entitled, "Research and Computer Applications." Using a service-learning approach, small groups of students partner with a community agency. Students examine the social problem being addressed by the program, conduct a literature review, write about research methodology, run data analyses to test their hypotheses, and formulate implications and recommendations. Students present their results and recommendations to the agency at the end of the semester through means of oral and written communication.

Project Timeline

The timeline of the *Research Partnership* model stretches from months before the beginning of the course to months after the conclusion of the course.

Steps for Implementation

Before the Course
1. The Instructor must develop professional relationships with administrators of community agencies.
2. The Instructor works with the community agency to prepare data in spreadsheet format, to understand variables, to clean the data, and to minimize missing data. An ideal dataset contains a client identification number, demographic data, service delivery data, and outcome data. IRB approval is not required as analysis is conducted on de-identified secondary data, the data is used for instructional purposes only, and results are presented only to the agency. If conference presentations or professional journal submissions emerge from the students' work, agency permission is obtained, and IRB approval is sought retrospectively.

During the Course
1. During the first and second class meetings, students are presented with project choices. Representatives from the community agencies come to speak with the class about their programs and data, and what they hope to gain. Students sign up to work with a particular dataset in groups of three to eight students. In so doing, an instructor may have two or three projects operating simultaneously. Regardless of the project, all students receive the same lectures and complete the same assignments. Each student must sign a "Data Agreement Form" which reminds students that the data remains the property of the agency, is to be kept confidential, and no further work can be done with the data without the explicit permission of the agency.
2. Throughout the semester, class time is spent in the classroom and computer lab. For most three-hour class periods, the first one to two hours is spent in lecture, discussion, and small-group activities. The remaining one to two hours is spent with the students on computers and the Instructor circulating to answer questions and provide reassurance.
3. A series of 12 *Research Partnership* (RP) assignments are completed by students during the one-semester course. With the exception of one assignment, each of the assignments is completed by each individual student. Students are encouraged to collaborate within their groups, but each student must do her/his own work.
4. For the last one to two class periods of the semester, students go to the agencies to make their final presentations. Findings must be communicated in such a way that they are understandable and palatable to agency staff.
5. As their final assignment, each student prepares a final report. This final report is a compilation of earlier assignments as well as several new sections. It has all the components of an empirical journal article. After grading and a final edit, written reports are submitted to the community agency for their use in decision-making around data collection and service delivery, and grant-writing. Only students whose final reports are of sufficient quality (receiving a grade of 90% or higher) are forwarded to the agency.

After the Course
1. Based on course performance, students are selected by the Instructor to prepare an Executive Summary of

their group's work. At the agency's request and with the Instructor's support, the student may participate in further data analyses, write a brief for the website, or make a presentation to the Board of Directors.

Outcomes/Assessment

The meeting of course objectives is measured at pre-test and post-test. On a 10-point Likert scale, students' scores have consistently shown more than a 4-point improvement between pre-test and post-test in the areas of knowing how to conduct descriptive and inferential statistics, knowing how to interpret univariate and bivariate findings, knowing how to report statistical findings in an understandable way, knowing how to use SPSS to analyze data, and understanding the role of the IRB.

Students' remarks on course evaluations show their appreciation for an instructor who is enthusiastic about

the material, able to build confidence in others, and ready to partner with students on projects to reach mutual goals. They also appreciate the use of structured and incremental learning opportunities. Students report that their motivation for learning is greatly enhanced through service-learning, and more specifically, through the direct application of research to practice.

Conclusion

Through the *Research Partnership* model, students gain exposure to community agencies and are given the invaluable opportunity of providing a vital service to a community agency. In turn, community agencies gain valuable research services at no charge. Participation in *Research Partnership* nudges community agencies another step toward evidence-based practice. The instructor too benefits as the use of this model affects all three pillars of most school's expectations for faculty performance: research, teaching, and service.

Service-learning in the United States history survey course

Earl F. Mulderink III
Southern Utah University

Keywords: United States history, survey course, community history, accountability, service tracking

Introduction

Over the past two decades, more educators have embraced the pedagogy of service-learning to connect classroom and community, deepen student learning, and promote a greater sense of civic responsibility. For ten years, students in my two-semester survey of United States history have been required to complete a service-learning project and report. Service-learning has been a highly effective—and even exciting—pedagogy according to many students at our regional comprehensive public university in a rural setting.

Project Description

Service-learning projects and reports are required in a two-semester sequence in United States history taught at the sophomore-level. These classes have no pre-requisites and are open to all students. Typically, about 40 students enroll each semester, first in History 2700, *United States History to 1877,* and then in History 2710, *United States History Since 1877.* At least one of these two courses is required of all history majors, and both are required for students seeking state licensure to teach. These courses urge future teachers to utilize active pedagogies and promote civic engagement.

At the outset of each class, a syllabus and supplementary materials emphasize the centrality of service-learning.

Students are encouraged to pursue projects that are personally meaningful to them while working within more explicit guidelines. Each student's project and report are worth 25% of their final grade, and they can work individually or with one or two others in a group (with all sharing the same grade). After completing their service projects, they are to submit a four- to five-page written report in an electronic format that addresses specific issues. Most importantly, the report must include a detailed explanation of what was learned or gained from this activity; this reflection component is central to the learning experience of service-learning.

Project Timeline

Over the semester, students are expected to devote a minimum of 20 hours to the service-learning project and report (although many put in more time). If a project involves two or three students, each is expected to contribute fully and equally. All proposals are subject to the instructor's approval (and constructive advice) and are due within the first five weeks of the semester. All service and reports are to be completed by the semester's end and "certified" by a signed "statement of accountability." This document solicits contact information and feedback from an outside client, partner, or "responsible person" who benefited from and cooperated with the service provider. Although students have great flexibility in scheduling their service projects, the final report asks them to provide details about tasks, timelines, and work processes.

Steps for Implementation

Students appreciate plentiful documentation, explicit guidelines, and firm deadlines. In addition to providing plentiful written and oral instructions to students, a proactive instructor provides periodic class discussions to offer encouragement, share ideas, and head off problems large and small. At the outset of the semester, students are informed of a wide array of potential projects and partners. Detailed forms and information sheets are distributed to cover most of the anticipated questions:

- **Class Syllabus**—Explains parameters and expectations for service-learning project and report
- **Potential Projects**—Lists relevant projects with contact information
- **Project Proposal**—Prompts student effort by end of Week 5 and is subject to instructor's comments and approval
- **Statement of Accountability**—Documents students' work and generates feedback from community partners
- **Reminders**—Distributed toward the end of the semester, this document reminds students about reports and reflection components

Outcomes/Assessment

Each project and final report is assessed by the instructor with an evaluation sheet and grade, and students are evaluated for what they learn more than for the service they provide. Students' self-assessments are often pertinent and eloquent. One future history teacher explained his reluctance to do service-learning and that his subsequent effort was "one of the hardest projects I have done." Thankfully, he appreciated the "learning experience" and concluded that the "service-learning project was supposed to help other people, but I think it helped me to become a better teacher in the long run." These types of reflections constitute the core of service-learning.

Because of the diversity of history service projects, the only formal assessment from partners comes through the "statement of accountability" that poses open questions. Over the past ten years we have compiled summative evaluations from diverse people, partners, and organizations in multiple communities across five states. In vital ways, the "outcomes" are displayed as finished service projects that serve a larger public. These include oral history projects completed with family members, seniors at care centers, and military veterans. Our local museums, historical organizations, churches, schools, libraries, and government agencies all contain evidence of students' history service projects. Students have written historical brochures, created exhibits, constructed web sites, celebrated History Day, and led walking tours, among other endeavors.

Students themselves often offer the best assessments of their own projects through self-reflection. One student compiled an impressive set of oral histories in which he learned more about World War Two. Besides gaining "knowledge [he] could not have acquired in a classroom," the student felt the war years come alive through interviews. Not only had this project enriched life, but he learned to value the sacrifices of men and women in military service. He wrote of getting "choked up" every time he drove past the local cemetery that contained graves of men he had interviewed and who had given the "ultimate sacrifice for their country." Students' statements like these underscore the experiential and meaningful aspects of service-learning.

Conclusion

History teachers at all levels should be cheered by students who acquire a deeper appreciation of history and community, along with greater self-awareness, through the pedagogy of service-learning. Students' own reflections illustrate the effectiveness of service-learning, particularly when they pursue individualized, personally-meaningful projects. Many students feel more connected to the history of their families and their communities, and they can better appreciate the diverse skills that historians use to accurately interpret the past.

History teachers at all levels should be cheered by students who acquire a deeper appreciation of history and community, along with greater self-awareness, through the pedagogy of service-learning.

Teaching the temporal dimension of service-learning projects

Roger Munger and Samantha Sturman
Boise State University

Keywords: time, project management, time management, reflection, meta cognitive skills, project planning

Introduction

How long will this take? This deceptively simple question is often very difficult to answer, especially if the student being questioned has little or no experience with the event in question. This temporal difficulty is further compounded by the fact that many students are notoriously poor judges of time. Service-learning projects, or any task for that matter, can fall victim to this phenomena. When students submit a project at the end of the term, they are often just relieved to have it finished. And, if they have not been keeping close records, they likely don't have an accurate (or even a ballpark) estimate of the actual time they spent working on the project. Without some reflection on and management of the temporal dimension of a service-learning project, students are likely to miss important deadlines, cram a project's workload into a single, stressful week(end) , and be unable to accurately answer a community-partner's question of "how long will this take?"

Project Description

In a persuasive writing course focused on promoting a socially responsible and environmentally sustainable society, undergraduate students partner with *green-minded* organizations in the local community to create documents to be used by the organization and/or the people it serves. In addition to learning rhetorical strategies writers can use to persuade readers to change their beliefs and behaviors, students learn strategies they can use to manage the temporal aspects of their service-learning projects, including building schedules, managing their time, and tracking their activities. Ultimately, one goal of the course is to provide students with the tools to successfully complete a project on time.

Steps for Implementation

Introducing project-management strategies to students occurs throughout the writing process. As students begin planning and outlining their documents, they learn about creating a schedule. When they begin drafting and revising, they learn about managing and tracking their time.

Creating a Schedule. Winging it is a strategy that is both appealing (it takes little effort) and familiar to students. However, at some point the duration and complexity of a project, especially one involving several collaborators in class and from the community, will require students to devote some well-spent time to creating a schedule. This requires students to think through the project from start to finish, reaching agreements on how to approach the project. When creating a schedule, students should do the following:

- Work backwards from the final project due date.
- Break the project into smaller, more manageable tasks and deliverables.
- Schedule ample time for people to review drafts and provide feedback.
- Include intermediate milestones, such as first draft completed, progress report submitted, and reviewer comments returned.
- Put the entire schedule in writing and, if a deadline is missed, immediately revise the remaining schedule.
- An effective schedule shows students what must be done, who must do it, and when it must be done: it's a roadmap to completing a project on time.

Managing Their Own Time. Time management is a critical skill for any project manager, but especially for students with little experience juggling the demands of a complex project. Projects invariably involve many deadlines, and to meet them all, each member of the project team needs to make the most of the time he or she has available. Below are three strategies students can use to effectively manage their own time:

- Make a list. Break a project task into several "to do" items that lead to the completion of the task. Begin each item with a verb (e.g., e-mail, research, call, draft) to reflect the action that must be taken. Next, prioritize each item and start with the top-priority items.
- Work when you are at your best. Most people have a time of day in which they work their best and fastest. Reserve this time exclusively for top-priority, most challenging items.
- When working, work. It's tempting to multitask. But, trying to do many things at once is not a good time-management strategy; rather, it insures that you accomplish a bunch of minor tasks and that nothing gets your best effort. Focus on each activity. Complete it. Then, move on to your next task.

When students are in control of their time, they can make informed and effective decisions when problems arise.

Tracking Their Activity. When estimating time (and budgets), a good project manager relies on his or her previous experience. Each completed project helps build on this experience base. Unless accurate records are kept, however, this experience is lost, and the project manager fails to learn from it. To begin accumulating the experience necessary to estimate time, students should do the following:

- Maintain an activity log during the project, detailing the date, duration, and type of activity.
- Based on the type of project, create a limited number of activity types (e.g., research, writing, revising/editing, project management, design) for describing activities in the log.
- Record time spent in half hour or hour increments. (Recording 150 hours for "doing project" is not very informative. Likewise, recording every two minute e-mail message or conversation is tedious and counterproductive.)

Experienced project managers can look at a specific project and be able to estimate how much time it will take for each step of the process. When students can do this, they can create effective schedules and efficiently manage their time.

Outcomes/Assessment

In addition to regular opportunities to reflect on the temporal elements of their projects, students reflected on the events of the project to build their experience base and better prepare for managing future projects. To help guide students in their analyses, they were asked to do the following:

- Using the activity log, determine total time spent as well as the percentage of total project time spent on each type of activity. Any surprises? What factors contributed to these numbers?
- Using the original project schedule, compare anticipated deadlines with actual completion dates. What factors led to changed deadlines? Which, if any, of these missed deadlines could have been predicted? Avoided? What critical tasks were left off the original schedule?

By reflecting on what this temporal data revealed about the effectiveness of the project team, students learned how to decrease time spent on activities of little value to a project and, instead, focus on high-value activities. Such student reflection along with their final documents and service-learning evaluations provided measures for success: 100 percent of the documents were delivered on time, and 71 percent of the students "strongly agreed" that they had gained practical experience that will appeal to employers.

Conclusion

Tracking and managing the temporal dimension of a project will not only lead to less stress for the project team but also it will help answer that inevitable question, "How long will this take?" By using the time-management tools provided here, students can begin to gain experience with successfully and efficiently completing service-learning projects.

THE ART OF SERVICE-LEARNING DISCOURSE

RICK ISAACSON
SAN FRANCISCO STATE UNIVERSITY

Keywords: visual rhetoric, persuasive advocacy, visual literacy

Introduction

Presentational speaking courses offer optimal avenues for service-learning advocacy. Community programs that we take for granted could not have established without the compelling use of persuasion to garner the support of legislators and funding agencies, and to mobilize voters and volunteers. But beyond such campaigns is the every day need for individuals dedicated to community service to advocate "in the trenches," to devise compelling messages to bring people into the circle of active community involvement.

Many of history's most memorable speeches share a common characteristic, a capacity to present a word picture to establish theme, meaning, and emotional impact through transporting imagery. This technique has historical roots in the classical rhetorical technique of ekphrasis. Leonard (1994) states that the ekphratic principle encourages the listener to "see a scene...in highly charged evocative language."

Project Description

Given the impact of visual rhetoric and a nationally declining command of evocative language to empower visually rendered discourse (Gitlin, 1996), I designed the Art of Service-Learning Speech for my presentational speaking courses. The assignment begins with this distribution of a wide assortment of fine art images, photographs, and commercial graphics compiled by past students and the instructor. Current students find additional images that relate to social or environmental concerns. A single or a related pair of images is selected by each student, images that inspire a new service theme or help support a subject already chosen.

Illustrating this assignment with the work of past students provides examples of the effective blending of iconic imagery and community oriented discourse. One example illustrates how a single image may have multiple applications, as it inspires the content of a text and a complementary theory of persuasion. A student used Picasso's The Old Guitarist from his Blue Period to craft both an introduction and conclusion and apply Schwartz's (1973) theory of resonance (using symbols to evoke commonly held audience experiences) for a speech on homelessness).

> Haven't you seen someone like this solitary, withered figure huddled in a doorway as the blue-violet shadows of evening fell? Painted in 1903, Picasso's, The Old Guitarist, could depict homelessness in our own time. The painting's somber blue shades connect us to the melancholy of the homeless.

> There still remains a touch of fragile nobility in the way the old man caresses his guitar. Picasso came to know the homeless of Barcelona. Today, I will provide you with surprising answers to the question, 'Who are the homeless on our own city streets?'

Continuing the thread of resonance, the speaker redisplayed Picasso's image to support the speech's conclusion. The artistic inventiveness applied to the two most vital elements of the address, enhances the credibility of the speaker, and thus the persuasiveness of the message (Verdeber, 2004).

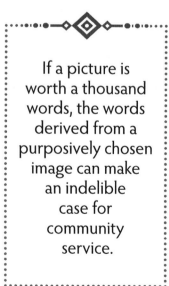

If a picture is worth a thousand words, the words derived from a purposively chosen image can make an indelible case for community service.

In the violet-blue shadows of evening, when a kindred soul of the old guitarist seeks refuge in a doorway, head listing, body slumped from fatigue and despair, don't avert your eyes. The man or woman may hold a cup, rather than a guitar, but examine the weather-beaten face with its life-map of deeply furrowed lines. Keep your assumptions and your heart open.

Contributing to the artistic construction of this speech is the development of a descriptive word bank, supporting the evocative character of ekphratic language. Before composing a text, students assemble a bank of descriptive words to capture the detail, scale, mood, texture, and action of the chosen image. Speakers find evocative words through thoughtful observation, reading critical commentary, and by consulting word resources. Speakers draw upon this word menu as the speech is written and edited.

In an address encouraging involvement with Amnesty International, a speaker displayed the powerful photograph which universally captured the bravery of student resistance during the 1989 protest in Tiananmen Square, an image that came to symbolically define the event. As most will recognize this image, note how much of the introduction is derived from the content of the photo. Language drawn from the speaker's word bank is underlined. The selected language clearly heightens the tension and impact of the moment.

> This was a battle of 'good versus evil,' a day when one man's faith moved mountains. The heat waves rose from the soft asphalt on the Chang'an Boulevard. The great city of Beijing shimmered like a mirage in a melting desert. The earth trembled beneath the deafening, metallic high pitch of engines, as if approaching herds of galloping ancient armies were compressed inside rows of Soviet-made tanks. The tanks came bringing death, crawling like colossal Paleolithic turtles.

> Standing before the gathered tanks, the world watched a single young man. He stood resolute on the boulevard where the blood of his fellow students had spilled the night before, now boiling under the scorching sun of this day when a young man walked into history. He carried his school bag, containing a few books and an unwavering courage to die for his beliefs. He stood immovable, turning the melting river of blood and asphalt into a pure mountain stream.

An old Chinese proverb states, 'A journey of a thousand miles begins with a single step.' We must never forget the importance of a singe step, for it can truly transform the world.

This assignment permits numerous options. An image may inspire the text of an introduction, conclusion, significant part of the body, or reinforce a persuasive concept. Integrating language with compelling imagery invariably produces the most richly crafted, tightly organized presentations of the semester. Recounting semester highlights, students most often recall service-learning presentations that rose to the level of artistic rhetoric. If a picture is worth a thousand words, those thousand words derived from the image can make an indelible case for community service.

Project Timeline

This speech is assigned early in the semester, as it establishes a precedent for incorporating more evocative and descriptive content in subsequent speeches. In a class meeting twice weekly, an initial day is used to describe the project and provide examples of past student presentations.

In the first session, students also brainstorm in small groups, producing potential speech topics and strategies from images supplied by the instructor and images that students bring to class, which suggest social and community themes. At the second meeting, students come with an image(s) that inspires a specific service oriented topic and a bank of words which provides a vivid and comprehensive description of the image. These ideas are shared class-wide, and feedback on potential development of suggested themes are offered. At the third meeting, students bring in sections of a speech text specifically inspired by their selected image(s). Because of the impact of introductions and conclusions, students are encouraged to work with an image that may drive both of these key segments, thus creating an aesthetic symmetry that adds to the impact and elegance of the speech. The speaking round begins at the next meeting. On the day of presentation, speakers submit a full-sentence outline, their word bank, and a description of the theory or concept of persuasion employed to lend impact to the speech.

Steps for Implementation

1. From the world of fine art, photography, commercial art, etc., select an image(s) that reinforces your chosen topic (if you have not chosen a topic, scanning through visual resources often inspires a compelling subject). This topic should focus on a persuasive appeal for community action or service on a local, national, or worldwide scale. Consider topics related to hunger, homelessness, the environment, human rights, health/illness, medical services, disease control, civil liberties, historical preservation, education and literacy, safety, peace movements, HIV, eradicating prejudice, animal rights, children's rights, etc. Remember that your objective should be to change or reinforce an attitude/and or behavior.

2. In addition to a full-sentence outline, develop a descriptive work or phrase bank inspired by your image(s) to make the eventual speech text more evocative. Think of words and phrases that express color, dimension, scale, textures, movement, emotion, etc. You will eventually draw from this word bank to enhance the evocative and transporting nature of your presentation.

3. Use your selected image(s) and your word bank to inspire the text of an introduction, conclusion, or significant section of the body of your persuasive message. Note how in the earlier two examples, Picasso's, *The Old Guitarist,* and the photo of Tiananmen Square, that the texts directly draw from the content of respective images.

A classic introduction contains an opening attention-gaining statement to generate interest, establishes the thesis and purpose of the persuasive message, states the importance of the message to the audience, previews the body of the speech, and concludes with a statement that connects the introduction to the body of the speech, the transition statement. A classic conclusion places the body and purpose of the speech in perspective to reinforce the main message, resonates in tone and rhythm with the introduction to create a harmonious, artistically crafted opening and closing statement, and concludes with a specific request for action. Consider employing a method of organization to coherently design your introduction and conclusion and utilize your image (e.g., are your image and text more adaptable to a problem/solution, compare/contrast, cause effect, chronological, or spatial pattern of organization)? Please note that these are classic suggestions for developing an introduction and conclusion. I am always open to original methods of devising an effective opening and closing of your message. Just have a good reason for drawing outside of conventional lines.

4. Determine whether a theory or concept of persuasion derived from the class text, handouts, discussions, or a past communication class, can enhance the persuasiveness of your message. Applied use of a communication concept or theory may enhance the persuasive appeal of the message. Identify this theory or concept in a side commentary apart from your speech outline.

5. If available, submit your chosen image(s) with your assignment. If your image is not accessible, please fully identify it with a full reference in your outline.

Outcomes/Assessment

Students submit progressive segments of this project. They first submit the initial images that they gathered, and identify their reasoning for the intended use for the final image or images selected. They also submit a word bank derived from the selected image(s). This word bank is assessed by the instructor for its depth and adequacy. The selected image(s) may be displayed as visual aids during the speech. The instructor includes the method and quality of this display as part of the evaluation of the presentation. A full-sentence outline of the central text, along with a rationale for employed theory is submitted at the conclusion of the speech and is assessed by the instructor and factored in the overall grading process.

Conclusion

In my experience, integrating aesthetic language with compelling, transporting imagery invariably produces the most richly crafted, tightly focused presentations of the semester. The use of evocative content also enhances a more dynamic delivery style, as the visual and narrative qualities of this speech reflexively encourage speakers to employ more animated and descriptive gestures to help convey suggested imagery. Increased and more flexible vocal variety also follow suit. Think of how expressive speakers are when relating a story that depicts personal qualities and intriguing settings.

Recounting semester highlights, students most often recall service-learning presentations that rose to the level of artistic rhetoric. If a picture is worth a thousand words, the words derived from a purposively chosen image can make an indelible case for community service.

References

Gitlin, Todd (1996, November 25). The Death of Eloquence. *San Francisco Chronicle*, pp. 11-14.

Leonard, George J. (1994). *The Art of the Commonplace.* Chicago, IL: University of Chicago Press.

Schwartz, T. (1973). *The Responsive Chord.* New York City, New York: Anchor.

Verdeber, R (2004). *The Challenge of Effective Speaking.* Belmont, CA: Wadsworth/Thomson Learning.

If a picture is worth a thousand words, the words derived from a purposively chosen image can make an indelible case for community service.

CONTRIBUTORS

Annie Abbott
Assistant Professor and Director of the
    Spanish and Illinois Program
Department of Spanish, Italian and Portuguese
University of Illinois at Urbana-Champaign
arabbott@illinois.edu

Raquel Meyer Alexander
Assistant Professor
Accounting and Information Systems
University of Kansas
raquela@ku.edu

Sean Anderson, PhD
Assistant Professor
Environmental Science and Resource
    Management Program
California State University Channel Islands
sean.anderson@csuci.edu

Scott P. Anstadt, PhD, LSCSW, IABMCP
Assistant Professor - Division of Social Work
College of Professional Studies
Florida Gulf Coast University
sanstadt@fgcu.edu

Paige Averett, PhD
Assistant Professor
School of Social Work
East Carolina University
averettp@ecu.edu

Maggie W. Baker
Coordinator, Service Learning
Center for Experiential Learning
Loras College
maggie.baker@loras.edu

Sharon M. Ballard, PhD, CFLE, CFCS
Associate Professor
Child Development and Family Relations
East Carolina University
ballards@ecu.edu

Elizabeth Anne Barber, PhD
Associate Professor
Leadership Studies, School of Education
North Carolina Agricultural and Technical State University
eabarber@ncat.edu

Clara H. Becerra, PhD
Assistant Professor of Spanish
Mount Union College
BECERRCH@mountunion.edu

CJ Gerda Bender, PhD
Faculty of Education
Manager, Curricular and Research
    Community Engagement (CRCE)
Department of Education
University of Pretoria
gerda.bender@up.ac.za

Deborah E. Bender, PhD, MPH
Professor, Department of Health Policy and Administration
Department of Health Policy and Administration
The University of North Carolina, Chapel Hill
dbender@email.unc.edu

Lynne Bercaw
Department of Education
California State University
lbercaw@csuchico.edu

Robert E. Bleicher
Associate Professor
School of Education
California State University Channel Islands
bob.bleicher@csuci.edu

Julia Blitz
Faculty of Health Sciences
Health Sciences
University of Pretoria
julia.blitz@up.ac.za

Barbara T. Bontempo, PhD
Professor
English Department
Buffalo State College
bontembt@buffalostate.edu

Merilyn C. Buchanan
Associate Professor
School of Education
California State University Channel Islands
merilyn.buchanan@csuci.edu

David B. Byrd, PhD
Professor, School of Accountancy and
    Director, Masters of Accountancy
Accounting
Missouri State University
DavidByrd@missouristate.edu

Sandra D. Byrd, CPA, PhD
Professor, School of Accountancy and Director, Low
    Income Tax Clinic; Public Affairs Professor
School of Accountancy
Missouri State University
sandrabyrd@missouristate.edu

Chris Liska Carger, PhD
Professor, Department of Literacy Education
Department of Literacy Education
Northern Illinois University
ccarger@niu.edu

Teena A. M. Carnegie
Associate Professor
Department of English: Technical Communication
Eastern Washington University
tamc4320@yahoo.com

Joanna J. Cemore, PhD
Associate Professor
Childhood Education and Family Studies
Missouri State University
joannacemore@missouristate.edu

Ann Marie Clark
Associate Professor
Curriculum and Instruction
Appalachian State University
clarkam@appstate.edu

Janice Clark Young, EdD, CHES
Associate Professor
Health and Exercise Sciences Department
Truman State University
jcyoung@truman.edu

Jon M. Clausen
Director of Educational Technology Programs
Educational Studies
Ball State University
jmclaus@bsu.edu

Susan Colby
Associate Professor and Assistant Chair
Department of Curriculum and Instruction
Appalachian State University
colbysa@appstate.edu

Manuel G. Correia
Assistant Professor
School of Education
California State University Channel Islands
manuel.correia@csuci.edu

Marcie Coulter-Kern
Associate Professor and Chair
Department of Psychology
Manchester College
mlcoulter-kern@manchester.edu

Lisa E. Cox, PhD, LCSW, MSW
Associate Professor of Social Work and Gerontology
School of Social and Behavioral Sciences; Social
    work and Gerontology Programs
The Richard Stockton College of New Jersey
lisa.cox@stockton.edu

Mo Cuevas
Social Work Program Director
Department of Social Work
West Texas A&M University
mcuevas@wtamu.edu

Karin deJonge-Kannan, PhD
Senior Lecturer of Linguistics and Co-Director,
    Master of Second Language Teaching Program
Department of Languages, Philosophy,
    and Speech Communication
Utah State University
karin.dejongekan@usu.edu

Timothy D. Dolan, MS, RID, NCIDQ, NCIDQ
    Certified # 016868, IIDA, IDEC
Assistant Professor
Department of Technology
Appalachian State University
dolantd@appstate.edu

Judy Donovan
Assistant Professor
College of Education
Minnesota State University, Mankato
jkdonov@gmail.edu

Marion Eppler, PhD
Associate Professor
Department of Psychology
East Carolina University
epplerm@ecu.edu

Amanda L. Espenschied-Reilly, MS, MA
Director of Service-Learning and Community Service
Service-Learning and Community Service
University of Mount Union
espensal@mountunion.edu

Tammy Faux, MSSW, PhD, LISW (MN)
Assistant Professor of Social Work
Social Work
Wartburg College
tammy.faux@wartburg.edu

Nancy Zachar Fett, LMSW
Associate Professor and Director of Social Work
Social Work
Loras College
nancy.fett@loras.edu

Billie J.A. Follensbee
Professor
Department of Art and Design, College of Arts and Letters
Missouri State
billiefollensbee@missouristate.edu

Connie M. Fossen, MSSW, EdD
Associate Professor and Field Director
Social Work Program
Viterbo University
cmfossen@viterbo.edu

Jacquelyn Frank
Assistant Professor/Coordinator,
    Gerontology Master's Program
School of Family and Consumer Sciences
Eastern Illinois University
jbfrank@eiu.edu

Marilyn D. Frank, MSW, PhD, LISW
Associate Professor
Department of Social Work
Minnesota State University, Mankato
marilyn.frank@mnsu.edu

Bobbi Gagne
Executive Director
Sexual Assault Crisis Team, Washington County, Vermont
sactwc@aol.com

Shari Galiardi
Service Learning Coordinator
Appalachian State University
galiardisl@appstate.edu

Sharyn Gallagher
Adjunct Instructor
Department of Continuing Studies
University of Massachusetts Lowell
Sharyn_Gallagher@uml.edu

Michael Glasser, PhD
Assistant Dean
National Center for Rural Health Professions
University of Illinois College of Medicine
michaelg@uic.edu

Joseph Goetz, PhD, AFC
Assistant Professor
Department of Housing and Consumer Economics
University of Georgia
goetz@uga.edu

Brenda Goodwin, MS, EdD
Assistant Professor
Department of Health, Physical Education, and Recreation
Missouri State University
BrendaGoodwin@missouristate.edu

Judith I. Gray
Associate Professor
Social Work
Ball State University
jgray2@bsu.edu

Cynthia Green Libby, DMA
Professor of Music
Department of Music
Missouri State University
cynthialibby@missouristate.edu

Lisa R. Grinde
Associate Professor
Department of Psychology
Loras College
Lisa.Grinde@loras.edu

Ann Gustad-Leiker, MA, LBSW
Executive Director
Center for Life Experiences
First Presbyterian Church
cfle@ruraltel.net

Ruthanne Hackman, PhD, MSW, LSW
School of Social Work
University of Pittsburgh
rhackman@att.net

Aileen Hale, PhD
English Department
Boise State University
aileenhale@boisestate.edu

Jeanette Harder, PhD, CMSW
Associate Professor and Program Chair
School of Social Work
University of Nebraska at Omaha
jharder@unomaha.edu

Jason Harris-Boundy, PhD
Assistant Professor, Management
College of Business
San Francisco State University
jchb@sfsu.edu

Elizabeth Hartung, PhD
Professor
Sociology and Anthropology Programs
California State University Channel Islands
elizabeth.hartung@csuci.edu

Robin Hasslen, PhD
Professor of Education
Education
Bethel University
r-hasslen@bethel.edu

Veronica House
Instructor and Service-Learning Coordinator
Program for Writing and Rhetoric
University of Colorado at Boulder
veronica.house@colorado.edu

Jane Hoyt-Oliver, LISW-S, PhD
Director, General Education and Professor of Social Work
General Education Program
Malone University
jholiver@malone.edu

Jenny Huq
Director, APPLES Service-Learning Program and
     Associate Director, Carolina Center for Public Service
APPLES Service Learning Program
The University of North Carolina, Chapel Hill
huq@email.unc.edu

Marsha Ironsmith, PhD
Associate Professor
Department of Psychology
East Carolina University
ironsmithe@ecu.edu

Rick Isaacson, PhD
Associate Professor and Internship and
     Service-Learning Director
Department of Communication Studies
San Francisco State University
isaacson@sfsu.edu or Risaac123@aol.com

Nicole L. Johnson
Assistant Professor
Department of Philosophy and Religious Studies
University of Mount Union
johnsonl@mountunion.edu

Jennifer Jones
Associate Professor
School of Teacher Education &
     Leadership, Literacy Education
Radford University
jjones292@radford.edu

Linda M. Kalbach, PhD
Assistant Professor
Education
Doane College
linda.kalbach@doane.edu

Patricia Proudfoot Kelly, EdD
Professor Emerita
Center for Research and Development
     in International Education
Virginia Polytechnic Institute and State University
kellyp@vt.edu

Laura J. Khoury
Associate Professor and Arab Studies Quarterly B.R Editor
Sociology and Anthropology Department
University of Wisconsin-Parkside
khoury@uwp.edu

Nancy King, PhD
Professor Emeritus
University Honors Program
University of Delaware
Nancy@NancyKingStories.com

Angela Lamson, PhD, LMFT, CLFE
Associate Professor
Child Development and Family Relations
East Carolina University
lamsona@ecu.edu

Darcy Lear
Lecturer and Coordinator of the minor
     program in Spanish for the Professions
Department of Romance Languages
University of North Carolina - Chapel Hill
lear@email.unc.edu

Melody Aye Loya, MSSW, PhD
Assistant Professor of Social Work and Field Coordinator
Department of Psychology, Sociology, and Social Work
West Texas A&M University
mloya@mail.wtamu.edu

Emma T. Lucas-Darby, PhD, MSW, LSW, NCGC
Professor, Department of Social Work
Department of Social Work
Carlow University
etlucas-darby@carlow.edu

Johnelle Luciani, RSM, MSW, PhD
Chair and Professor of Social Work
Social Work
Salve Regina University
lucianij@salve.edu

Elaine M. Maccio, PhD, LCSW
Assistant Professor
School of Social Work
Louisiana State University
emaccio@lsu.edu

Martin MacDowell, DrPH
National Center for Rural Health Professions
University of Illinois College of Medicine
mmacd@uic.edu

Mary Mahan-Deatherage
Director of Public Relations
Marketing and Public Relations
Katherine Shaw Bethea Hospital
mdeatherage@ksbhospital.com

Elizabeth Maier, PhD
Assistant Professor
Department of Justice Studies and Sociology
Norwich University
emaier@norwich.edu

Mark Malaby
Assistant Professor of Social Foundations of
     Education/Multicultural Education
Education
Ball State University
mmalaby@bsu.edu

Dina Mansour-Cole, PhD
Associate Professor of Organizational Leadership
Organizational Leadership
Indiana University Purdue University Fort Wayne
mansour@ipfw.edu

Nancy B. Marthakis, DO
Assistant Professor
Biology
Purdue University North Central
nmarthakis@pnc.edu

Donna McIntosh, MSW
Social Work Program
Siena College
McIntosh@siena.edu

Corinna McLeod, PhD
Associate Professor of English
English
Grand Valley State University
mcleodc@gvsu.edu

Monique Mironesco
Assistant Professor, Political Science
Social Sciences Division
University of Hawaii, West O'ahu
mironesc@hawaii.edu

Jean Mistele
Mathematics and Statistics Instructor
Department of Mathematics and Statistics
Radford University
jmistele@radford.edu

Verona Mitchell-Agbemadi
Director
Bethel University/Frogtown-Summit
    U. Community Partnership
v-mitchell-agbemadi@bethel.edu

Catherine Mobley
Associate Professor
Department of Sociology and Anthropology
Clemson University
camoble@exchange.clemson.edu

Brenda Moore
Assistant Professor and Department Head
Department of Social Work
Texas A&M - Commerce
Brenda_Moore@tamu-commerce.edu

Earl F. Mulderink, III, PhD
Professor of History and SUU Faculty
    Coordinator of Civic Engagement
History
Southern Utah University
mulderink@suu.edu

Roger Munger, PhD
Professor of English
English
Boise State University
rmunger@boisestate.edu

Nancy J. Nelson, PhD
Director, Africana Education Program
Eastern Washington University
nayonelson@hotmail.com

Pilar Pacheco
Assistant Director
Center for Community Engagement
California State University Channel Islands
pilar.pacheco@csuci.edu

Lance Palmer
Assistant Professor
Housing and Consumer Economics
University of Georgia
lpalmer@fcs.uga.edu

Alan Penczek
Adjunct Professor of Philosophy
Department of Philosophy
Stevenson University
apenczek@stevenson.edu

Laurie F. Peters, PhD, RN
Professor and Dean, School of Health Sciences
Health Sciences
Ivy Tech Community College, Kokomo
lpeters@ivytech.edu

Claudia M. Reder, PhD
Lecturer
English
California State University Channel Islands
claudia.reder@csuci.edu

Barbara Rich
Associate Professor and BSW Program Coordinator
School of Social Work
University of Southern Maine
rich@usm.maine.edu

Julie Richards, MSW, LICSW
Undergraduate Program Coordinator and Senior Lecturer
Department of Social Work
University of Vermont
julie.richards@uvm.edu

Janice G. Rienerth, PhD
Professor of Sociology
Department of Sociology and Social Work
Appalachian State University
rienerthjg@appstate.edu

Diane Robinson, BS, BA
Community Health Educator
Piedmont Health Services and Sickle Cell Agency
drobinson@piedmonthealthservices.org

Donald A. Rodriguez, PhD
Associate Professor and Program Chair
Environmental Science and Resource Management
California State University Channel Islands
donald.rodriguez@csuci.edu

Ingrid Rogers, PhD
Emeritus Professor of Modern Languages
Department of Modern Languages
Manchester College
ingridnrogers@gmail.com

Helen Rosenberg
Associate Professor
Sociology and Anthropology Department
University of Wisconsin-Parkside
Helen.Rosenberg@uwp.edu

Pete Sanderson, PhD
Professor of Computer Science
Mathematical Sciences Department
Otterbein College
Psanderson@otterbein.edu

David M. Sarcone, PhD
Associate Professor
International Business and Management
Dickinson College
sarconed@dickinson.edu

Julien Simon
Assistant Professor
World Languages and Cultures
Indiana University East
jjsimon@iue.edu

Thomas J. Smith, PhD
Assistant Professor
Department of Curriculum and Instruction,
    School of Education
North Carolina Agricultural and Technical State University
smithtg@ncat.edu

Scott Smithson, PhD
Associate Professor of Communication
    and Department Chair
Communication
Purdue North Central
ssmithson@pnc.edu

Caile E. Spear
Associate Professor
Kinesiology/COE
Boise State University
cspear@boisestate.edu

Laura Jacobsen Spielman
Assistant Professor, Mathematics Education
Department of Mathematics and Statistics
Radford University
lspielman@radford.edu

Nancy Francisco Stewart, PhD
Associate Professor
Department of Sociology and Social Work
Jacksonville State University
nfstewar@jsu.edu

Kyle Andrew Sturgeon
Program Director and Instructor
Architecture
Boston Architectural College
sturgeon.kyle@gmail.com

Samantha Sturman
Department of English
Boise State University
samanthasturman@gmail.com

Mary Sulentic Dowell
Assistant Professor, Reading Education
Department of Educational Theory, Policy
    & Practice; College of Education
Louisiana State University
sdowell@lsu.edu

Barbara A. Sylvia, MSW, PhD
Professor
Social Work
Salve Regina University
sylviab@salve.edu

Annemarie Vaccaro, PhD
Assistant Professor
College Student Personnel Program
University of Rhode Island
avaccaro@uri.edu

Ken Vollmar
Professor
Computer Science Department
Missouri State University
KenVollmar@missouristate.edu

Nataki S. Watson
Graduate Student
Counseling, School of Education
North Carolina Agricultural and Technical State University
nkwatson@ncat.edu

Madonna Weese,
Extension Specialist 4-H Youth Development
State 4-H Office
University of Illinois Urbana Champaign
mweese@illinois.edu

Gretchen Wehrle, PhD
Chair, Psychology and Sociology Department
  and Associate Director for Faculty
  Development, Dorothy Stang Center
Psychology and Sociology Department
Notre Dame de Namur University
gwehrle@ndnu.edu

Steve Willis, PhD
Associate Professor of Art Education
Department of Art and Design
Missouri State University
SteveWillis@missouristate.edu

Andi Witczak
Director
Center for Service Learning
University of Kansas
awitczak@ku.edu

Liz Wolvaardt
Faculty of Health Sciences
Health Sciences
University of Pretoria
liz.wolvaardt@up.ac.za

INDEX